At the
ALTAR
OF THE
Appellate
GODS

At the ALTAR OF THE *Appellate* GODS

Arguing before the US Supreme Court

—⁓⁓—

A Memoir

Lisa Sarnoff Gochman

RED ⚡ LIGHTNING BOOKS

This book is a publication of

Red Lightning Books
1320 East 10th Street
Bloomington, Indiana 47405 USA

redlightningbooks.com

Manufactured in the United States of America

First printing 2022

ISBN 978-1-68435-195-4 (hdbk.)
ISBN 978-1-68435-198-5 (web PDF)

CONTENTS

ACKNOWLEDGMENTS

TO DAVID HULSEY, RACHEL Rosolina, David Miller, and Vickrutha Sudharsan at Indiana University Press, thank you for taking a chance on an unknown author peddling a quirky memoir based on a decades-old United States Supreme Court case that no one understands. To Joseph Perry at Perry Literary, thank you for your patience and guidance through the process of finding the right publisher for my sui generis book.

To my beta readers, writing advisers, and cheerleaders, thank you for your comments, criticisms, wisdom, support, encouragement and, most of all, for your love and friendship through the years: Alexa Abrahams, Jeff Abrahams, Karen Abrahams, Mitch Abrahams, Diane Bark, Jeff Crespi, Deborah Crivelli, Amy Dash, Toby Davidson, Elissa Erly, Barbara Exposito, Barbara Fane, Karen Fiorelli, Janet Flanagan, Claire Palermo Flower, Lindsey Gange, Ashley Gochman, Jesse Gochman, Jordan Gochman, Steven Gochman, Jennifer Gottschalk, Mary Ellen Halloran, Carol Henderson, Dora Lopez, Carol Stanton Meier, Debra Owens, Barbara Quinn, Linda Rinaldi, Tom Smith, Allison Soffer, Lisa Spiegel, Dorothy Steinmetz, Geraldine Zidow, and Paul Zidow.

To Lori Linskey and Monica do Outeiro of the Monmouth County Prosecutor's office, thank you for graciously allowing me the time I needed to write this book.

To Judge Patrick DeAlmeida, Michael Dreeben, Edward DuMont, Dan Schweitzer, and Denise Simpson, thank you for your wise counsel during the *Apprendi* litigation and for racking your brains twenty years later for any useful bits of information you might have remembered about the Supreme Court argument. I truly could not have gotten through the argument, or this book, without you.

To Anne Paskow, thank you for assigning the *Apprendi* appeal to me. Good things do come in small packages.

To John J. Farmer Jr., thank you for allowing me to argue *Apprendi* before the Supreme Court of the United States. Your faith in my abilities gave me faith in my abilities.

To my family and friends who gathered from all corners of the United States in Washington, DC, in late March 2000 to watch the back of my head during my twenty minutes of fame, my gratitude for your love and unwavering support is immeasurable: Alexa Abrahams, Jeffrey Abrahams, Karen Abrahams, Mitchell Abrahams, Diane Bark, Ben Bark, Roseann Finn, Frances Gochman, Jesse Gochman, Jordan Gochman, Steven Gochman, Bob Luther, Michael Remez, Jill Riola, Alvin Sarnoff, Barbara Sarnoff, Allison Soffer, and Bob Soffer.

To my husband, Steven, and my son, Jordan, thank you for letting me share our family's stories with good friends and total strangers. Thank you for inspiring me to follow my first dream of arguing before the Supreme Court of the United States and my second dream of writing a book about my first dream. And thank you, most of all, for never letting me give up on those dreams. I love you both so much.

At the
ALTAR
OF THE
Appellate
GODS

PROLOGUE

"MS. GOCHMAN, WE'LL HEAR FROM YOU."

Never in my life have I heard any sound more intimidating than that of Chief Justice William H. Rehnquist's booming voice calling my name to begin my argument before the Supreme Court of the United States (SCOTUS) in Washington, DC. I gingerly rose from the high-back leather chair at counsel table, careful not to spill my glass of ice water all over my opening statement as I took one step to the lectern. Drawing a deep breath, I stood before the altar of the appellate gods, a mere mortal dressed in a simple black skirt and notched collar jacket, black patent leather cap toe pumps, and my grandma Eva's double strand of pearls with its gold filigree and ruby clasp. I was so close to the court's raised mahogany bench that when I faced Justice Ruth Bader Ginsberg seated on the far left, I could not see in my peripheral vision Justice Stephen G. Breyer seated on the far right. The majestic courtroom, its coffered ceiling soaring forty-four feet above my head, was utterly silent. Hundreds of eyes were fixed on me, waiting for me to speak. My throat tightened up as nerves seized me, and my first few words—"Mr. Chief Justice, and may it please the court"—came out muffled and a bit squeaky.

For the next twenty minutes on the morning of Tuesday, March 28, 2000, it was just me and the nine justices of the Supreme Court of the United States locking horns in a raucous verbal battle over the constitutionality of New Jersey's Hate Crime Statute in the landmark sentencing case of *Charles C. Apprendi, Jr., v. New Jersey*.[1]

That I had the honor of appearing in the highest temple of justice in the United States in the first place was nothing short of miraculous. I was a graduate of a second-tier New York City law school, toiling away as an anonymous state government attorney in a cramped, windowless office in Trenton, New Jersey. In the rarefied world of United States Supreme Court litigation, partners in elite private law firms and former SCOTUS law clerks with undergraduate and juris doctorate degrees from Ivy League universities are far more likely to argue a case in Washington, DC, than a commoner like me.

But even with a double-Ivy pedigree, it is nearly impossible for any attorney to argue before SCOTUS. When a lawyer vows to take his case all the way up to the Supreme Court of the United States, bet against him. The justices are very persnickety about the issues they choose to tackle. Every year, seven to eight thousand petitions for a writ of certiorari (a fancy Latin name for an order by which a higher court reviews a decision of a lower court) are filed by disappointed litigants with the Clerk's Office in Washington, DC. Of those thousands of petitions, the court grants and hears oral arguments in just eighty or so.[2] This means that, in any given year, only a very small number of the more than 1.35 million attorneys licensed to practice law across the United States will have the privilege of presenting their oral argument to the nine justices of the Supreme Court. I was one of those lucky few.

Actually, the word "lucky" is a misnomer. Crazy, meshuga, and "two tacos short of a combo plate" (as one New Jersey newspaper columnist once labeled my legal reasoning in an unrelated case) are more accurate descriptors of the grueling, pothole-riddled road to the Supreme Court. Quirky court rules must be followed to the letter, and hard-and-fast deadlines must be met without exception. The *Apprendi* litigation engulfed me for nine months while I wrote my merits brief and prepared for oral argument. And that was on top of my already burdensome caseload of New Jersey state criminal appeals. Family life was completely shunted aside. I barely saw my husband Steven and missed most of my nine-year-old son Jordan's school year. If the law is a jealous mistress, then SCOTUS is a woman scorned.

New Jersey's Hate Crime Statute particularly riled the United States Supreme Court justices. No one doubted that a state legislature could enact a law requiring enhanced punishment for criminal defendants convicted of hate crimes. The question before SCOTUS was thornier: Who was required by the United States Constitution to determine whether a crime was racially motivated, the jury or the sentencing judge?

Defendant Charles C. Apprendi Jr. was sentenced under the Hate Crime Statute to two additional years in state prison following a trial judge's finding that Apprendi's violent crime against the only Black family living in his neighborhood was motivated by racial bias. Apprendi challenged the constitutionality of this statute, arguing that only a jury of his peers was authorized by the Sixth and Fourteenth Amendments to the United States Constitution to make a factual finding that exposed him to additional punishment.

As the appellate attorney representing the state of New Jersey in *Apprendi*, I had spent the better part of the prior four years defending the constitutionality of the Hate Crime Statute before the New Jersey state appellate courts. A trial judge could make a finding of racial bias, I argued, because racial bias was the same as motive, and motive has long been a sentencing factor for the judge's consideration. The Supreme Court of the United States would have the final word on this significant federal constitutional issue, and the rapid-fire and often hostile questioning from the nine justices on the morning of March 28, 2000, revealed a deeply divided court.

But I only needed five votes to win.

—ᛗᛟᛞ—

CHAPTER 1

IF YOU HAPPENED TO HAVE occupied one of the 439 seats in the Supreme Court courtroom in Washington, DC, for the *Apprendi* argument on March 28, 2000, you would have witnessed but a sliver of a criminal case that began six years earlier. And that sliver might have seemed utterly confusing and out of context to you. Supreme Court arguments are not theatrical events staged for the audience's entertainment. Ushers do not hand out playbills summarizing the legal issues and listing the attorneys' biographies. There is no concession stand selling tubs of hot buttered popcorn and oversized boxes of Junior Mints. The whole shebang before the nine justices lasts only one hour, and arguing counsel cannot waste their limited time bringing the audience up to speed. Oral arguments are solely for the court's benefit, and the justices are well-versed on the facts of the case and the legal issues before they take their assigned seats on the bench.

The controversy underlying the *Apprendi* argument arose in Vineland, New Jersey, a rural Cumberland County township located two hours southwest of New York City and forty minutes southeast of Philadelphia. Founded as an alcohol-free utopian society in 1861 by Charles K. Landis, Vineland's population has always been predominantly white and Christian. In late November 1979, members of the Ku Klux Klan and the American Nazi Party joined forces to intimidate the small number of Black, Hispanic, and Jewish residents of Vineland. Barely three hours before the scheduled start of a "White Power" rally in Landis Park, however, the plan was foiled when police arrested the Grand Wizard and twenty-one other Klan members on weapons offenses.[1]

Fifteen years after the aborted Klan rally, Vineland remained predomin-antly white, with close to 40,000 white residents and 6,287 Black residents.[2] In July 1994, Michael Fowlkes Sr., his wife Mattie Harrell Fowlkes, and their three children (Philip, age fifteen; Dawn, age thirteen; and Michael Jr., age eight) moved into a three-story, single-family house on a quiet street sur-rounded by farmland in Vineland.[3] The Fowlkes family scarcely had time to settle into their newly constructed home when, on September 24, 1994, an unknown assailant fired a .22-caliber rifle at their house in the dead of night. Eight-year-old Michael Fowlkes Jr. awoke the next morning to find a bullet hole in his second-floor bedroom window. Michael had been sleeping, his father said, "maybe two feet from the window" when the bullet whizzed over the boy's twin-size bed and landed in the hallway.[4]

Within weeks, it became apparent that the September 24 shooting was not a random act of violence. Two more bullets struck the Fowlkes house on two different nights in November. One bullet tore through the molding of a window frame and was later recovered in the family room. The other bullet lodged in the stucco exterior. There were no witnesses to these three night-time shootings, and the police had no suspects. Michael Fowlkes Sr. told the police that he thought neighborhood juveniles were responsible, but his wife Mattie believed that her family was targeted because they were the only Black people in the area.

"If they're shooting at the house, they might come in," Mattie told the police. "I cannot live like this."[5]

Three days before Christmas, on December 22, 1994, at two o'clock in the morning, the unknown assailant struck again under the cover of darkness, this time taking aim at the two Black Santa Claus faces decorating the Fowlkeses' glass front doors. Eight bullets ripped through the Fowlkes home that night; one of those bullets lodged in thirteen-year-old Dawn's bedroom wall. "There was so much damage to the house," Michael Fowlkes Sr. lamented. Both front doors, the decorative half-moon window above the front doors, the interior staircase, and the downstairs foyer closet were destroyed. Awoken by the sound of shattering glass, Michael Sr. raced down his 180-foot-long gravel driveway to the edge of the street in time to see a gray Chevy pickup truck turning left onto the road, exhaust fumes suspended in the frigid night air.

A neighbor heard the gunfire, recognized the gray truck, and called the police. Less than thirty minutes later, white, middle-aged pharmacist Charles

C. Apprendi Jr. was arrested at his one-story house located one-half mile west of the Fowlkes home. The engine of Apprendi's gray Chevy pickup truck was still warm.

Tall and lanky, with wire-rimmed aviator prescription glasses, Apprendi's mild-mannered appearance was deceiving. His college nickname, "Nut-Nut," hardly hinted at his racist and violent impulses. Apprendi confessed to the police that he had driven past the Fowlkes house in his pickup truck over the prior months, surreptitiously observing Michael Fowlkes and his sons in their front yard clearing brush, planting shrubs, and stacking firewood to prepare for the bitter New Jersey winter months ahead. Watching a Black family happily settling into their new home infuriated Apprendi. He returned to the Fowlkes house on four separate nights, rolled down the window of his pickup truck, and fired his .22-caliber Ruger rifle, equipped with a laser sight and a silencer, into the facade of the house. Apprendi admitted to the arresting officer he was "giving them a message" that the Black family was unwelcome in his neighborhood.

Vineland police recovered an arsenal of weapons from every room of Apprendi's house: six .22-caliber automatic rifles; four automatic handguns; one single-barrel and one double-barrel shotgun; a Taser gun; crates of assorted-caliber bullets, including hollow-point rifle slugs; a canister of pepper gas; an ammo belt; homemade weapons silencers; rifle scopes, including one for night vision; a gas pellet gun; handcuffs; ankle cuffs; and a bulletproof vest. Two homemade pipe bombs were found in Apprendi's attic. One of these improvised explosive devices, Apprendi warned the police, could be easily triggered if jostled. The Atlantic City, New Jersey, bomb squad and the federal Bureau of Alcohol, Tobacco, and Firearms were called in, and both bombs were safely detonated in the open field behind Apprendi's house.

Unable to post bail set at half a million dollars, Apprendi was incarcerated at the Cumberland County Jail. Less than one month later, a Cumberland County grand jury indicted Apprendi on eight counts of the first-degree attempted murders of Michael Fowlkes Sr., Mattie Harrell Fowlkes, thirteen-year-old Dawn Fowlkes, and eight-year-old Michael Fowlkes Jr., as well as fifteen counts of related weapons offenses.[6] Each of the twenty-three counts stemmed from the four nighttime shootings between September 24 and December 22, 1994. If a jury found him guilty at trial of all twenty-three crimes charged in the indictment, Apprendi faced a maximum sentence of 150 years in the custody of a New Jersey state prison, plus fines totaling $882,000.

On July 24, 1995, six months after the indictment was filed, correctional officers from the county jail escorted Apprendi into the trial courtroom of the Honorable Rushton H. Ridgway in the Cumberland County seat of Bridgeton. Judge Ridgway enjoyed a reputation of being firm yet fair to the criminal defendants appearing before him, as well as to the prosecution. His windowless courtroom was in the original section of the historic 1909 courthouse.

Handcuffed and wearing a standard-issue orange jumpsuit, Apprendi stood silently at the defense table facing the judge. Standing next to Apprendi was Joseph D. O'Neill, the local private attorney Apprendi had hired to represent him in court. As a criminal defendant, Apprendi had two choices: he could plead not guilty to the indictment and demand that a jury of his peers determine his guilt, or he could waive his right to a jury trial and plead guilty to the crimes charged. Either way, it would then be up to Judge Ridgway to decide how many years Apprendi would spend in prison.

With Joseph O'Neill's legal advice, Apprendi avoided what was essentially a life sentence in prison by waiving his right to a jury trial and pleading guilty before Judge Ridgway to three of the twenty-three criminal charges listed in the indictment: one count of second-degree possession of a firearm for an unlawful purpose for the September 24 shooting (count three of the indictment), one count of second-degree possession of a firearm for an unlawful purpose for the December 22 shooting (count eighteen), and one count of third-degree unlawful possession of an antipersonnel bomb (count twenty-two).

In exchange for Apprendi's guilty pleas to these three counts of unlawful weapons possession, the Cumberland County Prosecutor's office agreed to dismiss the remaining charges, including each of the eight counts of the attempted murders of Michael Fowlkes Sr., Mattie Harrell Fowlkes, Dawn Fowlkes, and Michael Fowlkes Jr. This deal cut Apprendi's sentencing exposure by decades.

The negotiations were hammered out by Joseph O'Neill and Cumberland County First Assistant Prosecutor Robert J. Luther. As first assistant prosecutor, Luther was second-in-command in the prosecutor's office and handled a long roster of significant cases, including most of the homicides committed in the county. Due to the sensitive nature of bias intimidation crimes and the potential for enhanced sentencing under New Jersey's Hate Crime Statute, Luther kept control of the *Apprendi* case rather than assign it to a less experienced assistant prosecutor.

As part of the state's offer, Luther insisted that Apprendi enter a guilty plea to count twenty-two, which charged Apprendi with possession of one of the two improvised explosive devices the police had found in his attic. Luther firmly believed that if firing bullets into the Fowlkes home on four separate nights failed to drive the family out of Vineland, Apprendi's likely next step was to hurl one of his homemade bombs into the house.

Apprendi was sworn in under oath at the plea hearing and answered questions posed by his attorney about the September 24 and December 22, 1994, shootings to support an adequate factual basis for his guilty pleas. An adequate factual basis is a legal requirement of every guilty plea taken in trial courtrooms throughout the twenty-one New Jersey counties.[7]

"Mr. Apprendi," Joseph O'Neill began, "let me invite your attention back to September and December of 1994 and ask if on both of those dates you had in your possession a gun for an unlawful purpose, namely, to frighten some people in a house, people named Fowlkes, although you didn't know who they were at the time. Is that true? You discharged a weapon, didn't you, on both those occasions, September and December?"

Apprendi quietly answered, "Yes."

"And on the occasion of the second discharge of a weapon, you were apprehended by the police at that time and there was in your possession on your premises a bomb, is that also true?"

"Yes."

First Assistant Prosecutor Luther followed up with a series of his own questions to flesh out the details of both shootings. "Mr. Apprendi, on September 24, 1994, did you fire a rifle shot into the Fowlkes residence in the City of Vineland?"

"Yes."

"And you didn't hit anyone with that bullet, correct?"

"Yes."

"And did you fire a shot into the second-floor bedroom window at that time?"

"I'm not sure about the window, but everything else is correct."

"Well, at least you admit firing a rifle shot at the home on that date; is that correct?"

"Yes."

"And the location of this residence was about half a mile, three-quarters of a mile from your residence; is that correct?"

"Yes."

"All right." Luther continued, "And on December 22, 1994, did you fire several rifle shots into the residence located in the City of Vineland?"

"Yes."

"And your purpose on both occasions was to scare the people in the home; is that correct?"

Apprendi hesitated, unwilling to admit under oath in open court that when he fired bullets into the Fowlkes house on September 24 and December 22 his intent was to frighten the couple and their three school-age children sleeping inside. O'Neill did not want his client to incriminate himself further and argued to Judge Ridgway that Apprendi had already answered the prosecutor's question. The judge disagreed.

"Now it's quite clear to me," Judge Ridgway admonished O'Neill, "that Mr. Apprendi and any number of defendants are reticent when it comes to admitting their guilt. However, the law is the law. We've got to have a factual basis for the record."

O'Neill spoke privately with his client for a few moments, then turned to the judge apologetically. "I appreciate the court's indulgence, really, Judge. I know you have better things to do. I think we're ready."

O'Neill rephrased First Assistant Prosecutor Luther's question to make it more palatable for Charles Apprendi to admit his unlawful purpose for firing his rifle into the Fowlkes home on September 24 and December 22, 1994:

"When you discharged that weapon on each of those occasions," O'Neill asked Apprendi, "would it be fair to say that you did so not knowing whether anybody was inside the property, but recognizing that upon either hearing the sound of the discharge of the weapon or seeing the damage caused by the bullet, that would have possibly scared somebody? Can you accept that?"

Apprendi answered, "Yes."

O'Neill continued, "Do you acknowledge that what you did was for an unlawful purpose?"

"Yes."

Judge Ridgway interjected, "You know, whether it's to scare someone means to me that it puts someone in fear or to harass them and unless there's a contradiction to that from you or the defendant at this point, I will assume that's why it was done." The judge accepted Apprendi's guilty pleas to two counts of the crime of second-degree possession of a firearm for an unlawful purpose (counts three and eighteen) and one count of the crime of third-degree unlawful possession of an antipersonnel bomb (count twenty-two). The remaining counts of the indictment, including the most serious charges of first-degree attempted murder, were dismissed as part of the plea bargain.

The degree of the crime charged determines the maximum prison sentence for that crime. Following his guilty plea to the crime of second-degree possession of a firearm for an unlawful purpose as charged in count eighteen of the indictment, Apprendi faced an ordinary maximum sentence of ten years in a New Jersey state prison.[8] But Apprendi's racially motivated, hate-fueled shooting through the glass front doors of the only Black family in his neighborhood three nights before Christmas was no "ordinary" crime.

A key term of the plea agreement reserved the state's right to move before the trial court for extended-term sentencing on count eighteen under New Jersey's Ethnic Intimidation Act.[9] Originally enacted in 1981, the Ethnic Intimidation Act was one of the first laws in the United States to ban acts of racial and ethnic intimidation, such as burning crosses and defacing property with swastikas. In 1990, the New Jersey Legislature amended the Act by authorizing trial court judges to increase the sentencing range for the underlying criminal conduct by one degree if the judge found that the defendant had committed the crime "with a purpose to intimidate an individual or group of individuals because of race, color, gender, handicap, religion, sexual orientation or ethnicity."[10] This amendment was better known as New Jersey's Hate Crime Statute, and its application meant that if Judge Ridgway found that Apprendi's crime of second-degree possession of a firearm for an unlawful purpose on December 22, 1994, was racially motivated, the maximum prison sentence Apprendi faced would be doubled. Instead of facing up to ten years in a New Jersey state prison, Charles Apprendi now faced up to twenty years.

—ɯ—

CHAPTER 2

CHARLES APPRENDI'S VIOLENT HATE CRIMES against the Fowlkes family were abhorrent but not widely reported beyond the town of Vineland, New Jersey. I had no clue who Apprendi was when he pleaded guilty before Judge Rushton Ridgway in July 1995. Appellate attorneys like me come on board only after the defendant has been convicted of a crime and sentenced to prison. It was Robert Luther, the Cumberland County first assistant prosecutor, who filed the fateful motion asking the trial court to sentence Apprendi to an enhanced prison term under New Jersey's Hate Crime Statute. On the same sweltering July day that Apprendi pleaded guilty to count eighteen of the indictment charging him with second-degree possession of a firearm for an unlawful purpose for the December 22, 1994, shooting, First Assistant Prosecutor Luther put Apprendi on formal notice of the state's intention to seek harsher punishment for this crime because it was racially motivated.

Hate crime statutes do not punish racist thoughts. What they punish are crimes where the accused selected the victim because of that victim's race, creed, color, ethnicity, or sexual orientation, immutable characteristics that cannot be changed.[1] In other words, hate crime statutes ask what the defendant's motive was for committing the underlying offense against a class of vulnerable victims. Motive, good or bad, is highly relevant to the sentencing decision because it reveals the defendant's character at the moment the crime was committed. As the Supreme Court of the United States noted in *Wisconsin v. Mitchell*, "It is not uncommon for a defendant to receive a minimum sentence because he was acting with good motives, or a rather high sentence because of his bad motives."[2]

First Assistant Prosecutor Luther's ministerial act of filing the motion with the trial court did not yet authorize Judge Ridgway to increase Apprendi's sentence under the Hate Crime Statute. Before the sentencing provision of the statute could kick in, Luther first had to prove to Judge Ridgway by a preponderance of the evidence that Apprendi's crime was more likely than not motivated by racial bias. The "preponderance of the evidence" standard is the lowest burden of proof in law and the easiest to meet. Picture the scales of justice in perfect balance. All it takes is the added weight of one grain of sand on the prosecution's side to tip the scales in favor of the state. Luther needed only to prove that it was more likely true than not true that Apprendi had fired his rifle into the home of the Fowlkes family as they slept simply because he did not like the color of their skin.[3]

Six weeks later, First Assistant Prosecutor Luther, defendant Charles Apprendi, and his attorney Joseph O'Neill returned to Judge Ridgway's courtroom for a testimonial hearing on the state's motion to sentence Apprendi to an extended prison term pursuant to the Hate Crime Statute. No jury was present. The New Jersey Legislature specifically authorized the judge, not a jury, to determine whether a crime was racially motivated. Apprendi's fate rested solely in Judge Ridgway's hands.

The state's first witness was Vineland Police Detective Sergeant Dennis D'Augostine, who testified that Apprendi had voluntarily confessed to him that he had fired shots at the Fowlkes home "because there were Black people living there." Detective Sergeant D'Augostine had asked Apprendi how he knew a Black family lived in the house. "I had seen one of them outside," Apprendi admitted to the officer. "I was giving them a message" that he did not want Black people in his neighborhood.[4]

The state's next witness was Michael Fowlkes Sr., one of the victims of Apprendi's shooting sprees. Fowlkes told Judge Ridgway that his was the only Black family living in the area. The Fowlkes family did not know Charles Apprendi, and Charles Apprendi did not know the Fowlkes family. The first time Michael Fowlkes Sr. ever laid eyes on Apprendi was in the early morning hours of the December 22, 1994, shooting, just after Apprendi's arrest.

"I'd say it was 4:32 a.m.," Fowlkes testified. "And me and my wife were riding down the block heading west. And we saw the officers putting Charles in the police car."

Fowlkes described the front doors of his home as two large, rectangular panes of clear glass, each bordered by a six-inch, burgundy wood frame. The precise color of the door frame was important because Apprendi was raising the defense that he was high and drunk when the Fowlkeses' "glass and purple door caught my eye."

Trying to shore up his client's dubious "purple door" defense, Apprendi's attorney pressed Michael Fowlkes Sr. on cross-examination about the color of the six-inch-wide wood frame. O'Neill asked, "Now, the front door is, I think you said, a burgundy or purplish-reddish-brown-type of color?"

"No purple, no reddish," Mr. Fowlkes insisted. "The door is burgundy."

To counter the state's compelling evidence that Apprendi's crime was motivated by skin color, not door color, Apprendi presented seven character witnesses at the hearing. All but one of these character witnesses were white. Under friendly questioning by Joe O'Neill, each witness testified that Apprendi did not have a reputation in the community for racial bias against Black people.

"The only reputation Charlie ever had was being a little crazy," one of Apprendi's college classmates told the judge.

The relevance of these witnesses' opinions that Apprendi was not a racist was greatly diminished, however, by the uncontested fact that not one of them was with Apprendi on any of the four nights when he fired his rifle into the home of the Fowlkes family because they were Black or when he confessed to Detective Sergeant D'Augostine that he had seen the Fowlkes family outside in their yard and was "giving them a message" that they were unwanted in his neighborhood. So Apprendi did what criminal defendants often do when faced with irrefutable proof of guilt: he blamed his reprehensible behavior on self-intoxication.

"I wasn't thinking. I wasn't rational," Apprendi told Judge Ridgway. "I was under the influence of alcohol and drugs and didn't know what I was doing."

Apprendi testified that he had taken "very potent" opiates between 8:00 and 9:00 p.m. on December 21 to dull the pain caused by irritable bowel syndrome, followed by seven to nine vodka tonics at two different bars after midnight on December 22, 1994. On his way home, Apprendi drove past the Fowlkeses' house. Incensed by the Fowlkeses' purple front door, Apprendi claimed, he went home and grabbed his rifle. Apprendi insisted at the hearing that he did not see any Black Santa Claus faces decorating the front doors. He denied he was racist, claiming that he had falsely confessed that the shooting was racially motivated because the police were taunting him that "a pretty little thing like you is going to be taken advantage of in jail."

—⚏—

Three weeks later, correctional officers again escorted Apprendi from the Cumberland County jail and into Judge Ridgway's courtroom for a continuation of the hearing on the state's motion to sentence Apprendi to enhanced punishment under the Hate Crime Statute. First Assistant Prosecutor Luther showed the judge the .22-caliber rifle Apprendi had used when he opened fire on the Fowlkeses' home.

"Judge, this is not an ordinary scope on a rifle, it has a laser scope. And if the court would look at the wall over there, I've got the scope on right now. There's a red laser beam on the wall of the court showing that this type of weapon is deadly accurate. And I would submit that this shows that this defendant was not drunk or under the influence of drugs when he was firing it repeatedly at the Fowlkes residence on December 22, 1994." Charles Apprendi, Luther told the judge, "knew exactly what he was doing."

"Amen," Michael Fowlkes Sr. called out from his seat in the spectators' section of the courtroom.

Luther continued. "Judge, the defendant says there was no racial animus here. He was just driving by the Fowlkes's home and the purple door caught his attention. That's what he tells the court," the prosecutor said. "First of all, Judge, the door's not purple; it's burgundy. But even if the court thinks burgundy is similar to purple, the more important point is that most of that door was glass. There was only a six-inch wooden border around that door. The door and the house sit 180 feet from the roadway. So what was it that Mr. Apprendi saw on that door that caught his attention? Judge, it wasn't the color purple. It was the Black Santa Claus on the door that caught his attention."

Luther added that "the state doesn't have to prove Apprendi's history of racism. The state just has to prove that the criminal acts that this defendant committed were done with the purpose to intimidate based on race. And I think the state clearly has met that burden."

Judge Ridgway, as the finder of fact, ruled in the state's favor. The judge told the parties, "Quite frankly, I have difficulty believing that Charles Apprendi was attracted to the Fowlkeses' front door by the color. And that something went off in his intoxicated state of mind that he wanted to destroy the door." The judge recalled Apprendi's admission under oath at the plea hearing just two months earlier that his unlawful purpose for the shootings was to frighten the family sleeping inside the house.

"One need look no further than Apprendi's own statement to the police and to the court," the judge found, "to be satisfied that the crime was motivated by racial bias."

Judge Ridgway ruled that Apprendi was subject to an extended term of imprisonment under New Jersey's Hate Crime Statute. Instead of facing a maximum prison sentence of ten years, Apprendi now faced a maximum prison sentence of twenty years.

In anticipation of sentencing, Mattie Harrell Fowlkes gave to Judge Ridgway a four-page, handwritten victim-impact statement revealing the devastating emotional trauma her family had endured as victims of Apprendi's hate crime.[5]

"A bullet went through my eight-year-old baby's room. My son has not slept in that room since that day," Mattie Fowlkes wrote to the judge. "I don't teach my children to hate nor was I taught to hate. Everyone is entitled to their own opinions, likes and dislikes, but no one walking God's earth has the right to tell me or anyone else where to live." Mattie Fowlkes wondered, "How can someone hate another human being simply because the pigmentation of our skins is different?"

Referring to Mattie Fowlkes's letter, Judge Ridgway asked those in the courtroom to envision themselves in the victims' shoes:

"Can you imagine the terror of somebody living in their house and having shots fired at? Just because they had something they couldn't control, the color of their skin. It's frightening."

Michael Fowlkes Sr. gave an in-person victim-impact statement. He turned to Charles Apprendi sitting at the defense table in the courtroom and addressed him directly:

You can think anything that you want to think, Charles. But if you choose to act those thoughts out, then there is a price to pay. And that price is your freedom. You chose to do this. We didn't. We didn't know you. Didn't want to know you. But now, unfortunately, Charles, we are entwined for life. To watch those kids' faces—my three kids come down in that foyer and to see the bullet holes, glass, sprayed all over everywhere, that is an unforgettable sight, Charles. And, Charles, being that you did this, I wouldn't even wish that on you.

His family's dream home, Michael Fowlkes said, became a nightmare: "We all want a piece of the American dream, you know? And that first month in that house was a beautiful time. But now when people ride by they say, 'That's the house that the pharmacist shot at because they were Black.'" Michael Fowlkes asked Judge Ridgway to impose the maximum sentence of twenty years to punish Apprendi for "his heinous, terribly stupid acts."

Before deciding how long Apprendi's prison term would be, the judge offered Apprendi a final opportunity to speak on his own behalf.

"I'd like to apologize to Mr. Fowlkes and his family for what I really did," Apprendi said. "I realize that it is very wrong. I am honestly very sorry that I did this. I know I deserve to be punished for what I did."

Apprendi's remorse was fleeting.

"Race had nothing to do with this case, Your Honor," Apprendi protested. "None at all. There are so many lies and distortions and twisting of facts in this case that it would take me at least three hours to explain it to the court. My statement was not voluntary. I was just pounded by that detective. And then he goes on the stand and lies about it. I can't do anything about that," Apprendi complained. "As far as this Black Santa on the door, I never—this right now is the first time in the past nine months that I've ever heard of this fact about the Black Santa. I didn't see any Black Santa on the door." Apprendi insisted it was the purple front door that had "attracted my eye."

Judge Ridgway didn't buy Apprendi's excuses and sentenced him on count eighteen to an extended term of twelve years in state prison under New Jersey's Hate Crime Statute. This sentence was two years longer than the ten-year maximum prison term Apprendi faced if the Hate Crime Statute did not apply.[6]

The Fowlkes family felt that Apprendi's twelve-year sentence was a much too lenient "slap on the wrist."[7] Unsurprisingly, Charles Apprendi felt that his twelve-year prison sentence was too harsh. So Apprendi filed a formal notice of appeal with the Clerk's Office for the Superior Court of New Jersey, Appellate Division (the state's intermediate appellate court), in Trenton, the capital of New Jersey.

This is where I came in.

—ɯ—

CHAPTER 3

"MOM! WHERE ARE MY SNEAKERS?"

(*Oh, Jordan, not this again. If I'm late for work, I'll never find a parking spot.*)

"Did you check your bedroom closet?"

"Yes," Jordan yelled from upstairs.

He did not check his bedroom closet. His sneakers were exactly where he had put them away the night before. But, for my five-year-old, it was a lot easier to have Mom stop whatever she was doing, trudge up the steps, and look for his shoes than it was for him to slide open his closet door. Sneakers securely Velcroed on each foot, Jordan climbed into the back seat of my forest green Honda Accord for the car ride to kindergarten. We belted out songs from the Broadway musical *Les Miserables* the whole way there. I kissed my son goodbye and handed him his Power Rangers backpack. Jordan skipped into the classroom, already dreaming about the crustless peanut butter and strawberry jelly sandwich Dad had packed for his lunch.

I swapped out the *Les Miz* compact disc for Bruce Springsteen, drove out of the school parking lot, and began my hour-long commute to Trenton, New Jersey. By the fall of 1995, when Charles C. Apprendi Jr. was sentenced under the Hate Crime Statute, I had been a deputy attorney general with the New Jersey Office of the Attorney General, Division of Criminal Justice, Appellate Section, in Trenton, for nearly a decade. Before that, I was an assistant district attorney in the Appeals Bureau of the Bronx district attorney's office in New York City for close to three years.

My interest in criminal law was sparked during the summer between my first and second years of law school when I interned with the criminal trial division of the Legal Aid Society in Brooklyn, New York. I shadowed Stacey, a public defender with a crushing workload and a paltry annual salary. My first assignment was to draft a search-and-seizure motion in hopes of suppressing the vials of crack cocaine recovered from one of Stacey's clients during what appeared from the police report to be an illegal arrest. Search-and-seizure law is grounded in the Fourth Amendment to the United States Constitution and protects citizens from overreaching governmental authority. I had no idea then how prevalent search-and-seizure motions were. Criminal defendants probably file more pretrial motions based on Fourth Amendment claims than on any other type of legal argument. All I knew in the summer of 1982 was that this constitutional law stuff was *far* more interesting than anything I had learned in my first-year contracts and property classes.

Stacey didn't fit the stereotype of defense attorneys, who, by the early 1980s, were still portrayed on television by older, gray-haired, white gentlemen (think Perry Mason and Ben Matlock). Stacey was female and petite. So was I! Stacey had long, brown hair. So did I! I could be Stacey! As lawyers for the poorest criminals in the criminal justice system, public defenders are a bulwark against excesses by state and federal police, prosecutors, and judges. It is very taxing work. Their clients include murderers, rapists, and child molesters, the absolute worst of the worst, who may be mentally ill, threatening, and uncooperative. Public defenders are dedicated to what they do because they fervently believe that indigent criminals are entitled to the same quality defense of their constitutional rights afforded to wealthy, white-collar criminals with the means to pay costly legal fees charged by private counsel. That summer, I came to share that belief, and after close to forty years working for the other side, I still do.

I became a prosecutor and not a public defender after graduating law school for the simple reason that the Bronx district attorney's office offered me a job and the Legal Aid Society of New York did not. Three years later, when I moved to New Jersey and searched for a new position, I interviewed with the criminal Appellate Section of the Office of the Public Defender, a counterpart to New York's Legal Aid Society. One of the benefits of working for the Office of the Public Defender, said Lois DeJulio, the supervising attorney who interviewed me, was that if one of my cases happened to find its way to the Supreme Court of the United States, it would not be hijacked by a more senior attorney. *Ha!* I thought. *Fat chance of ever getting a case up to the United States Supreme Court.* The offer was tempting yet unrealistic. Ultimately, I chose to stay on the prosecution side and joined the Appellate Section of the Division of Criminal Justice within New Jersey's Office of the Attorney General.

My new office was on the sixth floor of the Richard J. Hughes Justice Complex in downtown Trenton. Nicknamed the "Death Star," the Hughes Justice Complex is a ten-story glass-and-steel structure comprising three separate buildings connected by a glass atrium. The two larger buildings are joined together at a right angle. Inside these two buildings are the offices where the state's business is conducted. Narrow, open bridges suspended high above the concrete lobby floor link these two office wings to the third building housing the New Jersey Supreme Court courtroom on the eighth floor and the New Jersey Appellate Division courtroom on the fifth floor.

Entering the glass atrium of the Hughes Justice Complex is like walking into a fog bank. Everything is murky and slightly damp. Thick layers of dust coat the exposed steel beams crisscrossing the high ceiling. Despite all of the glass, the Justice Complex feels claustrophobic. Barely any sunlight filters through the hermetically sealed, gray-tinted windows—not that my interior office had any windows. But I wasn't complaining. The windows in my former office in the Bronx district attorney's office were pocked by bullets fired years earlier by an angry resident of the apartment building across the alley.

My job at the Division of Criminal Justice in Trenton was pretty much like my former job in the Bronx. As the attorney representing the state of New Jersey in an appeal, I wrote legal briefs in response to the briefs filed by criminals convicted in the twenty-one New Jersey counties. I was one of about forty deputy attorneys general in the Appellate Section at the time. My appellate colleagues in the twenty-one New Jersey county prosecutors' offices also handle large numbers of criminal appeals.

The types of legal arguments raised on appeal by criminal defendants depend on what happened at the trial below. Defendants allege all sorts of perceived errors tainting their convictions and sentences. An appellate attorney might argue that the search of her client's car for drugs and firearms was illegal, a particular juror was biased and should have been removed from the panel, the judge improperly admitted prejudicial hearsay evidence, the assistant prosecutor's closing argument to the jury exceeded the bounds of permissible advocacy, the jury instructions were incorrect and confusing, the sentence imposed was too long, or all of the above.

Every week, like clockwork, dozens of appellate briefs and hundreds of trial transcripts are filed by attorneys on behalf of convicted defendants with the Superior Court of New Jersey, Appellate Division, which is the state's intermediate appellate court. And every week, copies of these briefs and transcripts are piled atop a two-tier, gray steel metal library cart for distribution to the attorneys in the Appellate Section in the Division of Criminal Justice. Hearing the squeaky wheels of the library cart slowly rolling down the hallways filled us with dread. Who among us would have yet another assignment added to our already overwhelming caseloads? We sent up silent prayers that, like the Angel of Death, the cart would pass by our offices without stopping. "Ask not for whom the assignment cart rolls; it rolls for thee."[1]

Regardless of the crimes committed or the issues raised in a defendant's appeal, my responsibility was to point out in sixty-five letter-size pages or less why there was no error at the defendant's trial or, if there was error, why it did not cast doubt on the defendant's convictions or sentence (called "harmless error"). After both parties file their respective briefs with the Clerk's Office of the Appellate Division, defense counsel and I report for oral argument, where two to three appellate judges pepper us with questions or look at us with blank stares as we take our turns standing at the podium.[2] The attorney for the defendant presents his argument first. Next up is the attorney for the state who presents the opposing viewpoint. The defense is then given one last chance to rebut the state's arguments.

Appellate arguments can be fairly dull to the casual observer. There are no jurors or witnesses, just judges and attorneys in the academic atmosphere of an austere appellate courtroom. The judges ask the attorneys questions, and the attorneys answer those questions to the best of their ability. It's very subdued. No one stands up and objects while an attorney presents her argument. Lawyers don't break down at the podium under withering cross-examination. There is no pounding on counsel table or gaveling from the bench. No one yells, "Order in the court!" or throws themselves on the mercy of the judge.

And, unlike jury trials, which conclude with the loud bang of the gavel, appellate arguments end with, well, nothing. When an appellate argument is over, the judge with the most seniority on the panel politely thanks counsel and says, "We will take this case under advisement." The attorneys depart the courtroom without knowing the outcome of the case. We then wait weeks or months for a decision from the intermediate appellate court to find out whether the defendant's convictions and sentence are upheld (I win) or whether the defendant gets a new trial or reduced sentence (I lose). While I wait, I write more responding briefs and argue more cases, resulting in more waiting. Sometimes, but not often, after the Appellate Division has issued its opinion, the Supreme Court of New Jersey will grant a petition filed by the losing party, and the case heads to the next appellate level for more briefing and another oral argument.

I am drawn to appellate litigation because I hate the sight of blood. I have been a prosecutor since 1984 and, in all that time, have managed never to see a dead body or attend an autopsy. Whenever I am required to view photographs of a particularly gruesome murder scene in order to respond to an appellate claim that the admission of these photographs at the defendant's trial was unduly prejudicial, I will ask a colleague with a strong stomach to look at them first and describe them to me so I know what to expect before I have to see them. And I learned the hard way never to open an unmarked manila envelope of loose photographs tucked inside a prosecutor's file lest they be the ones too gory to show to the jury.

I also prefer appellate litigation because trial litigation is barbaric. No matter how well prepared the trial prosecutor is, an unexpected turn of events beyond his or her control remains a constant threat. The judge might prohibit the state from introducing crucial evidence against the defendant. The state's star witness might recant his or her earlier statement to the police or blurt out something extraordinarily prejudicial despite prior warnings by the judge. And then there are the twelve jurors selected to sit in judgment of the defendant, each juror carrying into the deliberation room his or her own set of values and unique life experiences. There are far too many unforeseen variables at trial and way too many opportunities for things to go awry.

Not to mention that you must remain on constant high alert throughout a jury trial, regardless of how many weeks that trial drags on. No wondering what to cook for dinner while the judge reads complicated instructions aloud to the jury; no furtively checking email on your phone while opposing counsel cross-examines your witnesses. You must be ready to jump up from your seat at counsel table with the relevant objection the nanosecond the other side oversteps its bounds. That's a lot of pressure.

Appellate litigation, on the other hand, is predictable in its predictability, which suits me just fine. Assignments land on my desk in tidy packages containing little more than the defendant's brief and the trial transcripts. By the time a convicted criminal defendant files his or her appeal to the state's intermediate appellate court, the witnesses have testified, the jury has rendered its guilty verdict, and the physical evidence lending visual drama to the trial proceedings (bloodstained clothing, autopsy photographs, firearms, bullet fragments, semen-stained undergarments, decks of heroin, bank records, and videotaped confessions) has been returned to the evidence vault. All the live spectacle unfolding during a trial is memorialized by the court stenographer and reduced to black-and-white typewritten transcripts.

New Jersey judges have long compared these trial transcripts to "a dehydrated peach; it has neither the substance nor the flavor of the peach before it was dried."[3] Aside from coffee stains and the occasional smear of blood on a transcript from a surprisingly painful paper cut, there is no color at all. My goal is to breathe life back into these inert stacks of paper by weaving the witnesses' testimony into a gripping narrative and crafting a persuasive rebuttal to the defendant's legal arguments. And all this must be accomplished without misrepresenting the trial record or the law. No twisting or embellishing the facts, no ignoring case law that undercuts my legal argument. A prosecutor's job is to seek justice, not to obtain criminal convictions or win on appeal at all costs.

Trial attorneys often regard their appellate colleagues as some strange breed of reclusive legal whizzes. As for me, only the reclusive part is true. That's because I suffer from impostor syndrome. My high-achieving, perfectionist personality often lies to me. In those unsettling moments, I am sure that my cover will be blown and I will be exposed as an incompetent fraud. An assistant prosecutor in the heat of trial who suddenly appears in the doorway of my office asking, "Can I run something by you?" sends chills down my spine. That prosecutor didn't just stop by to shoot the breeze. He's looking for a quick answer to a complex legal problem. If he's at the point where he's seeking help from an appellate attorney, he needs an answer *now!* And I want to help; I really do. But I'm frozen with fear that I won't know the answer off the top of my head or, worse, I'll give him the wrong advice.

Yet stick me in front of a panel of judges, and I have little fear. I've entered the courtroom prepared to do battle and my lawyer persona takes charge. My body language conveys confidence, my voice is tinged with authority, and I successfully manage to keep my impostor syndrome self-doubt at bay—until, of course, the argument is over and the perfect answer I *should* have given rings out in my head, clear as a bell, during the car ride home.

CHAPTER 4

I NEVER KNOW WHAT TYPE of criminal appeal will land on my desk. I've handled everything from murders and sexual assaults to arson and insurance fraud. I once had a case where a jockey was convicted of fixing standardbred harness races at a local track.

Anne Paskow, the chief of the Division of Criminal Justice's Appellate Section, employed a not-so-scientific method to divvy up the endless stream of defendants' briefs filed with the intermediate appellate court. Defense briefs were rated by the complexity or novelty of the issues raised combined with the number of attendant trial transcripts. The more experienced attorneys were assigned the more challenging appeals. On March 27, 1996, the defense brief in *State of New Jersey v. Charles C. Apprendi, Jr.*, Appellate Division Docket No. A-1587-95T2, was assigned to me. Paskow rated Apprendi's brief "A plus" for the importance, novelty, and difficulty of the constitutional arguments raised and "short plus" for the brevity of the transcripts. Stacked one on top of another, the three transcripts of Apprendi's plea, extended-term, and sentencing hearings measured a mere two inches thick.

Because Charles Apprendi was challenging the constitutionality of a New Jersey statute, his brief raised an issue of statewide importance, hence its "A plus" rating. No one in my office, including me, however, had an inkling that this issue would one day pique the interest of the Supreme Court of the United States. Few cases do. Would Anne Paskow have assigned the *Apprendi* appeal to me had she known it would end up before SCOTUS? I've never asked her because I don't want to know the answer. Not that I wasn't up to the monumental task, at least in my own mind. (The flip side to my impostor syndrome is my often-overinflated ego.) But coveted United States Supreme Court cases were usually rewarded to deputy and assistant attorneys general with more seniority than me.

The novel issue raised by Apprendi's brief was intriguing. His attorney Joseph O'Neill argued that, because Judge Ridgway's finding of racial bias bumped up Apprendi's maximum sentence for a second-degree offense (between five and ten years) into the statutory sentencing range reserved for first-degree offenses (between ten and twenty years), racial bias was not a sentencing factor at all but an additional element of an entirely new first-degree offense. Unless a jury found that his client's crime was racially motivated or his client expressly pleaded guilty to this fact, O'Neill wrote, the judge could not sentence Apprendi to an additional two years in prison. The crux of O'Neill's claim on appeal was the distinction between a sentencing factor and an element of an offense. I had never come across this issue before and had much to learn before I could start writing my responding brief.

It all starts with the text of the Bill of Rights to the United States Constitution. The jury trial clause of the Sixth Amendment provides, "In all criminal prosecutions the accused shall enjoy the right to . . . trial, by an impartial jury." The due process clause of the Fourteenth Amendment provides, "No State shall make or enforce any law which shall abridge the privileges and immunities of citizens of the United States; nor shall any state deprive any person of life, liberty, or property without the due process of law." Together, these two clauses require the state to prove each and every element of the crime charged, including the defendant's unlawful intent (*mens rea*) and his or her unlawful action (*actus rea*), before the defendant may be convicted of that crime following a jury trial or a guilty plea.

And the state must prove each element of the crime beyond a reasonable doubt, the most onerous evidentiary standard in law. New Jersey judges instruct jurors sitting on criminal trials that "proof beyond a reasonable doubt is proof, for example, that leaves you firmly convinced of the defendant's guilt. In this world, we know very few things with absolute certainty. In criminal cases the law does not require proof that overcomes every possible doubt."[1] But the jury better be pretty damn sure the defendant is guilty beyond all reasonable doubt before voting to convict him of a crime that might send him to prison for decades.[2]

In contrast, sentencing factors are circumstances that trial judges consider in setting an appropriate term of imprisonment within a statutorily prescribed range of years after the defendant has been found guilty of an offense by a jury or guilty plea. A criminal defendant like Charles Apprendi convicted in New Jersey of a second-degree crime faces an ordinary term of imprisonment between five and ten years. The sentencing judge balances aggravating and mitigating factors personal to that defendant to determine where within the five-to-ten-year statutory range the appropriate prison term should fall. Aggravating sentencing factors found by the judge (for example, the gravity and seriousness of the psychological harm Apprendi inflicted on his victims) push the prison term toward the highest end of the statutory sentencing range of ten years. Mitigating sentencing factors found by the judge (for example, Apprendi's agreement to compensate the Fowlkes family for the physical damage to their home) push the prison term toward the lowest end of the statutory sentencing range of five years.

The judge must find the existence of an aggravating sentencing factor by a preponderance of the evidence before it may be included in the sentencing calculation.[3] "Preponderance of the evidence" is the least onerous evidentiary burden in law. Under this one-grain-of-sand burden of proof, the state must establish that a fact (again, for example, the gravity and seriousness of the psychological harm Apprendi inflicted on his victims) is more likely true than not true.[4] If the evidence is in equipoise, the state's evidentiary burden has not been met.

The "preponderance of the evidence" standard was the one used by Judge Ridgway when he determined that it was more likely true than not true that Apprendi's crime was racially motivated. The result of the judge's factual finding pushed the sentencing range for Apprendi's second-degree conviction into the sentencing range reserved for a first-degree conviction. O'Neill argued on appeal, as he did at trial, that only a jury could make the finding of racial bias that led to enhanced punishment, and it had to do so under the rigorous "beyond a reasonable doubt" standard of proof.

Although Apprendi's argument was pending before the New Jersey state courts, it raised important questions of federal constitutional law: did the

Sixth and Fourteenth Amendments of the United States Constitution permit Judge Ridgway to increase Charles Apprendi's sentence for the crime of possession of a firearm for an unlawful purpose beyond the ordinary maximum term of ten years in state prison based on his finding, by a preponderance of the evidence, that Apprendi's crime was racially motivated? Or did this finding of fact, which bumped the sentencing range for Apprendi's second-degree crime into the sentencing range for a first-degree crime, have to be found by a jury beyond a reasonable doubt? No one had challenged the constitutionality of New Jersey's Hate Crime Statute in the appellate courts before. This was my initiation into the "sentencing factor versus element of the offense" debate that would preoccupy most of my waking hours (and some of my sleeping hours, too) for the next four years.

— ɯ —

New Jersey court rules gave me thirty days to file my responding brief in the state's intermediate appellate court, but I was far too busy chiseling away at other assignments to tackle the *Apprendi* appeal right away. I needed an extension of time. I called Apprendi's attorney Joseph O'Neill to ask for his consent to an additional thirty days. Joe and I had never had a case together before, so this was our very first phone conversation. We had no idea then what was in store for us. With Joe's kind permission, the new due date for my brief was Tuesday, May 28, 1996, the day after the long Memorial Day weekend. I barely made my new deadline.

As counsel for the state, I emphasized in my responding brief that it didn't matter at the plea stage what Apprendi's motive was for firing his rifle into the Fowlkes house, because it's been the law of the land since 1894 when the United States Supreme Court held in *Pointer v. United States* that motive is not constitutionally required to be an essential element of any state or federal crime.[5] "The presence or absence of a motive for the commission of the offense charged is always a legitimate subject of inquiry. . . . but it is not in any case indispensable to a conviction."[6] Often it is simply impossible to uncover any adequate motive for a crime, such as murder, but that impossibility does not prevent the state from prosecuting the defendant for killing another human being.[7] What the state is required to establish under the rigorous "beyond a reasonable doubt" standard is the accused's criminal intent.[8]

The Cumberland County Prosecutor's Office met its burden of proving Apprendi's purposeful criminal intent, I wrote, when Apprendi admitted under oath before Judge Ridgway that he possessed the .22-caliber rifle with the purpose to scare the Fowlkes family by firing bullets into their home in the middle of the night. A person acts purposefully if he or she means to act in a certain way or cause a certain result.[9] Apprendi's action (his *actus rea*) was possessing the rifle; his purposeful intention (his mens rea) was to scare the Fowlkes family. But Apprendi did not have to admit *why* he wanted to scare them. The "why" was Apprendi's motive, "the moving course, the impulse, the desire" that induced Apprendi to scare the family because they were Black.[10]

In 1996, there were no New Jersey or United States Supreme Court decisions directly on point. Coming close to what I needed was a ten-year-old SCOTUS decision, *McMillan v. Pennsylvania*.[11] In *McMillan*, SCOTUS addressed mandatory minimum sentences, the length of time a prisoner must serve before he or she becomes eligible for release on parole.[12] Charles Apprendi was challenging his twelve-year maximum sentence, not a mandatory minimum sentence, but the reasoning of *McMillan* was nonetheless helpful to my position.

McMillan examined Pennsylvania's Mandatory Minimum Sentencing Act, which authorized trial judges to sentence anyone convicted of a violent felony (such as murder, rape, robbery, and aggravated assault) to a mandatory minimum prison sentence of five years if the judge found by a preponderance of the evidence that the defendant visibly possessed a firearm during the commission of the crime.[13] Defendant Dynel McMillan shot his victim after a fight over a monetary debt and was convicted by a jury of aggravated assault. The jury was not asked to make a separate finding as to whether McMillan visibly possessed a firearm during the commission of the aggravated assault. It was the sentencing judge who found under the "preponderance of the evidence" standard that McMillan visibly possessed a firearm. The judge then imposed the mandatory minimum prison term of five years as authorized by the Pennsylvania statute.

McMillan argued to the United States Supreme Court that a judicial finding of visible possession of a firearm violated his Sixth Amendment right to a jury trial and his Fourteenth Amendment right to due process of law because the judge's finding increased his mandatory minimum prison term from zero to five years. Because of this increased mandatory prison term, McMillan asserted, visible possession of a firearm was an element of the crime for which he was being sentenced and which the jury must find beyond a reasonable doubt before the five-year mandatory minimum term could be imposed.

Writing on behalf of the majority of the court, then Justice William Rehnquist (before he was sworn in as chief justice three months later) rejected McMillan's claim. Using a multipronged approach, the *McMillan* court held that visible possession of a firearm was a sentencing factor the judge could find by a preponderance of the evidence. A multipronged approach looks at all relevant aspects of an issue. The *McMillan* court considered that the Pennsylvania statute did not create any presumptions of guilt, the statute did not relieve the prosecution of its burden of proving McMillan's guilt of aggravated assault beyond a reasonable doubt, the statute did not create a separate offense calling for a separate penalty, and the statute did not change the definition of any crime.[14] Pennsylvania's Mandatory Minimum Sentencing Act, Justice Rehnquist said, "gives no impression of having been tailored to permit the visible possession of a firearm finding to be a tail which wags the dog of the substantive offense."[15] (Coincidentally, while I was in the thick of the *Apprendi* litigation, the movie *Wag the Dog*, starring Robert DeNiro and Dustin Hoffman, was released in theaters. I was sorely disappointed to learn that the movie had nothing to do with mandatory minimum sentences.)

The Supreme Court in *McMillan* refused to draw a constitutional line between a sentencing factor and an element of the offense with a one-size-fits-all, bright-line rule. In contrast to a multipronged approach, a bright-line rule is an objective test that resolves a legal issue in a straightforward, predictable, and even-handed way.[16] With a bright-line rule, everything is black or white; there are no gray areas. For example, when a criminal suspect unequivocally invokes his constitutional right to speak with a lawyer during police interrogation, all questioning must stop until counsel has been made available to the suspect.[17] Period, end of story.

A multipronged approach, in contrast, offer litigants wiggle room to advocate their positions. Under a multipronged approach, I wrote in my brief, the Hate Crime Statute was constitutional under *McMillan* because there was no indication that the New Jersey Legislature had drafted the statute to evade the "beyond a reasonable doubt" requirement; the statute did not create any presumptions of guilt or relieve the prosecution of its burden of proving Apprendi guilty of second-degree possession of a firearm for an unlawful purpose beyond a reasonable doubt; and the statute became applicable only after Apprendi was duly convicted of that crime following his guilty plea.

One of the factors considered by the *McMillan* court, however, gave me pause. Unlike the Pennsylvania statute, which increased the mandatory minimum sentence, New Jersey's Hate Crime Statute increased the maximum sentence. Justice Rehnquist noted in *McMillan* that the argument that visible possession of a firearm under the Pennsylvania statute was an element of the offense "would have at least more superficial appeal if a finding of visible possession exposed McMillan to greater or additional punishment."[18] In other words, allowing the judge to find a fact resulting in a mandatory minimum sentence was fine, but the court might not look so kindly on a law, such as New Jersey's Hate Crime Statute, where judicial fact-finding increased a defendant's maximum sentence above the statutory limit.

I asserted in my brief to the Appellate Division that relying on this single factor to strike down New Jersey's Hate Crime Statute as unconstitutional would, in effect, create a bright-line rule, a result specifically rejected by the *McMillan* court. I had to acknowledge, though, that the two-year increase in Apprendi's maximum sentence gave his claim "more superficial appeal." But, I countered, racial bias was the same as motive, and motive has always been treated by the New Jersey and federal courts as a traditional sentencing factor that a judge may find by a preponderance of the evidence. Under *McMillan*, I concluded, New Jersey's Hate Crime Statute was constitutional.

I filed my responding brief in *Apprendi* with the Clerk's Office of the Appellate Division in June 1996 and wouldn't revisit the case until just a few days before oral argument was scheduled. Filing an appellate brief is like handing in a final exam. I am an expert on whatever subject I am addressing at the moment I am addressing it, but as soon as I turn in my test paper, it's over, and I'm on to the next subject. It's the same with appellate briefs. All the information I painstakingly researched for the assignment I most recently worked on—all the salient facts, all the pertinent legal discussions—must be immediately purged to make room for the new fact pattern and legal principles relevant to the next assignment on the conveyor belt. After nearly four decades of practicing criminal appellate litigation, my memory bank is full.

CHAPTER 5

THE WHEELS OF APPELLATE LITIGATION turn slowly in New Jersey. More than eight months after filing my responding brief with the Appellate Division's Clerk's Office, the *Apprendi* oral argument was finally held at 9:30 a.m. on Tuesday, February 4, 1997, in the Superior Court of New Jersey's Appellate Division courtroom on the fifth floor of the Hughes Justice Complex in Trenton. A few days before the argument, I opened my brief, amazed I had ever known this stuff. To prepare for oral argument, I had to become an expert all over again on the federal constitutional issues implicated by the sentencing enhancement provision of New Jersey's Hate Crime Statute.

At least the *Apprendi* argument would be heard in the same office building where I worked. Appellate Division arguments are scheduled in one of several county courthouses throughout the state. My daily commute from home to Jordan's elementary school to Trenton was long, but it was a lot better than driving north past the evil-smelling oil refineries on the New Jersey Turnpike in bumper-to-bumper traffic during the morning rush hour. One time on my way to an appellate courtroom in northern New Jersey, I was stuck in a miles-long traffic jam when a local news reporter announced on the car radio that "argument in the case of *State of New Jersey versus Samuel Manzie,* the teenager who pleaded guilty to murdering his young neighbor in Jackson Township, New Jersey, will begin within the hour."[1] *Manzie* was my case, and it did not begin within the hour, because I was still sitting in traffic.

To reach the Appellate Division courtroom inside the Hughes Justice Complex, I had to cross one of the two narrow, open concrete-and-glass bridges suspended five floors above the lobby. When I started at the Division of Criminal Justice in May 1987, I heard a rumor that the Hughes Justice Complex was designed by the engineering firm responsible for a hotel in Kansas City, Missouri, where similar walkways had collapsed six years earlier, killing more than one hundred partygoers and injuring hundreds more. This rumor was patently untrue, but, as a public building, the Hughes Justice Complex was built by the lowest qualified bidder, so I sprinted across the fifth-floor walkway to the relative structural safety of the Appellate Division courtroom for the *Apprendi* argument.

Joseph O'Neill and I appeared before a panel of three appellate judges: Burrell Ives Humphreys, Edwin H. Stern, and Barbara Byrd Wecker. In New Jersey, three appellate judges sitting on a panel instead of two can indicate several things: the case presents a pressing legal issue of statewide importance; the case started out with a two-judge panel, but a third judge was added to break a stalemate between the first two judges; or absolutely nothing at all. Based on the questioning by each of the three judges, my guess was that one of the first two options applied here. Judges Humphreys and Stern appeared to side with my argument; Judge Wecker appeared to side with Joe O'Neill's argument. It's foolish, though, for an attorney to presume she won her case based on the judges' questioning at oral argument. Sometimes you think a judge is leaning in your direction, only to be disillusioned when the decision is issued and you realize the judge was stringing you along the entire time. I left the Appellate Division courtroom fairly confident I had won, but you just never know.

Most New Jersey Appellate Division opinions are released about three weeks following oral argument. After six months, there was still no word from the *Apprendi* court. Finally, on August 19, 1997, the Appellate Division panel issued its *Apprendi* opinion. The court upheld the constitutionality of New Jersey's Hate Crime Statute and affirmed the twelve-year sentence Judge Ridgway had imposed following Apprendi's guilty plea. (I won.) Cumberland County First Assistant Prosecutor Robert Luther contacted the Fowlkes family in Vineland to inform them of the news.

Most New Jersey Appellate Division opinions are also "unpublished," meaning their holdings are of no precedential value to anyone other than the parties to the specific case addressed in that opinion. Then there are opinions written for publication, meaning their holdings are binding on all lower trial courts throughout New Jersey. The *Apprendi* decision was published, indicating the statewide importance of the federal constitutional issue raised by the defendant.

Writing for a two-judge majority, Judge Humphreys found that "the flaw in the defendant's argument is that the New Jersey Legislature has not made racial bias an element of the crime" of second-degree possession of a firearm for an unlawful purpose.[2] The judge agreed instead with the state's position that Apprendi's bad motive was a traditional sentencing factor and not an element of the offense.[3] Consequently, the appellate judge wrote, as long as a defendant is convicted of a crime by his plea of guilty or the jury's verdict, the United States Constitution permits the sentencing judge to impose an extended term of imprisonment when the judge is satisfied by a preponderance of the evidence that the crime was committed because of racial bias.[4]

Judge Humphreys acknowledged that Apprendi's claim had "superficial appeal" under SCOTUS's *McMillan* decision because the Hate Crime Statute exposed Apprendi to greater and additional punishment by bumping up his sentence of imprisonment following his guilty plea to a second-degree crime (five to ten years) into the sentencing range reserved for first-degree crimes (ten to twenty years). But, the appellate judge concluded, "this one factor standing alone does not place the statute on the 'impermissible side of the constitutional line.'"[5] Judge Stern joined Judge Humphrey's majority decision.[6]

The third member of the panel dissented. "I disagree with the majority's conclusion that it is permissible to treat a defendant's purpose in committing a crime as a mere sentencing factor rather than as an element of the crime itself," wrote Judge Wecker. To do so, she said, "is to deprive the defendant of two fundamental constitutional rights: the right to trial by jury and the right to be convicted of a crime only upon proof of guilt beyond a reasonable doubt. Those guarantees are at the heart of our constitutional system of government."[7] Under *McMillan*, the dissenting judge believed, New Jersey's Hate Crime Statute "falls on the impermissible side of the constitutional line, and violates both the United States and the New Jersey Constitutions."[8] Judge Wecker succinctly concluded, "I would reverse."[9]

Judge Wecker's dissenting opinion offered her personal expression of disagreement with Judges Humphreys and Stern, but dissenting opinions do not create legal precedent. Wecker's dissent was not binding on the *Apprendi* litigation or any future criminal case where a defendant faced enhanced sentencing under the Hate Crime Statute. It nonetheless had a significant procedural impact on the next step in the appellate process.

In New Jersey, when the judges on an intermediate appellate panel unanimously agree on the outcome of a case, the losing party must file a petition for certification to the state Supreme Court if he or she wants the final judgment of the Appellate Division reviewed and, hopefully, reversed. Filing a petition for certification offers no guarantee, however, that the losing party will get its day before the state Supreme Court. The Supreme Court of New Jersey exercises its discretion sparingly in deciding whether to grant or deny a petition.[10] But there is an exception to this rule. When an Appellate Division judge writes a dissenting opinion, New Jersey court rules grant the losing party the automatic right to take its case directly to the Supreme Court of New Jersey on the issue addressed by the dissenting judge.[11] Charles Apprendi did not have to file a petition and hope that the Supreme Court of New Jersey granted certification. His case would be heard as of right by the state's highest appellate court on the basis of Judge Wecker's dissent.[12]

—◊◊◊—

Initially, it appeared that the litigation in the Supreme Court of New Jersey would be a replay of the litigation in the Appellate Division. Joe O'Neill filed a brief arguing that the Appellate Division majority had reached the wrong conclusion; I filed a responding brief arguing that the Appellate Division majority had reached the right conclusion. Same old wine in a brand-new bottle. But my win in the Appellate Division offered me no assurance of a win in the Supreme Court of New Jersey.

And then the benevolent appellate gods smiled down on me.

On March 24, 1998, three months after I filed my *Apprendi* brief with the Supreme Court of New Jersey but before oral argument was scheduled, the Supreme Court of the United States waded into the "sentencing factor versus element of the offense" waters in *Almendarez-Torres v. United States,* a decision strongly supporting my position that motive was a traditional sentencing

factor.[13] Defendant Hugo Roman Almendarez-Torres pleaded guilty in a
Texas federal district courtroom to unlawfully returning to the United States
after he was deported. Almendarez-Torres admitted during his plea hearing
that his initial deportation followed his three convictions in the United States
for aggravated felonies. At the later sentencing hearing, Almendarez-Torres's
attorney argued that, because the federal indictment charging his client with
unlawful entry following deportation did not mention the three prior aggravated felonies, Almendarez-Torres was guilty of "simple" unlawful reentry
under section (a) of the federal criminal statute.[14] In turn, the attorney argued,
Almendarez-Torres could not be sentenced to more than two years in prison,
the maximum penalty authorized by section (a).[15]

The federal district court judge rejected this argument, finding that the
three prior convictions for aggravated felonies qualified Almendarez-Torres
for a maximum prison term of up to twenty years under a different section of
the same statute. Almendarez-Torres was sentenced to seven years in federal
prison due to his three prior convictions.[16] After an unsuccessful appeal to the
federal circuit court, Almendarez-Torres's case was heard by the United States
Supreme Court in October 1997.

Five months later, in March 1998, SCOTUS upheld the constitutionality of
the federal statute authorizing the trial judge to increase Almendarez-Torres's
sentence above the two-year maximum for "simple" unlawful reentry because
of Almendarez-Torres's prior criminal history.[17] The Supreme Court held
that the statute did not define a separate crime based on the defendant's recidivism.[18] The court rejected Almendarez-Torres's call for a bright-line rule
"that any significant increase in a statutory maximum sentence would trigger
a Constitutional 'elements requirement.'"[19] SCOTUS opted instead to follow the multipronged approach of *McMillan v. Pennsylvania*.[20] In a majority
opinion written by Justice Stephen Breyer, the court held in *Almendarez-
Torres* that a criminal defendant's prior commission of a serious crime was
"as typical a sentencing factor as one might imagine."[21] A defendant's criminal
history could be considered by a trial judge under the "preponderance of the
evidence" standard in imposing an enhanced sentence above the ordinary
statutory term.[22]

The 5-4 decision in *Almendarez-Torres* birthed unusual alliances of justices cutting across the ideological spectrum. Justice Breyer, the author of

the majority opinion, was among the Supreme Court's more liberal justices, but the four justices who joined him in the majority were among the court's conservative core: Chief Justice Rehnquist and Associate Justices Sandra Day O'Connor, Anthony Kennedy, and Clarence Thomas.

The Supreme Court's archconservative, Justice Antonin Scalia, rejected the majority's reasoning. Justice Scalia wrote in his dissenting opinion in *Almendarez-Torres* that only a jury could make the factual finding that subjected a criminal defendant to a prison term greater than the statutory maximum for the underlying crime.[23] Joining Justice Scalia were liberals John Paul Stevens, David Souter, and the "Notorious RBG" herself, Ruth Bader Ginsburg.[24] Regardless of their differing ideologies, five members of the Supreme Court united to form the majority opinion in *Almendarez-Torres*, and in the legal world, the majority rules, even if it's by just a single vote.

The timing of the *Almendarez-Torres* opinion was extraordinary. It's rare for a United States Supreme Court opinion directly addressing your argument to be decided while your case is pending before the state Supreme Court. And the law established in *Almendarez-Torres* favored New Jersey. SCOTUS said it was okay for a judge to increase a defendant's sentence above the statutory maximum term based on the traditional sentencing factor of a prior criminal conviction. Substitute the word *motive* for *prior criminal conviction*, I thought, and New Jersey's Hate Crime Statute was clearly constitutional.

Buoyed by the *Almendarez-Torres* opinion, I immediately jotted off a supplemental letter to the Supreme Court of New Jersey to alert the justices to the new SCOTUS decision supporting the state's position. And then I waited. Seven more months would pass before oral argument in *State v. Charles C. Apprendi, Jr.* would be held in the Supreme Court of New Jersey.

—※—

On October 6, 1998, Matthew Shepard, an openly gay freshman at the University of Wyoming, went for a beer at a dive bar in Laramie, Wyoming. Two high school dropouts, Russell Henderson and Aaron McKinney, pretended to befriend Shepard as part of a plan to rob him. Henderson and McKinney lured Shepard into their pickup truck and, after stealing $20 from Shepard's wallet, drove their victim about a mile out of town to a remote field. McKinney pistol-whipped Shepard's face and head repeatedly with the butt of a Smith & Wesson revolver, bludgeoning his skull. McKinney and Henderson then lashed Shepard with a clothesline to a crude log fence in near-freezing temperatures and drove away. Eighteen hours later, a teenager spotted Shepard hanging from the fence, initially mistaking the college student for a fallen scarecrow. Shepard's face was so badly swollen from the beating that his parents barely recognized their son in the hospital. Shepard never regained consciousness and died six days later on Monday, October 12, 1998. Matthew Shepard had been the victim of a vicious, homophobic hate crime.

By sheer coincidence, oral argument in *State v. Charles C. Apprendi, Jr.* in front of the seven justices of the Supreme Court of New Jersey was scheduled for Tuesday, October 13, the morning after Matthew Shepard died. Focusing on the hate crime aspect of the *Apprendi* case, local and national media outlets flocked to the courtroom on the eighth floor of the Hughes Justice Complex in Trenton to watch the argument. Shepard's murder had put New Jersey's Hate Crime Statute squarely in the spotlight. The clerk of the Supreme Court of New Jersey, Stephen W. Townsend, called me at home early that morning to let me know that Chief Justice Deborah Poritz was permitting a single television camera and a single still camera to be set up in the courtroom to record the proceedings. Media outlets would share these recorded images. The *Apprendi* case was garnering national attention, and I was proud to be representing the state of New Jersey in its efforts to root out and punish hate crime.

I sprinted across the suspended walkway to the eighth-floor courtroom and took my seat at the counsel table reserved for respondents. The presence of the lone television camera trained on arguing counsel did not distract me, and I soon tuned out the soft clicks of the photographer's still camera to concentrate on the court proceedings. Arguing on behalf of his client, Joseph O'Neill stepped up to the podium first. As the losing party in the Appellate Division, Joe faced an uphill battle to begin with. His case was made that much more difficult by the recent decision in *Almendarez-Torres* in which SCOTUS found that not every fact increasing a defendant's sentence above the statutory maximum was an element of the crime that must be proved to the jury beyond a reasonable doubt.

O'Neill was undeterred by the *Almendarez-Torres* opinion. He argued to the New Jersey high court that the question whether a defendant committed a crime with a purpose to intimidate is a factual issue, not a legal issue.[25] "That requires a jury finding," O'Neill said.[26]

Supreme Court of New Jersey Justice Stewart Pollack pointed out to O'Neill that the provision in the Hate Crime Statute calling for an extended prison term operates only at sentencing.

"That's clear," O'Neill replied, "but that doesn't make it right. This court's duty is to correct it. A defendant should be able to enjoy all his constitutional rights. The only way to find intent would be to put it before a jury."[27]

Justice Daniel O'Hern asked O'Neill what was so morally offensive about having a judge impose the extended term instead of a jury. O'Neill responded, "You're depriving somebody of something that next to life is most important—liberty."[28]

The Office of the Public Defender, the organization representing indigent adult and juvenile clients charged with criminal and juvenile offenses in New Jersey's state courts, had joined the *Apprendi* case in the Supreme Court of New Jersey as amicus curiae in support of defendant Charles Apprendi. An amicus curiae "friend of the court" brief is written by an organization or individual who is not a party to the case but has expertise in its subject matter and a strong interest in its outcome. The Office of the Public Defender often appears as a friend of the court in the Supreme Court of New Jersey to present a comprehensive and statewide view in cases where the criminal defendant is represented by private counsel. Joseph O'Neill had a duty of loyalty to his client and he was there solely to represent Charles Apprendi. Assistant Deputy Public Defender Jacqueline E. Turner was there on behalf of all potential criminal defendants across New Jersey who might someday be subject to enhanced punishment under the Hate Crime Statute.

"New Jersey," Turner advised the court, "is the only state in the country where the decision to impose stiffer penalties on someone involved in a hate crime is left in the hands of a judge. In all other states, juries decide whether the defendant's conduct warrants a longer sentence."[29] Turner continued, "I'm not saying you can't punish hate. I'm just saying: Do it right."[30]

The justices' questions to O'Neill and Turner focused on the *McMillan* and *Almendarez-Torres* cases. This boded well for me, as both SCOTUS decisions supported my position that motive was a traditional sentencing factor and not an element of second-degree possession of a firearm for an unlawful purpose. When it was my turn, I argued to the New Jersey justices that the Hate Crime

Statute did "not relieve the prosecutor of proving guilt of the underlying crime . . . . The Legislature merely called on judges to impose lengthier sentences when they find that a defendant committed a crime based on biases, such as race, ethnic origin, religion, sex, or sexual orientation." Such crimes, I noted, were singled out for additional punishment "because the Legislature deemed them so offensive, so damaging."[31]

Appellate judges are infamous for their skill in treating one party with disfavor, only to turn on a dime and treat opposing counsel with equal disfavor when it's their turn at the podium. But I had the law on my side, and my argument went smoothly. I left the courtroom thinking about the cruelty and violence inflicted on the Fowlkes family and on Matthew Shepard simply because of the color of their skin or whom they loved. I was optimistic that the court would uphold the constitutionality of New Jersey's Hate Crime Statute. Once again, there was nothing else to do but await the court's decision as the *Apprendi* litigation inched along.

—⚬⚬—

Five months later, on March 24, 1999, while I was still waiting for the Supreme Court of New Jersey to reach a decision in *Apprendi*, the once-benevolent appellate gods threw me a curveball.

A year to the day that *Almendarez-Torres* was decided, SCOTUS issued its opinion in *Jones v. United States*, muddying the waters of the "sentencing factor versus element of the offense" debate before the court and putting New Jersey's Hate Crime Statute on shaky ground.[32] At issue in *Jones* was a federal criminal statute enacted by Congress making it a felony to carjack a vehicle while in possession of a firearm.[33] This crime was punishable by a maximum term of fifteen years in federal prison, unless the victim suffered serious bodily injury, in which case the maximum sentence rose to twenty-five years in prison. If the victim died, the maximum sentence rose to life in prison. The federal government presented evidence to the jury that defendant Nathaniel Jones and his two cohorts had carjacked the victims' vehicle at gunpoint. The unanimous jury found Jones guilty beyond a reasonable doubt of the federal crime of carjacking.

One of the victims, a man named Mutanna, suffered a perforated eardrum with numbness and permanent hearing loss when Jones's codefendant stuck the gun into Mutanna's left ear and later struck Mutanna on the head. But the jury was never asked to find whether Mutanna had suffered serious bodily injury, and its guilty verdict did not reflect this fact. It was the sentencing judge who found in a subsequent court hearing that the government's allegation that the victim had suffered serious bodily injury was more likely true than not true under the "preponderance of the evidence" burden of proof. Jones was sentenced to a maximum term of twenty-five years in federal prison.[34]

Jones's attorney argued to the United States Supreme Court that the federal carjacking statute defined three distinct crimes, rather than one single crime with a choice of three maximum penalties. Absent a jury finding of serious bodily injury, counsel asserted, Jones could not be sentenced to more than fifteen years in federal prison for carjacking. Five justices (John Paul Stevens, Antonin Scalia, David H. Souter, Ruth Bader Ginsburg, and Clarence Thomas) agreed with Jones's position. The court held in a majority opinion authored by Justice Souter that serious bodily injury to the victim was an element of the crime of robbery, and carjacking was a type of robbery. Serious bodily injury thus was an element of the federal carjacking statute that must be determined by a jury under the stringent "beyond a reasonable doubt" standard of proof before Jones could be subjected to an enhanced prison term of twenty-five years.[35]

Unlike Congress, the New Jersey Legislature has always required the jury to decide under the reasonable doubt standard whether the victim of a violent crime suffered serious bodily injury or death. The *Jones* opinion thankfully did not impact New Jersey's carjacking statute. The future of New Jersey's Hate Crime Statute, however, was not as certain. Without naming any state or federal statute in particular, the *Jones* majority strongly signaled its mistrust of criminal sentencing laws that authorized a judge to rely on any factor other than recidivism to increase a defendant's prison term above the statutory maximum for the underlying crime. The Hate Crime Statute was one of these questionable criminal sentencing laws.

Jones, like *Almendarez-Torres*, was a 5-4 decision. This time, though, Justice Thomas switched sides. When he realigned himself with the four dissenting justices in *Almendarez-Torres* (Stevens, Scalia, Souter, and Ginsburg), a new five-member majority emerged in *Jones*. Having lost Thomas as an ally, the justices who had formed the majority in *Almendarez-Torres* (Rehnquist, O'Connor, Kennedy, and Breyer) now found themselves in the minority.

If it's rare when one SCOTUS opinion directly addressing your argument is issued while your case is pending before the state Supreme Court, what are the odds of two SCOTUS opinions? And I'm not referring to an area of criminal law that the justices consider with some regularity, such as Fourth Amendment search-and-seizure. At the time the *Apprendi* appeal was assigned to me in late March 1996, there was little SCOTUS case law remotely addressing the novel federal constitutional argument raised by Apprendi's attorney. Now, in 1999, as *Apprendi* was pending before the Supreme Court of New Jersey, SCOTUS issued not one but *two* opinions (*Almendarez-Torres* and *Jones*) directly addressing the "sentencing factor versus element of the offense" debate. The odds of this SCOTUS doubleheader playing out at the same time *Apprendi* was pending in the Supreme Court of New Jersey were astronomical.

The Supreme Court of New Jersey took immediate notice of the *Jones* opinion and ordered Joe O'Neill and me to file supplemental briefs within two weeks setting forth our respective views of the impact of *Jones* on the Hate Crime Statute. *Jones* put a serious crimp in my argument that factors bumping up a criminal defendant's punishment into the next-highest sentencing range could be determined by the trial judge under the "preponderance of the evidence" standard. Now it was I, not Joe, who faced the uphill battle.

But all was not lost, at least not yet. The Supreme Court in *Jones* did not overrule its holding in *Almendarez-Torres*. A defendant's prior criminal history could still be considered by a trial judge as a traditional sentencing factor, even if the judge's finding bumped up the defendant's sentence into a higher sentencing range.[36] I could continue to argue that motive, like a prior conviction, was a traditional sentencing factor that could be found by the judge under the "preponderance of the evidence" standard. But there was a hitch.

Buried in footnote 6 of the majority opinion in *Jones* was a proposed bright-line rule that "any fact (other than prior conviction) that increases the maximum penalty for a crime must be charged in an indictment, submitted to a jury, and proven beyond a reasonable doubt."[37] If adopted by SCOTUS, this bright-line rule would replace the multipronged approach the court had employed in *McMillan* and *Almendarez-Torres*. The *Jones* court did not, however, apply this proposed bright-line rule in its analysis of the federal carjacking statute, so its articulation of this rule was what judges and lawyers call *dictum*. Dictum is an aside in a court decision that is not essential to the legal holding of that particular case and has no precedential value for future cases. "Dictum settles nothing, even in the court that utters it."[38] Although this proposed bright-line rule was relegated to a footnote in *Jones*, the fact that it was mentioned at all meant it was too important to be ignored.

My challenge was to persuade the Supreme Court of New Jersey in *Apprendi* to follow the multipronged approach of *Almendarez-Torres* and not adopt the bright-line rule proposed in footnote 6 of *Jones*. The federal carjacking statute in *Jones*, as I explained in my supplemental brief to the court, dealt with two facts (serious bodily injury and death of the victim) that New Jersey had long treated as elements of the offense that must be found by a jury beyond a reasonable doubt. The Hate Crime Statute, on the other hand, dealt with a fact that New Jersey had long treated as a traditional sentencing factor (motive) that may be found by the trial judge under the lower "preponderance of the evidence" burden of proof.

I had been so sure after the *Almendarez-Torres* decision was issued that the Supreme Court of New Jersey would uphold the constitutionality of New Jersey's Hate Crime Statute. Following *Jones*, I was far less confident. A colleague offered her sympathy: "If you're going to lose in the state Supreme Court," Catherine Foddai told me, "it might as well be because the Supreme Court of the United States ruled against you."

Cathy made an excellent point, but her words did not cheer me up.

—⁓—

The Supreme Court of New Jersey gives the attorneys in a pending case twenty-four hours' notice before its written decision is issued. The parties are not informed, however, of what the opinion will say or which side will prevail. This lack of information is frustrating for the crime victims, the attorneys, and the defendants left waiting until the text of the decision is officially released by the court the following morning at 10:00 a.m. There are no leaked bootleg copies of the opinion available to any of us, either. But this twenty-four-hour window gives the prosecutor's office sufficient time to alert the victims of a defendant's crime ahead of the release of the decision to the public and to the media. No crime victim should first learn from the six o'clock news that the Supreme Court of New Jersey has issued a decision in his or her case.

On June 23, 1999, three months after SCOTUS decided *Jones*, the Division of Criminal Justice finally got word that the Supreme Court of New Jersey would release its decision in *Apprendi* the next morning. I immediately called First Assistant Prosecutor Robert Luther at the Cumberland County Prosecutor's Office to let him know to expect the opinion the following day. Luther in turn contacted Michael and Mattie Fowlkes at their home in Vineland. We each spent an anxious night waiting to learn whether the Supreme Court of New Jersey would find that racial bias was a traditional sentencing factor under *Almendarez-Torres* (I win) or whether racial bias was an element of the crime of second-degree possession of a firearm for an unlawful purpose under *Jones* (I lose).

At ten o'clock the next morning, the Supreme Court of New Jersey issued its opinion upholding the constitutionality of the enhanced sentencing provision of New Jersey's Hate Crime Statute and affirming the judgment of the Appellate Division. I had won.

Writing for the 5-2 majority, New Jersey Supreme Court Justice Daniel O'Hern found that the bright-line rule proposed in footnote 6 of *Jones* did not apply to Apprendi's Sixth Amendment constitutional claim because the suggested rule was dictum that did not control New Jersey courts.[39] State courts must follow United States Supreme Court precedent, but they are not bound by United States Supreme Court dictum. The Supreme Court of New Jersey instead applied the multipronged approach of *McMillan* and *Almendarez-Torres*.[40]

Right off the bat, though, the court rejected my argument that the state legislature's placement of the Hate Crime Statute among the sentencing provisions of the Code of Criminal Justice indicated that a finding of a biased purpose to intimidate under the Hate Crime Statute was always meant to be a sentencing factor.[41] Justice O'Hern ruled otherwise, finding that the state legislature cannot circumvent the prosecution's "beyond a reasonable doubt" burden of proof by excising elements from the definition of the crime and placing them in a sentencing statute.[42] But that was just one prong of the multipronged test.

Four of the factors considered in *Almendarez-Torres* and *McMillan*, Justice O'Hern held, supported the conclusion that the Hate Crime Statute was constitutional. First, the Hate Crime Statute did not shift the burden of proof to Apprendi by creating a presumption of guilt on the fact of bias motivation. Second, unlike the wide differential in sentencing between a nominal fine and life in prison, the ten-year differential in sentencing Apprendi faced was relatively narrow. Third, the statute did not create a separate crime of bias intimidation calling for a separate penalty. And, fourth, "the statute gave no impression of having been tailored to permit the bias finding to be 'a tail that wags the dog of the substantive offense.'"[43]

The Supreme Court of New Jersey also agreed with the state's argument that Apprendi's biased motive or purpose to intimidate, like a prior conviction, was a traditional sentencing factor that could be found by a judge under the lower "preponderance of the evidence" burden of proof.[44] Justice O'Hern noted that the New Jersey Legislature had simply taken one factor that was always considered by sentencing courts to bear on punishment and constitutionally dictated the precise weight to be given that factor under the circumstances outlined in the Hate Crime Statute.[45] Justice O'Hern observed, "There is no real question as to this actor's purpose in shooting into his neighbors' home."[46] New Jersey's Hate Crime Statute, the justice said, "obviously requires a delicate balance of constitutional rights. We do not punish thought. We do punish more severely crimes involving particularly vulnerable victims."[47]

Justice O'Hern further noted that evidence of racial bias is extremely prejudicial to a criminal defendant. New Jersey's Hate Crime Statute erected a procedural barrier that guaranteed the jury would not hear witness testimony or view tangible evidence of a defendant's racial bias. Had Apprendi succeeded on appeal, this barrier would have come crashing down. All the damaging evidence presented to Judge Ridgway proving that Apprendi had shot at the Fowlkes house to "give them a message" that Black people were not welcome in his neighborhood would instead be presented to a twelve-member jury. This situation would create, as Justice O'Hern observed, "an added risk of prejudice for defendants. It would open trials to evidence of former acts of bias on the part of the actor."[48] In other words, Mr. Apprendi, be careful what you wish for.

Justice O'Hern made an unusual admission in the *Apprendi* opinion. He acknowledged that the New Jersey Supreme Court's conclusion that the Hate Crime Statute was constitutional might not survive SCOTUS's scrutiny. Justice O'Hern wrote, "Any disposition that we make is necessarily tentative in the sense that the final word on this subject will have to come from the United States Supreme Court."[49] O'Hern was referencing a recent amendment to the federal sentencing guidelines creating a hate crime penalty enhancement applicable to all federal crimes.[50] Similar to New Jersey's Hate Crime Statute, the Violent Crime Control and Law Enforcement Act of 1994 authorized federal trial judges to increase a defendant's sentence if the judge found the defendant intentionally selected the victim because of the race, creed, or other characteristic of the victim.[51] Justice O'Hern predicted that "eventually the United States Supreme Court will have to resolve the issue that we face in this case."[52]

Justice O'Hern was right. The United States Supreme Court did not have to wait, however, for a defendant sentenced to a hate crime penalty enhancement under the federal sentencing guidelines to resolve the "sentencing factor versus element of the offense" debate. New Jersey's native son Charles C. Apprendi Jr. was knocking on SCOTUS's door with the state's Hate Crime Statute in hand.

CHAPTER 6

I AM QUITE CERTAIN THAT in June 1999 when the Supreme Court of New Jersey issued its opinion upholding the constitutionality of the Hate Crime Statute, not one of the nine justices on the Supreme Court of the United States in Washington, DC, had heard of Charles C. Apprendi Jr., let alone was remotely aware that Apprendi had been sentenced to two additional years in a New Jersey prison for committing a hate crime. SCOTUS does not seek out cases to decide. Even if New Jersey Supreme Court Justice Daniel J. O'Hern personally called United States Supreme Court Chief Justice William Rehnquist and said, "Hey, Bill, listen, I just wrote an opinion about New Jersey's Hate Crime Statute. It's a doozy of an issue and I think you might want to look at this one," SCOTUS could not consider the case. Article III of the United States Constitution permits only the parties to the actual controversy to appear before SCOTUS.

As the criminal defendant sentenced under New Jersey's Hate Crime Statute, Charles Apprendi had standing to ask SCOTUS to declare the statute unconstitutional. A litigant asks SCOTUS to hear his or her case by filing a written petition for certiorari with the Supreme Court Clerk's Office in Washington, DC, setting forth the reasons why he or she thinks the issue is of such vital and national importance that intervention by the United States Supreme Court is imperative. The mere act of filing a petition for certiorari is no guarantee that the court will hear the case. Less than 1 percent of the petitions filed each year are granted. And a successful petition would merely get Apprendi's foot in the massive bronze doors of the United States Supreme

Courthouse. Granting Apprendi's petition would mean that SCOTUS wanted to study the merits of Apprendi's substantive arguments more closely. Apprendi would then have to file a supplemental merits brief setting forth the facts and applicable legal precedents in greater detail to convince the Supreme Court that he should win on the substantive argument presented. But first Apprendi had to seek the court's permission to hear his case.

Supreme Court Rule 13.1 gave Apprendi ninety days from the date the New Jersey Supreme Court opinion was released to file his certiorari petition with SCOTUS.[1] This ninety-day deadline is firm. If Apprendi filed his certiorari petition one day late, the Clerk's Office would refuse to accept his petition.[2] On September 17, 1999, seven days shy of his ninety-day deadline, Joseph O'Neill filed forty copies of his petition for certiorari on behalf of his client, Charles C. Apprendi Jr., and served me, as counsel representing the state of New Jersey, with three copies. As required by Supreme Court Rule 33.1, O'Neill's certiorari petition was printed in booklet format, measuring 6.25 inches by 9.25 inches, with an eggshell white cover. I don't recall whether Joe O'Neill called to let me know he was filing a certiorari petition, but it wouldn't have been out of the ordinary had he given me a heads-up. We were adversaries in name only. As with most of my opposing counsel, Joe and I got along well both in and out of court. And we shared the sneaking suspicion that the *Apprendi* litigation was destined for the Supreme Court of the United States.

In most cases, SCOTUS gives the responding party the option of submitting a short, standard waiver form in lieu of a formal brief.[3] This waiver form states, "I DO NOT INTEND TO FILE A RESPONSE to the petition for a writ of certiorari unless one is requested by the Court."[4] The state of New Jersey files waiver forms in opposition to most certiorari petitions. It is too expensive and time-consuming for the state to respond in full to every cert petition filed by New Jersey state inmates. There's not much risk to the state by submitting a waiver letter. The Supreme Court will not grant a petition filed by a criminal defendant without first considering the government's responding argument. If the Supreme Court wanted further input from the state on the merits of Charles Apprendi's petition, it would order us to file a formal brief in response.[5]

But Division of Criminal Justice Appellate Section Chief Anne Paskow and I agreed that filing a standard waiver form in answer to Apprendi's petition would be an inadequate response under the circumstances. We knew

No. _____

In The
Supreme Court of the United States

————————◆————————

CHARLES C. APPRENDI, JR.,
Petitioner,

v.

STATE OF NEW JERSEY,
Respondent.

————————◆————————

On Petition For A Writ Of Certiorari
To The Supreme Court Of New Jersey

————————◆————————

PETITION FOR WRIT OF CERTIORARI

————————◆————————

JOSEPH D. O'NEILL, ESQ.
Counsel of Record
CHARLES I. COANT, ESQ.
JOSEPH D. O'NEILL, P.A.
30 West Chestnut Avenue
P.O. Box 847
Vineland, New Jersey 08362
Phone: (856) 692-2400

RICHARD G. SINGER, ESQ.
217 North Fifth Street
Camden, New Jersey 08102
Phone: (856) 225-6181

COCKLE LAW BRIEF PRINTING CO., (800) 225-6964
OR CALL COLLECT (402) 342-2831

Petition for Writ of Certiorari in *Apprendi v. New Jersey*.

SCOTUS was going to pay extremely close attention to this one. Apprendi's petition presented an important question of federal constitutional law that was the subject of ongoing debate in the United States Supreme Court. During the eighteen months immediately prior to the day Apprendi filed his petition for certiorari, SCOTUS had twice grappled with the "sentencing factor versus element of the offense" debate, first in *Almendarez-Torres* and then in *Jones*. Both cases were 5-4 decisions, and Justice Thomas was the swing vote in each case. There was no clear consensus in the United States Supreme Court.

Other significant considerations made the *Apprendi* case the perfect vehicle for SCOTUS to take up this contentious issue. The case was "clean," meaning there were no procedural or jurisdictional barriers preempting United States Supreme Court review under Article III of the federal Constitution. Equally important was that the Hate Crime Statute had been enacted by the New Jersey Legislature, and SCOTUS owes no deference to state legislatures. SCOTUS owes deference solely to its own coequal branches of the federal government, Congress and the executive branch. For this reason, SCOTUS is hesitant to strike down statutes enacted by Congress as unconstitutional.

The federal carjacking statute in *Jones* presented this very problem, leading the court to apply the "doctrine of constitutional doubt," a legal principle that comes into play when a federal statute is unconstitutional under one interpretation but constitutional under a different interpretation. The United States Supreme Court has a duty to adopt the constitutional interpretation rather than to strike down as unconstitutional the offending portion of the federal statute enacted by Congress.[6]

SCOTUS reiterated this long-standing principle in *Jones*: "Where a statute is susceptible of two constructions, by one of which grave and doubtful constitutional questions arise and by the other of which such questions are avoided, our duty is to adopt the latter."[7] By construing the subsections of the federal carjacking statute setting forth the enhanced sentences for serious bodily injury and death of the victim as elements of the crime of carjacking and not as sentencing factors, the *Jones* court avoided striking down the federal carjacking statute as unconstitutional.[8]

But SCOTUS owed no such deference to the New Jersey Legislature. The federal constitutional question of "sentencing factor versus element of the offense," which the justices sidestepped in *Jones* under the doctrine of constitutional doubt, had just been handed to them on an eggshell white, 6.25-inch-by-9.25-inch

No. 99-478

Supreme Court of the United States

CHARLES C. APPRENDI, JR.,

Petitioner,

v.

STATE OF NEW JERSEY,

Respondent.

**On Petition for Writ of Certiorari to the
Supreme Court of New Jersey**

RESPONDENT'S BRIEF IN OPPOSITION

JOHN J. FARMER, JR.
  Attorney General of New Jersey
LISA SARNOFF GOCHMAN
  Deputy Attorney General
  Attorney of Record
DIVISION OF CRIMINAL JUSTICE
R.J. HUGHES JUSTICE COMPLEX
  P.O. Box 086
TRENTON, NEW JERSEY 08625
(609) 292-9086

October 20, 1999

Respondent's Brief in Opposition to Petition for Writ of Certiorari in *Apprendi v. New Jersey.*

paper platter by Charles C. Apprendi Jr. The justices could remove their proverbial kid gloves and deal with the federal constitutional issue presented in *Apprendi v. New Jersey* head-on.

I had thirty days to file either a waiver form or a full response opposing Apprendi's petition.[9] If I filed a waiver form, I risked that the all-but-inevitable order from SCOTUS would grant me less than thirty days to file a full response or that the strict deadline imposed would conflict with fast-approaching due dates in unrelated New Jersey state appeals. Many of my colleagues thought that submitting a waiver letter would be sufficient; so rarely does the Supreme Court grant certiorari that filing a full and formal response absent an order from the court seemed like overkill. But the *Apprendi* case just felt different, more urgent, given the recent decisions in *Almendarez-Torres* and *Jones*. So Anne Paskow and I abandoned the Appellate Section's default position of submitting a waiver letter in opposition to Apprendi's cert petition, and, on October 20, 1999, I filed with SCOTUS the requisite forty copies of my formal booklet brief with a Halloween orange cover.[10]

Halloween orange befitted a brief filed in late October, but the choice of color for the cover was not mine. There are so many different colors assigned to the booklet briefs filed by the various parties at the different stages of United States Supreme Court litigation that the court has compiled a helpful color chart for reference.[11] Covers for petitions for certiorari are eggshell white, and covers for responses to petitions for certiorari are Halloween orange.[12] If certiorari is granted, covers for the merits briefs have their own color palette: robin's egg blue for petitioners' briefs on the merits, ruby red for respondents' briefs on the merits, adhesive bandage tan for the joint appendix, celadon green or Kelly green for friend of the court briefs (depending on which party the brief supports), and daffodil yellow for reply briefs.[13] For Chief Justice Rehnquist, "this color-coding comes in very handy when you have a stack of eight or ten briefs in a particular case and can locate the brief you want by its color without having to read the covers of each."[14]

New Jersey's attorney general at the time my Halloween orange brief was filed was John J. Farmer Jr., a former federal prosecutor. In New Jersey, the attorney general is nominated by the governor and confirmed by the New Jersey Senate. As the chief legal officer for the state of New Jersey, Attorney General Farmer's powers included prosecution of serious statewide criminal activity and appeals through the Division of Criminal Justice. Attorney General

Farmer officially represented the state of New Jersey in the *Apprendi* litigation. I was merely "counsel of record," and my name was listed below Attorney
General Farmer's on the state's Halloween orange brief opposing Apprendi's
eggshell white certiorari petition.

SCOTUS's decision to grant or deny certiorari is guided by the considerations set forth in Supreme Court Rule 10.[15] This gatekeeping rule explains
that "review on a writ of certiorari is not a matter of right, but of judicial
discretion."[16] As Chief Justice Rehnquist has explained, "We receive nearly
7,000 petitions for certiorari every Term, and can grant only a tiny fraction of
them. A high degree of selectivity is thereby enjoined upon us in exercising
our certiorari jurisdiction, and our Rule 10 embodies the standards by which
we decide to grant review."[17]

Certiorari is granted "only for compelling reasons," such as when "a state
court or a United States court of appeals has decided an important question
of federal law that has not been, but should be, settled by this Court."[18] Given
this rule, it would have been disingenuous (legalese for "*Liar!*") for me to
argue in response to Charles Apprendi's petition that the issue addressed by
the Supreme Court of New Jersey did *not* present "an important question of
federal law that has not been, but should be, settled by" SCOTUS. Justice
Daniel O'Hern of the Supreme Court of New Jersey slammed the door on
that argument when he wrote in his majority opinion upholding the constitutionality of the Hate Crime Statute that "any disposition that we make is
necessarily tentative in the sense that the final word on this subject will have
to come from the United States Supreme Court."[19] I had to find some other
way to make this invitation to SCOTUS to take up Apprendi's case (no pun
intended) unappealing.

I emphasized instead that New Jersey's Hate Crime Statute punishes a
defendant's motive and not his criminal intent. SCOTUS had long recognized motive as an important factor in setting an appropriate sentence.[20] By
equating a suspect's motive with other traditional sentencing factors, I hoped
to persuade SCOTUS that New Jersey's Hate Crime Statute was constitutional under the recent case of *Almendarez-Torres* in which SCOTUS held
that a prior criminal conviction was a traditional sentencing factor.[21] The
Supreme Court of New Jersey, I noted in my responding brief, had "faithfully
applied the constitutional calculus formulated by this Court in a series of
decisions addressing the so-called 'sentencing factor versus element of the

offense' debate."[22] Citing Supreme Court Rule 10(c), I argued that state courts' adherence to United States Supreme Court precedent "means that the issue decided by the state court may implicate federal constitutional provisions, but ultimately fails to present 'an important question of federal law that has not been, but should be settled by this Court.'"

Both the petition and the opposing brief contain perhaps the only words a Supreme Court justice or his or her law clerk will read before deciding that the case is not "cert worthy" and tossing the petition onto the ever-growing "denied" pile. This is the "Question Presented." So significant is the Question Presented that the Supreme Court demands it "be set out on the first page following the cover, and no other information may appear on that page."[23] The Question Presented was Apprendi's best shot at grabbing the court's attention and my best shot at convincing the court that Apprendi's petition was not cert worthy.

As a general rule, Questions Presented are drafted to elicit a yes or no answer from the justices. In his brief on petition for a writ of certiorari to the Supreme Court of the United States, Joseph O'Neill phrased his Question Presented so that the answer would be "no" if the court agreed with him:

QUESTION PRESENTED

Whether this Court should decline the invitation of the New Jersey Supreme Court to decide whether New Jersey's hate crime law, *N.J.S.A.* 2C:44-3e, unconstitutionally provides for an extended term of imprisonment increasing the maximum possible penalty by ten years, based on proof by a preponderance of the evidence, rather than on proof beyond a reasonable doubt, and denies the defendant's rights to notice by indictment and trial by jury?[24]

I prefer the answer to the Question Presented to be "*Yes!!*" with an exclamation point or two. The more resounding the yes, the better. Not bound by O'Neill's Question Presented, I rephrased the one in the state's opposing brief in a more positive and encouraging light, hoping the Supreme Court's answer would be "*Yes!!*" and the petition would be denied:

QUESTION PRESENTED

Whether existing United States Supreme Court precedent firmly supports the conclusion reached by the Supreme Court of New Jersey that the extended term sentencing provision of the Hate Crime Statute, *N.J.Stat.Ann.* 2C:44-3e (West

1995), preserves a defendant's federal constitutional rights to due process of law, notice by indictment and trial by jury?[25]

I admit I wrote this Question Presented before falling under the spell of the Oxford comma, which is the final comma inserted in a list of three or more items. For example, the sentence "I love my dogs, Bosco and Ovaltine" might mean I have two dogs, one named Bosco and the other named Ovaltine, and I love them both. Inserting an Oxford comma in the same sentence between the word *Bosco* and the word *and* clarifies that I love my dogs and I love chocolate milk.

Using an Oxford comma is purely a stylistic choice. But given a second chance to file my formal brief in response to Apprendi's petition for certiorari, I would insert an Oxford comma between the word *indictment* and the word *and* toward the very end of my Question Presented. This small but mighty punctuation mark would emphasize that New Jersey's Hate Crime Statute preserved three independent federal constitutional rights: one, the right to due process of law; two, the right to notice by indictment; and three, the right to trial by jury. Being a grammar geek is an essential component of appellate practice. Prominently displayed atop my filing cabinet at work is a mug, a birthday gift from my friend Geraldine, who knows me well, cautioning that "I am silently correcting your grammar."

—m—

It was only in my professional role as counsel of record on behalf of the state of New Jersey that I hoped SCOTUS would deny Charles C. Apprendi Jr.'s petition. I certainly did not want to give the justices the opportunity to strike down New Jersey's Hate Crime Statute as unconstitutional after I had successfully defended its constitutionality in the state appellate courts. On a personal level, though, I wanted one of my cases to go to the United States Supreme Court so badly.

Two years earlier, in September 1997, I had won an unrelated appeal in the Supreme Court of New Jersey that I strongly believed SCOTUS might want to consider under the nascent "special needs" exception to the Fourth Amendment warrant requirement. In *State in the Interest of J.G., N.S., and J.T.*, the Supreme Court of New Jersey upheld the constitutionality of two state statutes mandating preconviction HIV/AIDS blood testing of adults and juveniles charged with sex offenses.[26] The case balanced the rights of a ten-year-old rape victim to obtain timely medical information regarding her alleged assailants' HIV status against the privacy interests of the three juveniles charged with but not yet convicted of sexual assault. I thought the novel Fourth Amendment privacy issue at stake had an excellent chance of being considered by SCOTUS if an attorney for any of the three juveniles in the case filed a petition for certiorari. Not one did.

Three months later in December, my husband Steven, our son Jordan, and I made our annual winter trip to Washington, DC, to see family and friends and tour a few of the city's many museums and national monuments. As we waited in the visitors' line on the steps of the United States Capitol, I turned to face the United States Supreme Court building on the opposite side of First Street and confidently predicted to my husband, "I am going to argue there one day."

There was absolutely no reason for me to be so sure that I would ever appear before SCOTUS. I wasn't thinking about any case in particular, let alone *Apprendi*, when I uttered this ridiculously arrogant prediction. In December 1997, the *Apprendi* decision issued by the New Jersey state intermediate appellate court was barely four months old, and it would be another month before I filed my *Apprendi* brief with the Supreme Court of New Jersey. SCOTUS, meanwhile, had heard oral argument in *Almendarez-Torres* in October 1997, but by late December of that year, as I stood on the steps of the Capitol, there was still no decision from the court. The "sentencing factor versus element of the offense" debate was a mere blip on the SCOTUS horizon at that point. I was simply disappointed that *State in the Interest of J.G., N.S., and J.T.* was not the case taking me to Washington, DC.

Any shred of hope I had of appearing before SCOTUS now hinged on Charles C. Apprendi Jr.'s petition for certiorari. On October 20, 1999, I filed my Halloween orange booklet brief in response to Apprendi's certiorari petition, outwardly concerned that SCOTUS would grant Apprendi's petition and inwardly praying it would. And then, as before, I waited.[27]

CHAPTER 7

THANKSGIVING IS MY FAVORITE HOLIDAY. It's all about family and freshly baked pumpkin muffins and deep-fried turkey and all eighteen minutes and twenty seconds of "Alice's Restaurant Massacree" without the pressure of shopping for the perfect present or the nagging feeling that I inadvertently left someone off my gift list. On Friday morning, November 26, 1999, I folded linen napkins hot out of the dryer and packed away the good china in the basement. Another overindulgent Thanksgiving dinner was in the books. But my distracted mind was 155 miles southeast in Washington, DC, where I knew that Charles C. Apprendi's certiorari petition was listed on the United States Supreme Court's appellate docket that day. In their private, wood-paneled conference room inside the courthouse in Washington, DC, the nine justices were sitting around their large, rectangular conference table discussing *my case*!

A United States Supreme Court term extends from the first Monday in October to the end of the following June after the court has released all its decisions for that term. During this nine-month session, the court conferences cases between two and four times each month. This is when the justices decide which cases to hear from the thousands of petitions filed by aggrieved civil and criminal litigants each term.

At the Friday, November 26, 1999, conference, Justice Stephen Breyer, then the most junior associate justice, closed the door of the conference room after his eight more senior colleagues entered. Aside from the justices themselves, no one—not law clerks, not support staff—was present. In an exception to the usual majority rule, only four votes, not five, are needed to grant an applicant's certiorari petition. Who, if any, of the nine justices, I wondered, would vote to grant Apprendi's petition and return the "sentencing factor versus element of the offense" debate to the court's oral argument calendar? Would it be Rehnquist, O'Connor, Kennedy, and Breyer, the four justices favoring the case-by-case approach approved in *Almendarez-Torres*? Or Stevens, Scalia, Souter, and Ginsberg, the four justices leaning toward the bright-line rule suggested in footnote 6 of *Jones*? Some combination of the eight? None at all? And where did Justice Clarence Thomas, the swing vote in *Almendarez-Torres* and *Jones*, fall along this spectrum?

"Whether to grant certiorari," Chief Justice Rehnquist observed, "is a rather subjective decision, made up in part of intuition and in part of legal judgment."[1] I had no clue what any of the justices was thinking or how they were voting. And, unfortunately for me, the results of this clandestine meeting would not be publicly announced until the following Monday morning at exactly ten o'clock. That was three very long days away.

Deep down in my appellate bones, though, I knew the Supreme Court of the United States would take this case. There was no obvious reason for the court *not* to grant Apprendi's petition. The justices had recently tackled the "sentencing factor versus element of the offense" debate in *Almendarez-Torres* (a prior conviction is a sentencing factor) and *Jones* (death and serious bodily injury are elements of the federal crime of carjacking) but failed to reach a consensus. *Apprendi* was a perfect vehicle for the justices to finesse the distinction between a sentencing factor and an element of a crime. I sensed I was standing on the brink of something big. Steven, Jordan, and my parents, who were visiting from Florida, humored me as we stood in the kitchen facing southeast toward the hulking, white marble Supreme Court building 155 miles away on Capitol Hill and offered up prayers to the appellate gods that SCOTUS would grant Apprendi's petition.

Back in the late fall of 1999, SCOTUS did not release its list of certiorari grants and denials on its website. I was wholly dependent on the telephone for this information. At exactly ten o'clock on Monday morning, November 29, 1999, after a nail-biting weekend of not knowing whether certiorari in *Apprendi* was granted or denied, I sat alone in my office in the Hughes

Justice Complex in Trenton with the door closed against the intrusions of well-meaning colleagues who were as anxious as I was to learn the outcome of the court's vote. Toes flat on the floor, my heels bouncing frantically up and down, I stared at the telephone, willing it to ring, as I waited for the call from Andrea Hampton, my contact at the National Association of Attorneys General (NAAG). Founded in 1907, NAAG is "the nonpartisan national forum for the 56 state and territory attorneys general and their staff."[2] As part of its mission, NAAG assists state appellate litigators who appear before the United States Supreme Court. Andrea Hampton received the physical certiorari lists as soon as they were released by the Supreme Court and would let me know the result of the justices' Friday, November 26 conference.

At exactly ten o'clock, nothing happened. Silence. Agonizing silence.

Calm down, I told myself. *Andrea probably hasn't even gotten the cert list yet.*

The seconds ticked by at a glacial pace. I checked my watch. 10:01. My heels bounced faster, joined by the staccato tapping of my fingernails on the metal desk. I checked my watch again. 10:02. *Surely Andrea has the cert list by now,* I thought. Still nothing. 10:03. I couldn't hear my own thoughts above the din of my fingernails drumming maniacally on the desk. 10:04. *Oh my God, why is this taking so long?* 10:05. I forgot how to breathe.

The piercing ring of the telephone at 10:06 echoing through my office scared the crap out of me. The ten-digit number on the caller ID started with 202, the area code for Washington, DC, where NAAG is headquartered. I reached for the receiver with my heart thumping wildly in my throat.

"Hello, this is Lisa Gochman at the Division of Criminal Justice."

"Good morning, Lisa, it's Andrea Hampton at NAAG. How are you today?"

"I'm fine, Andrea. How are you?" I strained to stay polite, but it was hard to maintain my composure as the shrill voice in the back of my head silently screamed, *Cut to the chase, Andrea. Cut to the chase!*

Hampton's cheerful "I'm good, Lisa, thanks!" reply was followed by an interminable split-second pause. (*Tell me already, Andrea! For God's sake, just tell me!*) I'd never been so close to having a case go up to the Supreme Court of the United States, and odds were I'd never be this close again. If certiorari was denied, the *Apprendi* litigation would abruptly end, and my hopes of arguing in the Supreme Court would be over. This was, I knew, a one-shot deal for me.

"The court granted the certiorari petition in *Apprendi versus New Jersey* this morning," Hampton told me.

These were the thirteen little words I had longed to hear, but now I wasn't certain I had heard them correctly. I asked Hampton, "Are you sure? Are you sure?" She offered to check the case list again. Another interminable split-second passed. (*Oh, great. Now Andrea thinks I'm an idiot.*)

"Yes, certiorari was granted in *Apprendi versus New Jersey.*"

She was sure.

Two hundred and forty-one certiorari petitions were considered by the justices during their conference on Friday, November 26, 1999. Review was granted in just five. *Apprendi* was the only criminal petition granted that day; the other four grants were in civil cases.[3] Because the votes of the individual justices on a certiorari petition are not made public, I did not know who voted to grant Apprendi's petition, and, frankly, I did not care. My case was heading to the United States Supreme Court regardless of who voted to get it there.

"Andrea," I said, "I have a million questions for you, but I'm too flabber-gasted to remember what they are. I'll have to call you back."

"Of course, Lisa. I'll be here."

I barely had time to process Andrea Hampton's stunning news before my office phone rang again. The 202 area code popped up a second time on my caller ID.

"Hello, this is Lisa Gochman at the Division of Criminal Justice."

"Good morning, Ms. Gochman. This is Deputy Solicitor General Michael Dreeben." The Office of the Solicitor General, located in Washington, DC, is part of the United States Department of Justice. The Office of the Solicitor General is the federal counterpart to the Appellate Section in New Jersey's Division of Criminal Justice. New Jersey Attorney General John J. Farmer Jr. and his deputies and assistants represented the state government in criminal prosecutions before the state appellate courts, including the Supreme Court of New Jersey; Solicitor General Seth Waxman and his deputies and assistants represented the United States government in criminal prosecutions before the federal appellate courts, including SCOTUS. Deputy Solicitor General Dree-ben himself argued more than one hundred United States Supreme Court cases during his thirty-plus-year career with the federal government. Aside from the attorneys within the Office of the Solicitor General and a small cadre of private lawyers with dedicated Supreme Court appellate practices, however, arguing a case in the United States Supreme Court is nearly impossible. Which is why the very first thing Michael Dreeben said to me after identifying himself on the phone was "Congratulations, Lisa. You won the lottery!"

As the attorney in charge of the criminal docket before SCOTUS, Deputy Solicitor General Dreeben had a vested interest in Charles C. Apprendi Jr.'s petition. Dreeben's office had represented the United States government before SCOTUS in both *Almendarez-Torres* and *Jones*. The solicitor general's office had prevailed in *Almendarez-Torres* (a prior conviction is a traditional sentencing factor) but lost in *Jones* (serious bodily injury and death are elements of the federal crime of carjacking). *Apprendi v. New Jersey* was officially the next Supreme Court case in the evolving "sentencing factor versus element of the offense" debate. If SCOTUS declared New Jersey's Hate Crime Statute unconstitutional, the ripple effect of its precedent might imperil dozens of federal criminal statutes with comparable sentencing enhancement provisions, as well as the federal sentencing guidelines. The solicitor general's office would reach a decision in a few weeks, Dreeben told me, whether to file a friend of the court brief on behalf of the state of New Jersey.

"I grew up in New Jersey," Dreeben said before we hung up. "I'm happy to assist my home state in the *Apprendi* litigation." (Dreeben and I had another small-world connection. His son had been engaged to the daughter of a friend of mine from college. Sadly, the engagement was broken off when both kids graduated from preschool.)

I immediately called my husband to share the surreal news. "Steven! I'm going to the United States Supreme Court!"

"Lisa! You're going to the United States Supreme Court!"

We danced our little happy dances in our respective offices.

"What do you have to do next on the case?" Steven asked.

"I have absolutely no idea," I admitted. "But I probably should let Anne know about this."

Anne Paskow, the chief of the Appellate Section, did not share in my joy that the United States Supreme Court had granted Apprendi's petition.

"This is not good news," Paskow said somberly. "You and I both know if the justices believed the state Supreme Court decision in *Apprendi* was correct, there would be no practical reason for SCOTUS to revisit it."

Denying the petition would have, in effect, upheld the constitutionality of New Jersey's Hate Crime Statute. The grant of certiorari hinted that four or more justices were troubled by the Supreme Court of New Jersey's decision. Chances were they had voted to hear the *Apprendi* case intending to reverse, not affirm, the Supreme Court of New Jersey and, by doing so, to declare New Jersey's Hate Crime Statute unconstitutional.

But in that moment, I had no interest in divining the reasons why Apprendi's petition was granted or trying to forecast what the ultimate outcome might be. From a professional perspective, I should have been thoroughly dismayed that certiorari had been granted. After all, I had successfully shepherded the *Apprendi* litigation through both levels of the New Jersey state appellate courts. But all I selfishly cared about was that one of my cases was heading to the Supreme Court of the United States.

Paskow had argued a case before SCOTUS several years earlier and was familiar with the perils and pitfalls of Supreme Court litigation. "It's going to be a roller coaster ride," she warned me.

"That's fine with me," I replied.

I love roller coasters. Nothing beats the adrenaline rush of cresting the lift hill of a colossal steel coaster. Nothing, that is, except going to the Supreme Court of the United States.

I practically skipped back to my office. Win or lose, my case (*my case!*) would be heard by the nine justices of the United States Supreme Court. I couldn't begin to imagine the gratification that Joe O'Neill, a small-town lawyer from southern New Jersey, must have felt. After all, it was his certiorari petition the court had granted. Joe was the rare exception to the rule to bet against any lawyer who vows to take his case all the way up to the Supreme Court of the United States. I called Joe to congratulate him. His assistant immediately put me through to him.

"Congratulations, Joe! This is so unbelievable!"

"Thanks, Lisa," Joe replied. "I guess we'll see each other in Washington, DC!"

I was in a daze. I went out to the parking lot at the Hughes Justice Complex at lunchtime, the very same lot I had parked in each and every day for the past thirteen years, but I could not remember where I had left my car a mere three hours earlier.

—ɷ—

By voting to grant Charles C. Apprendi Jr.'s petition, four or more justices had lifted me out of the pit of obscurity that is the Petition Clerk's Office of the United States Supreme Court and promoted me to the elite Merits Clerk's Office. A few days later, I received a letter on official United States Supreme Court letterhead from William K. Suter, clerk of the Supreme Court, advising that "the Court today entered the following order in the above stated case: 'The petition for certiorari is granted.'" A second letter, this one sent by Denise J. McNerney, assistant clerk for merits cases, cautioned, "Inasmuch as this case will be argued in the March Session, please note that requests for extensions of time to file briefs on the merits are not favored." The words *are not* appeared in bold.

Holy moly, I thought. *This shit just got real.*

Denise McNerney was responsible for overseeing attorneys' filings with SCOTUS after certiorari was granted. She became an invaluable lifeline as I navigated what was for me the Byzantine world of United States Supreme Court litigation. Over the next several months, I called McNerney with a multitude of questions about Supreme Court rules, deadlines, brief formatting, and oral argument logistics. These were probably the same questions McNerney had answered hundreds of times before for other equally panicky first-timers. She patiently answered each of my inquiries. If McNerney was sitting on the other end of the phone rolling her eyes at my naïveté, nothing in her voice gave it away.

Enclosed with McNerney's letter was a twenty-one-page, 8.5-inch-by-5.5-inch booklet with a khaki tan cover. *Guide for Counsel in Cases to Be Argued before the Supreme Court of the United States* was written by the clerk of the Supreme Court, William K. Suter, to assist attorneys preparing cases for argument before the Supreme Court, "especially those who have not previously argued here."[4] Attorneys making their debut before SCOTUS, Clerk Suter wrote, "were to be assured that some first-time arguments have been far superior to presentations from counsel who

Office of the Clerk
Supreme Court of the United States
Washington, D. C. 20543-0001

November 29, 1999

Lisa S. Gochman, Esq.
Division of Criminal Justice
R.J. Hughes Complex
P.O. Box 086
Trenton, NJ 08625-0086

Re: 99-478 - Apprendi, Jr. v. New Jersey

Dear Ms. Gochman:

The Court today entered the following order in the above stated case:

"The petition for a writ of certiorari is granted."

The following items are enclosed: Memoranda describing the procedures under the Rules, a Specification Chart, and the Guide for Counsel. Inasmuch as this case will be argued in the **March Session**, please note that requests for extensions of time to file briefs on the merits **are not** favored.

If you have any questions, please feel free to telephone me.

Sincerely,

WILLIAM K. SUTER, CLERK

Denise J. McNerney
Assistant Clerk - Merits Cases
(202) 479-3032

Enclosures

GUIDE
FOR
COUNSEL

IN CASES TO BE ARGUED

BEFORE THE

SUPREME COURT OF
THE UNITED STATES

October Term 1999

have argued several times."[5] Clerk Suter's words were meant to allay the fears of rookies like me, but they had the opposite effect. Math is not my strong suit, but even I could figure out that if *some* first-time presentations are far superior, then *most* first-time presentations are far *inferior*. I was not assured.

There was much practical advice for the uninitiated scattered throughout *Guide for Counsel*, ranging from the scheduling of oral argument to courtroom seating for guests. But I was captivated by the stranger UBIs (useful bits of information) worthy of inclusion in the *Handbook for the Recently Deceased* from the movie *Beetlejuice*. For example, *Guide for Counsel* laid down these rules of engagement for the civilized warfare of oral argument:

> *Never under any circumstance* interrupt a Justice who is addressing you. Give your full time and attention to that Justice—do not look down at your notes and <u>do not look at your watch or at the clock located high on the wall behind the Justices.</u> If you are speaking and a Justice interrupts you, cease talking immediately and listen.[6]

The first four words of this quote are italicized as they originally appeared in the booklet. "Never" means never. Don't even *think* about interrupting a justice. I underlined the middle sentence to highlight the ticking elephant in the courtroom—the large, round, analog clock suspended high above the chief justice's head. If you tell me not to look at something, I'm going to look. It's human nature. But I mustn't look; *Guide for Counsel* says so.

Guide for Counsel also suggested I pack light:

> It has been said that preparing for oral argument at the Supreme Court is like packing your clothes for an ocean cruise. When packing for the cruise, you should lay out all the clothes you think you will need, then return half of them to the closet. When preparing for oral argument, eliminate half of what you initially planned on covering. Your allotted time evaporates quickly, especially when numerous questions come from the Court. Be prepared to skip over much of your planned argument and stress your strongest points.[7]

There is so much wrong with this advice.

First off, it is impossible for me to pack light. My pocketbook alone is the size of a fully grown German shepherd. On one four-day trip to Walt Disney World, my suitcase was ten pounds over the airline's weight limit, costing me $35 in surcharges. Second, I'm not fond of cruises. Just plop me on a tropical beach with my prescription snorkel mask and leave me there for a week, please. Most importantly, United States Supreme Court litigants wouldn't have to "pack light" and could easily get their points across if the justices would *just stop asking so many questions!*

Another pearl of wisdom included in *Guide for Counsel* was to "know your client's business." Clerk Suter offered this anecdote to illustrate his point:

> One counsel representing a large beer brewing corporation was asked the following by a Justice during argument: 'What is the difference between beer and ale?' The question had little to do with the issues, but the case involved the beer brewing business. Counsel gave a brief, simple, and clear answer that was understood by everyone in the Courtroom. He knew the business of his client, and it showed. The Justice who posed the question thanked counsel in a warm and gracious manner.[8]

(That's all well and good, but excuse me, Justice So-and-So, your question, which, as you candidly admit, has little to do with the issues before you, is cutting into my precious time at the lectern. Plus, I purposely took that arcane piece of information out of my suitcase and left it at home because you told me to pack light!)

The wild roller coaster I was strapped into was swiftly climbing the near-vertical lift hill. I secured my lap bar, raised both hands high in the air, and squeezed my eyes tight as the coaster nosedived into its first corkscrew turn, bound for Washington, DC.

CHAPTER 8

LAMPPOSTS ON THE UNITED STATES Supreme Court grounds rest atop bronze turtles, the court's unofficial mascot. The turtles are said to symbolize the slow, deliberate pace of justice. Yet compared to the crawl of appellate litigation in New Jersey, things move apace in the Supreme Court of the United States.

Supreme Court Rule 25.1 gave Apprendi's attorney Joe O'Neill a mere forty-five days from the order granting his petition for certiorari to file his merits brief, making his brief due on January 13, 2000. Joe had preexisting scheduling conflicts and asked the Clerk's Office for a fourteen-day extension of time to file his merits brief, which I thought was a perfectly reasonable request and did not oppose. But O'Neill's application for a two-week postponement was denied by the Clerk's Office in a tersely worded letter: "Your request dated December 13, 1999, for an extension of time for filing petitioner's brief on the merits is denied. The Clerk will entertain no additional requests for an extension of time." Supreme Court Rule 25.2 gave me only thirty days after the filing date of Joe's merits brief to file my response. If Joe could not get an extension of time, there was absolutely no reason to expect that I could count on getting one.

As the *Apprendi* litigation ramped up into overdrive that winter, I reluctantly relinquished my stint as prop mistress (or, as I prefer, "prop goddess") for a local theater company's presentation of *Scrooge*, the musical version of Charles Dickens's *A Christmas Carol*. The annual production was a family affair: Jordan was a cast member, Steven was on the stage crew, and I scoured the aisles of arts-and-crafts stores and thrift shops for inspiration to create ornate props that could be seen from the upper balcony of the theater. I hot-glued oversized fake diamonds, emeralds, and rubies to the outside of a homely aluminum water pitcher from which the Ghost of Christmas Present would pour the milk of human kindness; I designed a sky-high, three-tier cake from Styrofoam disks, white royal icing, and red pom-pom ribbon for the engagement party scene; and I draped Cheapside with tattered Christmas garlands and festooned the Fezziwigs' mantel with gold and silver satin ornaments. But now, with inflexible United States Supreme Court deadlines fast approaching, I didn't dare devote the time, energy, and creativity required for evening rehearsals and weekend performances.

With no time to spare, I began researching and writing my responding brief weeks before Apprendi's merits brief was filed. After two rounds of litigation in the state courts, I was intimately familiar with the facts and the law. But where my substantive arguments in the New Jersey courts relied on both New Jersey state and federal cases, substantive arguments before the United States Supreme Court rely almost exclusively on United States Supreme Court precedent. The justices are "unimpressed with arguments that depend on the decisions of lower federal courts or state courts."[1] I could not file with the Supreme Court of the United States what I had filed with the New Jersey courts. I had to write an entirely new brief for an entirely different audience, and the brief could not exceed nine thousand words, including footnotes, within fifty 6.25-inch-by-9.25-inch booklet-size pages. Every word I wrote in my United States Supreme Court merits brief had to be carefully weighed. There was no room for gratuitous adjectives or flowery language.

Based on the voting history of each justice in *Almendarez-Torres* and *Jones*, I had good reason to anticipate that the *Apprendi* court would be split 4-4 with Justice Thomas as the swing vote. Except for Justice Thomas, the voting blocs in both *Almendarez-Torres* and *Jones* remained consistent. One bloc included Chief Justice Rehnquist and Justices O'Connor, Kennedy, and Breyer. The other bloc included Justices Stevens, Scalia, Souter, and Ginsberg. Justice Thomas had joined the former voting bloc in *Almendarez-Torres* (a prior conviction is a traditional sentencing factor) and the latter voting bloc in *Jones* (death and bodily injury to the victim are elements of the federal offense of carjacking). I was pretty sure I had Rehnquist, O'Connor, Kennedy, and Breyer on my side, so my primary goal in writing my merits brief was to persuade as many members as possible in the opposing bloc that motive was a traditional sentencing factor. But if Stevens, Scalia, Souter, or Ginsberg wouldn't budge, I held out hope of nudging Justice Thomas, the swing vote, over to my side. I needed only five votes to win. I was, as Tom Goldstein (publisher of Scotusblog.com) advises first-timers before the Supreme Court, "trying to hit singles, not home runs."[2]

And I wrote that entirely new brief on my own. On the few prior occasions when a case handled by the Appellate Section of the New Jersey Division of Criminal Justice reached the United States Supreme Court, several deputy attorneys general collaborated on the merits brief. That custom ended with the writing of the merits brief in *Apprendi v. New Jersey*. Anne Paskow did not assign any of my colleagues to assist me, and I preferred this arrangement. By nature, appellate attorneys are not team players. We want total control over our cases, no surprises, and no competing egos.

To write my merits brief, I set up camp in a carrel in the Office of the Attorney General's library on the sixth floor of the Hughes Justice Complex. In late 1999, the state's attorneys' computers in New Jersey had basic email and word processing capability, but we did not yet have internet access to the search engines Westlaw and LexisNexis to expedite the legal research process. Finding a published decision from the New Jersey or federal courts required us to pull the physical reporters (the thick, bound volumes in which judicial opinions are printed in chronological order) off one of the shelves in the library. A born-and-bred New Yorker, I knew little about New Jersey geography upon arriving in Trenton in 1987. When I told a former colleague from the Bronx district attorney's office that the library overlooked the river, she naturally asked, "Which river?" I had no idea. (It is the Delaware River.)

I also spent countless hours in mind-numbing misery standing in front of the photocopying machine making two copies of every United States Supreme Court case and law review article I might possibly need, one copy for my office in Trenton and one copy for my house, so when I bolted upright in bed at two o'clock in the morning, freaking out that I couldn't remember which justice wrote which opinion, I had only to walk downstairs to the pile of photocopied cases on my dining room table, microwave some chamomile tea in my official SCOTUS mug, and start reading.

One Saturday afternoon in December, Steven dropped me off at the Hughes Justice Complex while he and Jordan, now nine years old, visited the planetarium in the New Jersey State Museum in downtown Trenton with Jordan's Cub Scout pack. The Hughes Justice Complex is a depressing place to spend a Saturday afternoon. Government workers, by and large, do not venture into their offices on weekends. We make a fraction of the salaries earned by lawyers in private practice, but we aren't expected to show up regularly for work on weekends either. But I was drafting the merits brief in *Apprendi* and needed the word processing program available to me only on my desktop computer at the office. I signed in with the security guard at the first-floor main entrance so he would be aware I was working in my office on the sixth floor of the otherwise empty building.

The individual hallways and offices in the Hughes Justice Complex do not have their own light switches. The controls for all the tubular fluorescent ceiling bulbs in the back half of the Appellate Section where my office was located were in a locked room in a separate area of the building off-limits to Division of Criminal Justice employees. I had no way to turn on the overhead lights. It was just me and the lone Hughes Justice Complex security guard—me, all the way up on the sixth floor in my windowless office, and the security guard six flights below in the lobby. Only the weak light emitted by the computer screen illumnated my otherwise pitch-black office.

The Appellate Section was creepy in the dark. Aside from the rows and rows of windowless offices, there was an unlit storage area bordered by open metal shelves, each shelf creaking under the weight of hundreds of old and current appellate files. Each file represented a crime committed by someone who may still be serving time in prison. Most of the crimes were violent, some unspeakably so. During my career, I have handled many ghastly murder appeals: the twelve-year-old girl raped and bludgeoned by her fourteen-year-old neighbor, the middle-aged gas attendant stabbed two dozen times in a botched robbery, the young widow whose head was split open by an axe-wielding serial rapist who broke into her bedroom in the middle of the night, the eighteen-month-old toddler internally decapitated when his babysitter shook him so hard his spinal cord detached from his brain stem, the seven-year-old boy starved to death by his adoptive parents. These are just a sampling of the horrors lurking inside the hundreds of files I hurried past to reach my office.

For every defendant convicted of murder, there is a victim, and that victim leaves behind family, friends, and colleagues mourning an untimely death and searching for closure that likely will never come. In my capacity as appellate counsel, I officially represent the citizens of the state of New Jersey, but what keeps me going, appeal after god-awful appeal, is knowing I have done everything in my power as a prosecutor to keep a murderer or a rapist or a child abuser behind bars so that the traumatized victim and his or her family might sleep a little bit easier at night. In one of my homicide appeals, the child victim's unique first name was spelled differently in each trial transcript. I called the assistant county prosecutor who had successfully tried the case for the correct spelling of the young girl's name. The victim deserved this small dignity, even in death.

The Fowlkes family may have been spared physical injury from Charles Apprendi's .22-caliber bullets, but Mattie Harrell Fowlkes's victim-impact letter to Judge Rushton Ridgway revealed the deep and lasting psychological pain her young son suffered as a result of Apprendi's violent and targeted racist assault. "A bullet went through my eight-year-old baby's room," Mrs. Fowlkes had written to the judge. "My son has not slept in that room since that day." The Fowlkes family was foremost on my mind at every step of the *Apprendi* litigation in state and federal courts.

I hunkered down inside my dark and windowless office for hours drafting my merits brief, too unnerved to walk alone past the shadowy storage area again. I didn't dare get up from my desk to go to the bathroom. I did make sure, though, to email my boss, Anne Paskow, to let her know I was diligently working in the office that Saturday afternoon, all alone in the dark, like a blind mole rat.

We were all blind mole rats in the Appellate Section, endlessly digging through piles of criminal defendants' briefs but barely making a dent. As representatives of the state of New Jersey, we must respond to every single one of these documents. And they never, *ever* stop coming. There were days when my sole source of exercise was the walk from the outdoor parking lot to the elevator bank in the lobby of the Hughes Justice Complex. Some days, if the wait for the elevator was too long, I would lug my briefcase up the six flights of steps from the lobby to my office, until the day I realized that the filthy, poorly lit stairwell would be a terrible place to suffer a heart attack. No one would find me until the next fire drill when hundreds of state employees trampled my decomposing body as they frantically evacuated the building.

—⚭—

Steven and Jordan picked me up at the Hughes Justice Complex when their scouting adventure ended late in the afternoon. The winter sun had set by then, and, without any natural light filtering through the tinted windows, the hallways of the Appellate Section were now as dark as my unlit office. I was very happy to get out of that building and go home.

CHAPTER 9

THE *APPRENDI* LITIGATION IN THE United States Supreme Court began on September 17, 1999, the day Apprendi filed his petition for certiorari, and ended on June 26, 2000, the day the United States Supreme Court issued its decision. This nine-month time frame inconveniently spanned my son Jordan's third-grade school year. As a full-time working mother, I prided myself on staying involved in Jordan's education and after-school activities. I carpooled Jordan to religious school, attended all his Little League baseball games, and would have watched all his youth basketball league games, except I was a tad too enthusiastic in the stands and Jordan had banned me from future attendance.

The Supreme Court of the United States, however, does not give a hoot about the day-to-day family obligations of counsel. My merits brief was due on February 14, 2000, and it was fruitless for me to waste a single second thinking about requesting an extension of time. I was incredibly fortunate that my husband Steven readily assumed the bulk of the parental and household duties so I could stay laser-focused on the *Apprendi* litigation. And Jordan was an excellent student who didn't need much coaxing to do his homework, even if you couldn't decipher his penmanship. But I do recall one concerning conversation I had that school year with Jordan's third-grade teacher.

"Mrs. Dolci," I asked, "why isn't Jordan required to memorize his multiplication tables? He goes through the same mental gymnastics every time I quiz him."

Mrs. Dolci blamed it on the "new math." This confused me. How on earth did the multiplication tables change in the thirty-two years since I attended elementary school?

"We teach our students to conceptualize groups of objects and add up the groups," Mrs. Dolci said.

This explained why every single time I quizzed Jordan on three times three, he would count on his fingers while chanting aloud, "Three plus three is six, plus three is nine." Every single time I quizzed Jordan on four times four, he would count on his fingers while chanting aloud, "Four plus four is eight, plus four is twelve, plus four is sixteen." So every single time, I would respond with exasperation, "Jordan, four times four is sixteen! *It's always going to be sixteen!*"

My irritation with my third-grader's "new math" at home was a symptom of the magnitude of the project I had taken on at work. I bore full responsibility for every aspect of the state's merits brief in *Apprendi* and it was a daunting job. This was the downside to having complete control over my case. My colleagues were occupied with their own heavy caseloads, so I couldn't ask them to put their work aside to assume tasks I had eagerly agreed to handle myself.

One of my ambitious yet impractical ideas was to find every out-of-state criminal statute with a sentencing enhancer similar to New Jersey's Hate Crime Statute. I wanted to advise SCOTUS of the expected upheaval in sentencing law nationwide if the Hate Crime Statute was struck down as unconstitutional. A loss in the United States Supreme Court might reverberate far beyond New Jersey if the court used its decision in *Apprendi* to adopt the bright-line rule proposed in footnote 6 of *Jones*. Adoption of the proposed rule would require prosecutors to prove to a jury beyond a reasonable doubt *any* factor (apart from a prior criminal conviction) increasing the sentence above the statutory penalty range. But I had neither the time nor the resources to pull the penal codes of forty-nine other states off of the library shelves and figure out by myself which of the thousands of criminal statutes might be affected by a loss in *Apprendi*. I turned to attorneys general across the country, trying to persuade one to draft a friend of the court brief that other states could join in support of New Jersey. It was in their best interest to get on board to save their own sentencing laws.

Friend of the court briefs are often filed in support of a sister state's merits brief in the United States Supreme Court as a show of solidarity when the pending litigation impacts other states' laws. I had no idea at the time whether such visible support would make any difference to the eventual outcome of the *Apprendi* case, but it wouldn't have hurt to have the backing of other jurisdictions. The National Association of Attorneys General provided me with a two-page "Party Memo—on the Merits" to enlist reinforcements. Anything with the word *party* in the title should have been a lot more entertaining. It was, instead, a basic form I filled out with pertinent information about the *Apprendi* case pending before SCOTUS: due dates, contact information, the legal arguments the state of New Jersey planned to make, and the potential negative impact on other state criminal statutes with analogous penalty enhancers if New Jersey's Hate Crime Statute was declared unconstitutional. The memo was faxed to attorneys general and solicitors general offices in all states and territories.

It was a tough sell. I spoke to many attorneys but was repeatedly told that their states' hate crime statutes were not drafted in the same manner as New Jersey's Hate Crime Statute. I patiently explained each time that the heart of the sentencing issue in *Apprendi* was not restricted to hate crime statutes, but I had no luck convincing a single state to file a friend of the court brief for other states to join. I was frustrated that not one state came to New Jersey's assistance.

There were requests, however, from nonprofit interest groups seeking permission to file friend of the court briefs in support of New Jersey. I was unfamiliar with some of these groups and asked Deputy Solicitor General Michael Dreeben for guidance. He told me it was the policy of the Office of the Solicitor General to consent to any group wishing to file an amicus brief in the Supreme Court, unless the person making the request is (and these are my words, not Michael Dreeben's) obviously nuts. "Withholding consent," Dreeben counseled, "gives the impression you have something to hide."

One group who filed a Kelly green amicus brief in support of New Jersey was the Anti-Defamation League (ADL). Founded in 1913, the ADL is one of the nation's oldest civil and human rights organizations. Its stated mission "is to protect the Jewish people and to secure justice and fair treatment for all."[1] In its amicus brief, the ADL cited the Federal Bureau of Investigation's Hate Crime Statistics Act Report, which documented nearly eight thousand hate-motivated crimes across the country in 1998 alone. The majority of these hate crimes were race-based (58%), followed by religion, sexual orientation, and ethnicity. "Hate-motivated crimes," wrote the ADL, "are among the most destructive of the public safety and happiness."[2]

Quoted in the ADL's amicus brief was Brian Levin, a professor of criminal justice and the director of the Center for the Study of Hate and Extremism at California State University in San Bernardino. An internationally renowned authority on hate crimes, Professor Levin himself filed a separate Kelly green friend of the court brief in support of New Jersey on behalf of multiple organizations: the Brudnick Center on Violence and Conflict, a public policy research center at Northeastern University in Boston; the California Association of Human Relations Organizations, a statewide consortium of human rights groups; the Center for Democratic Renewal, formerly known as the National Anti-Klan Network; the Center on Hate and Extremism, a non-partisan national public policy and educational organization; Hatewatch, an internet blog associated with the Southern Poverty Law Center; the National Association of Human Rights Workers, a human relations commission advocating hate crime laws and tolerance programs; and the Northwest Coalition for Human Dignity, a regional group promoting hate crime legislation. These academic and civil rights groups supported the enactment and enforcement of sentence enhancement provisions against individuals convicted of bias-motivated crimes.

Professor Levin quoted in his own amicus brief another noted authority on hate crimes, James Weinstein, a constitutional law professor at the Sandra Day O'Connor College of Law at Arizona State University, to underscore the qualitative difference between hate crimes and other offenses. "The effect of Kristallnacht on German Jews," Weinstein posited, "was greater than the sum of the damages to the buildings and assaults on individual victims."[3]

The Office of the Solicitor General also filed an amicus brief with a putty gray cover in support of New Jersey. With Solicitor General Seth Waxman on the brief were Assistant Attorney General James K. Robinson, Deputy Solicitor General Michael Dreeben, Assistant Solicitor General Edward DuMont, and Department of Justice attorney Nina Goodman.

Eleven months earlier, the federal government lost its case in *Jones* when SCOTUS held that serious bodily injury and death of the victim were elements of the offense of carjacking. Now the solicitor general was fighting to save other federal statutes with similarly questionable sentencing enhancers. As the solicitor general explained in his amicus brief in *Apprendi*, "Because various federal criminal laws authorize the imposition of enhanced sentences on the bases of facts found by the court at sentencing, see *e.g.,* 21 U.S.C. 841(b) (drug type and quantity), the United States has a strong interest in the outcome of this case."[4]

The solicitor general's "strong interest" in the outcome of the *Apprendi* case thus lay not in the narrow question whether motive was a traditional sentencing factor but in the much broader question whether *any* factor increasing the maximum term a defendant faced could be found by a judge under the low "preponderance of the evidence" burden of proof. Federal drug laws left it to the jury in the first instance to determine under the "beyond a reasonable doubt" burden of proof whether a defendant possessed or distributed illegal drugs. These same federal laws, however, did not require the jury to determine the type or quantity of the drugs. These facts were left to the sentencing judge to find under the lower "preponderance of the evidence" standard, and the judge's factual findings dictated the length of the defendant's maximum term of imprisonment. Solicitor General Waxman argued in his amicus brief that "Congress's very separation of those factors, such as type and quantity of particular drugs, into separate sentencing provisions demonstrates a judgment that they are not essential to a finding of criminality."[5]

In contrast, in New Jersey, the type of illegal drug (cocaine or heroin, for example) and quantity of those drugs (grams or ounces, for example) have always been treated as elements of the crimes of possession and distribution of controlled dangerous substances that the jury must find beyond a reasonable doubt.[6] There was no need for me to defend the constitutionality of these state drug statutes, because their constitutionality was unaffected by *Jones*. I stood a better chance of prevailing in *Apprendi* if SCOTUS concentrated on the narrow question of the traditional role of motive in sentencing a criminal defendant. The solicitor general's exploitation of *Apprendi* to advocate for the constitutionality of federal statutes that, in my mind, impermissibly treated elements of the offense as sentencing factors was troublesome. By expanding the argument to include any and all federal criminal statutes with potentially unconstitutional sentencing enhancers, it seemed to me, the Office of the Solicitor General had filed a "frenemy of the court" brief in support of New Jersey.

—⁊⁊⁊—

On January 7, 2000, William S. Suter, the clerk of the United States Supreme Court, sent a letter to Stephen W. Townsend, the clerk of the Supreme
Court of New Jersey, requesting him "to certify and transmit immediately
the entire record in *Apprendi v. New Jersey*." State court records include all
transcripts of the court proceedings, all briefs and memoranda filed by the
parties, and all judicial orders entered in the state trial and appellate courts for
SCOTUS's reference and examination. The physical record in a capital murder prosecution alone can fill dozens of Bankers boxes. Many of the thousands
of pages of documents stored inside these boxes are likely unrelated, however,
to the narrow legal issue raised in the Question Presented. The justices and
their law clerks don't want to sift through reams of paper searching for the relevant documents they need, so the court makes the parties do this work for
them. Supreme Court Rule 26 requires the parties to file a joint appendix at-
taching only those documents that are germane to the Article III controversy
pending before the court.

As counsel for petitioner Charles Apprendi, Joseph O'Neill was responsible for preparing and printing the joint appendix. But the joint appendix was
due to be filed with the court the same day as Joe's merits brief, so I agreed
to compile the appendix.[7] I'm sure Joe thought it would be easier for me to
put the joint appendix together, as I worked for a large government entity,
and his was a small, four-person law firm. The phrase "the vast resources of
the attorney general's office" is often bandied about by judges and criminal
defense lawyers as if state attorneys are interchangeable and have unlimited
financial and technical support at their disposal. But I remember, in a time
before word processors, when the attorney general's office ran out of yellow
legal pads and the attorneys had to supply their own. So much for the "vast
resources" of the New Jersey attorney general's office.

Some of the documents pertinent to the *Apprendi* litigation (the two state
appellate court opinions and the transcripts of the extended-term motion
and sentencing hearings held before the trial court) had been appended to
Joe O'Neill's certiorari petition and were not required to be reprinted in the
joint appendix. Only minor wrangling between Joe's law associate Charles
Coant and me was needed before we agreed on the remaining documents for
inclusion in the joint appendix: the twenty-three count Cumberland County

indictment filed against Charles Apprendi, the transcript of the plea hearing held before Judge Ridgway, the state's motion for the imposition of an extended-term sentence pursuant to the Hate Crime Statute, and the judgment of conviction entered by the trial court on the day that Apprendi's twelve-year sentence was imposed.

Supreme Court Rule 26.3 requires fifty copies of the joint appendix (with its requisite adhesive bandage tan cover) to be filed with the Clerk's Office. The initial costs are borne by the petitioner, so a shorter record meant less financial outlay for Joe, who, I knew by this point in the protracted proceedings, was representing his client for free.[8] Not unexpectedly, after three levels of litigation in the Cumberland County trial court, the New Jersey intermediate appellate court, and the New Jersey Supreme Court, Charles Apprendi was running low on funds to pay his mounting legal bills. Joe O'Neill agreed to continue representing Apprendi on a *pro bono* basis. *Pro bono publica* is Latin for "for the public good" and generally refers to free legal services offered to indigent litigants in both civil and criminal cases. Joe was not about to abandon his client or to forfeit his chance to argue a case before the United States Supreme Court.

On January 13, 2000, Joe O'Neill filed forty copies of his merits brief with its robin's egg blue cover in the United States Supreme Court Clerk's Office. Assisting Joe on the brief was his law firm associate Charles Coant, and Richard G. Singer, a criminal law professor and former dean of New Jersey's Rutgers School of Law–Camden. Also filed with the Clerk's Office that same day were two celadon green friend of the court briefs submitted on Apprendi's behalf. One amicus brief was jointly filed by the National Association of Criminal Defense Lawyers, the Families against Mandatory Minimums Foundation, and the Association of Federal Defenders. The second amicus brief was filed by the Rutherford Institute, a nonprofit civil liberties organization. All three briefs argued that New Jersey's Hate Crime Statute was unconstitutional because it permitted the state to determine facts doubling the statutory maximum prison sentence without notice in the indictment and without proving those facts to a jury beyond a reasonable doubt. I had thirty days to respond to every argument raised by Charles Apprendi and amici in all three briefs.

The pressure of United States Supreme Court litigation was taking its toll on me. Sleep was elusive, and when I did sleep, I had recurring work-related stress nightmares masquerading as high school–related stress nightmares.

I dreamed about final exams in subjects, such as calculus and physics, I hadn't studied for and couldn't fake my way through. I couldn't open my locker to get my textbooks because I couldn't remember the combination to the lock. And then there were the more literal nightmares. In one, Associate Justice John Paul Stevens ice-skated in long, graceful strides around an oval rink, his black silk judicial robe fluttering gently behind him. In another, I stood inside the courtroom of the Supreme Court in Washington clutching the lectern for dear life and stammering "Homina, homina, homina" like Ralph Kramden in *The Honeymooners* while Chief Justice William Rehnquist stared at me, aghast.

And if drafting the legal substance of the merits brief wasn't challenging enough, the format of the booklet brief had to conform to the idiosyncratic printing specifications set out in Supreme Court Rule 33.1:

- The text must be double-sided and "reproduced with a clarity that equals or exceeds the output of a laser printer."
- The text "shall be typeset in a Century family (*e.g.*, Century Expanded, New Century Schoolbook, or Century Schoolbook) 12-point type with 2-point or more leading between lines."
- The typeface of footnotes must be 10-point type with 2-point or more leading between lines.
- The paper used must be "opaque, unglazed, and not less than 60 pounds in weight, and shall have margins of at least three-fourths of an inch on all sides."
- The text field, including footnotes, must not exceed 4⅛ inches by 7⅛ inches.
- The document must be bound firmly in at least two places along the left margin (saddle stitch or perfect binding preferred) "so as to permit easy opening." Spiral, plastic, metal, and string bindings are not permitted.

New Jersey state court briefs are downright lackluster in contrast. They are formatted in 12-point Courier New, the font most resembling old-fashioned typewriting; they are produced on single-sided, plain white, letter-size copier paper; and they are held together in the top left corner by a giant staple. The fanciest we get in New Jersey is underlining a word for emphasis.

Tina Stanley, my administrative assistant, was an integral part of the merits-brief-writing process. Two decades ago, word processing was nowhere near as user-friendly as it is today, plus we were working with the Supreme Court's

No. 99-478

In The
Supreme Court of the United States

CHARLES C. APPRENDI, JR.,

Petitioner,

v.

STATE OF NEW JERSEY,

Respondent.

**On Writ of Certiorari to the
Supreme Court of New Jersey**

BRIEF FOR RESPONDENT

JOHN J. FARMER, JR.
 Attorney General of New Jersey
LISA SARNOFF GOCHMAN
 Deputy Attorney General
 Counsel of Record
DIVISION OF CRIMINAL JUSTICE
R.J. HUGHES JUSTICE COMPLEX
P.O. Box 086
TRENTON, NEW JERSEY 08625
(609) 292-9086

Counsel for Respondent

Merits brief for respondent in *Apprendi v. New Jersey*.

unfamiliar printing specifications. Stanley's work was impeccable, and, best of all, she remained calm whenever I made yet another revision to the merits brief. And I was always revising my merits brief. I had submitted drafts to my supervisors at the Division of Criminal Justice, to the National Association of Attorneys General, and to the Office of the Solicitor General. I also sent drafts to every state attorney who expressed the slightest bit of interest in writing a friend of the court brief on New Jersey's behalf. Of course, everybody had something to say about my merits brief, even if it was simply to point out, as one state attorney from California did, that I had miscalculated the number of years between the publication dates of two Supreme Court decisions. Thank goodness someone caught my embarrassing subtraction error before the final draft was filed with SCOTUS.

Tina Stanley and I also had to anticipate the Y2K computer virus wiping out all our hard work at the stroke of midnight on January 1, 2000. The day before, Friday, December 31, 1999, Stanley printed out a paper copy of the most recent draft of my merits brief, ready to retype it from scratch in case computer systems around the world crashed one time zone after the other as the year changed from 1999 to 2000.

The job of printing the merits brief was left to one of the few printing companies in the country specializing in United States Supreme Court booklet briefs. In the olden days, attorneys depended on private couriers or the United States Postal Service to mail handwritten drafts (assuming their office hadn't run out of yellow legal pads) to the printing company. The printer would then typeset the document before sending it back to the attorney for proofreading. The brief was physically shuttled back and forth until the attorney was satisfied with the printed version or ran smack up against the court-imposed deadline. This process was frustrating, time-consuming, and ripe with opportunity for typographical errors. Fortunately, my office had the word processing capability to meet SCOTUS's formatting specifications, giving me a few extra days to fine-tune my arguments and double-check my math. As it was, although my brief wasn't due until February 14, 2000, it needed to be in final form with a few days' lead time to send a computer disk to the printer for printing, binding, and filing in the Clerk's Office of the United States Supreme Court in Washington, DC.

Given how few petitions for certiorari are granted by SCOTUS each year, the competition for the contract to print the state's merits brief was fierce.

Cockle Legal Briefs in Nebraska was eager for New Jersey's business and sweetened its proposal by offering me free Omaha Steaks. Unfortunately for me, I couldn't accept the steaks because they were bigger than a bagel and more costly than a cup of coffee, the rough parameters of what a New Jersey state employee may accept as a gift from an outside contractor. Anything more extravagant might raise the inference that the gift or benefit was offered to influence the performance of the government employee's duties or to reward the employee for the discharge of his or her official duties. So when Cockle Legal Briefs generously offered me free Omaha Steaks if I retained their services, I resisted the temptation and courteously declined.

For past petitions and merits briefs, my office had contracted with Byron S. Adams, a legal printing company in Washington, DC, and we opted to do so again. On February 10, 2000, I mailed a camera-ready hard copy of my merits brief with a backup computer disk to the printer. Four days later, on February 14, 2000, the printing company filed the requisite forty copies of my merits brief with the Clerk's Office in DC in the matter of *Apprendi v. New Jersey*, Supreme Court Docket No. 99-478; served three additional copies of the printed brief on petitioner Charles Apprendi's attorney Joseph O'Neill; mailed one courtesy copy to each counsel of record on all five amicus briefs; and sent me seventeen copies. The cost of printing a total of sixty-five copies of the merits brief plus postage and courier service was $863.50. The cover of the brief was ruby red, the perfect color for Valentine's Day.

But there wasn't time to revel in this once-in-a-lifetime achievement. At the very moment an employee of Byron S. Adams Press was hand-filing my merits brief in the Supreme Court of the United States in Washington, DC, I stood before the Supreme Court of New Jersey in Trenton to argue an unrelated search-and-seizure case.[9] Four weeks later, I was back before the Supreme Court of New Jersey to argue an unrelated death penalty case.[10] In between, I chipped away at the backlog of other assignments and tried to recall what my son looked like.

On March 16, 2000, one month after my ruby red merits brief was filed in Washington, my office was served with Apprendi's twenty-page daffodil yellow reply brief. By now, Apprendi had mustered the big guns on his side. With Joseph O'Neill on the reply brief were Jeffrey T. Green and Timothy D. Hawkes, attorneys from Sidley Austin, a Washington, DC, law firm with a dedicated United States Supreme Court appellate practice. Green and Hawkes participated in the *Apprendi* litigation through Sidley Austin's pro bono program, which assists indigent criminal defendants in cases before the Supreme Court at no cost to the defendants.

Reading any defense attorney's reply brief is distressing. Reply briefs highlight every fact I allegedly misrepresented and expose every perceived flaw in my legal analysis. Joe O'Neill and company's reply brief declared that my argument was "unsupported" and "too broad," "suggesting a clear distinction" between motive and intent "where there is none."[11] And that was just the first page. The reply brief homed in on the weak spot in my argument: How could motive be a traditional sentencing factor when it behaved like an element of the offense by bumping up the defendant's custodial sentence for the underlying crime into a separate and higher statutory sentencing range? My merits brief, O'Neill wrote, "never comes to grips with that fundamental distinction."[12] Ouch.

When my initial panic subsided, I remembered that my merits brief had, in fact, addressed the fundamental distinction between a sentencing factor and an element of the offense. Motive, I had argued, was on the same footing as a prior conviction. Both were traditional sentencing factors. If, as the Supreme Court held in *Almendarez-Torres*, a prior conviction could be relied on by the sentencing judge to enhance the defendant's prison term, then bad motive could, too. But Supreme Court rules do not permit the respondent to file a reply brief in response to the petitioner's reply brief. Charles C. Apprendi Jr. would have the last word on the subject until oral argument. And oral argument was less than two weeks away.

CHAPTER 10

WHEN THE *APPRENDI* CERTIORARI PETITION was granted in November 1999, my supervisors at the Division of Criminal Justice assured me that I would *not* be the person to argue before the United States Supreme Court on behalf of the state of New Jersey. That rare honor would be awarded to one of the state's attorneys with far more seniority. But I really, really wanted to argue this case. After nearly four years of often intense litigation, *Apprendi* was part of my DNA.

My parents had been hounding me for weeks to shore up the travel arrangements for Washington, DC, as if I had any control over SCOTUS's calendar. On January 7, 2000, I finally received a letter from the Supreme Court Clerk's Office saying oral argument in *Apprendi* was scheduled for Tuesday, March 28, 2000. I was excited to give my folks a firm date. I called my parents in Florida so they could book their flights and reserve hotel accommodations in DC to watch the argument.

"Mom, I heard from the court. The *Apprendi* argument is scheduled for Tuesday morning, March 28."

Mom was not pleased. "That's terrible timing, Lisa," she scolded. "That's when the cherry blossoms are in bloom. We'll never find a hotel room."

The two-week cherry blossom season in Washington, DC, typically starts in late March and peaks in early April. The annual National Cherry Blossom Festival attracts throngs of tourists from around the world who descend on the nation's capital to walk among the three thousand pink Japanese cherry trees lining the Tidal Basin near the Jefferson Memorial.

"Gee, Mom," I kidded her, "I'll call Chief Justice Rehnquist personally and ask him to change the date of the oral argument."

Needless to say, I did not place that phone call. And we had no trouble booking hotel rooms at the Hyatt Regency on Capitol Hill, which was conveniently located within walking distance of the United States Supreme Court building.

By late January, the question of who would argue *Apprendi* on behalf of the state of New Jersey was still up in the air, and I was lobbying my supervisors hard for the honor. By then, I had argued seventeen cases in the Supreme Court of New Jersey, one in the New York Court of Appeals, and countless others before the intermediate appellate courts in both states. I felt ready for Washington, DC. But the ultimate decision was left to New Jersey Attorney General John J. Farmer Jr. On the last Friday afternoon in January, I received a phone call from Attorney General Farmer's secretary, Elise Hartpence, asking me to come up to the general's spacious, sunlit office on the eighth floor of the Hughes Justice Complex in Trenton overlooking the icy Delaware River.

As one of more than four hundred line attorneys in the New Jersey Office of the Attorney General, my name was listed too low down on the organizational chart to merit any direct interaction with all but a few of the thirteen attorneys general I served under during my twenty-six-year career with the state. I had not yet met Attorney General Farmer and probably never would have but for the mind-boggling fact that SCOTUS had granted certiorari in one of my assignments. As I entered his office, Attorney General Farmer greeted me warmly and extended his hand to shake mine, then motioned for me to take a seat across from his desk. I immediately felt at ease in his presence. He spoke to me not as his subordinate but as his equal.

"Lisa, let me tell you something," he said, leaning back in his office chair, hands folded behind his head. "The role of attorney general is largely political, and the buck really does stop at my desk." I wasn't sure where he was heading with this, so I remained quiet and listened.

"I never get to do any courtroom lawyering anymore," Farmer told me. "I'm in meetings all day long. I miss the challenge and excitement of litigation."

He was torn: "I hate the idea of usurping a high-profile case from a line attorney, but this is my only opportunity to argue before the United States Supreme Court."

On balance, the attorney general said, arguing before the United States Supreme Court won out. And who could blame him? Rank has its privilege and John Farmer far outranked me. He truly could not have been any nicer, though, as he took away *my* only opportunity to argue before the United States Supreme Court.

"General Farmer," I asked, "would it be possible for me to second-seat you during the argument?" Second-seating meant I would help prepare the attorney general for his appearance before the United States Supreme Court and sit next to him at counsel table during the argument in Washington, DC.

"Of course, Lisa," Attorney General Farmer replied. "I'm going to need your full assistance in preparing for the argument."

This was a decent compromise. I would witness my case argued in the United States Supreme Court by the attorney general of New Jersey without the intense pressure of handling the argument myself. I gave General Farmer a draft of my not-yet-finalized merits brief, returned to my office, and let out a sigh of relief.

The following Tuesday morning, Attorney General Farmer summoned me back upstairs.

"I read your brief over the weekend," he told me. "The issues in this case are far more complex than I realized, and I won't have sufficient time to get up to speed. I want you to handle the oral argument." As the attorney most familiar with the litigation, he said, I was best suited to argue *Apprendi* before the United States Supreme Court. Attorney General Farmer would second-seat me.

"Are you sure? Are you sure?" I asked incredulously.

He was sure.

I left the general's office in a daze, deliriously happy and terrified all at once. I was deliriously happy because John Farmer had chosen *me* to argue *Apprendi* in the Supreme Court of the United States! I was also terrified because I am well aware of my limitations as an appellate litigator. My writing skills far surpass my oratory skills. Public speaking scares me to death. I'm okay facing a panel of judges when in my "lawyer zone," but please don't make me turn around and address the audience seated in the spectators' gallery behind me.

And I don't always come up with the right word on the spot. Occasionally, I create a spontaneous portmanteau by combining two synonyms to form a new word: *glad* plus *happy* equals *glappy*. I've also been known to blurt out unintentional spoonerisms by transposing the initial sounds of two words, like *gooing chum*. How mortifying would it be to look Chief Justice Rehnquist in the eye as I began my argument with "May it cleate the Port"?

Years ago, my husband and I were eating brunch (itself a portmanteau mashing together the words *breakfast* and *lunch*) in a restaurant in Florida. I was delighted that my banana pancakes had chunks of banana inside each pancake, as well as liberally strewn across the top.

"There's pancake in the batter!" I squealed.

Steven looked at me with concern. "What are you talking about?" he asked.

"*There's pancake in the batter!*" I defiantly repeated. I didn't understand why Steven didn't understand what I was saying.

Naturally, I didn't mention any of this to Attorney General Farmer.

My real fear, though, was that I would awaken on the morning of the oral argument with a migraine headache. I've suffered from migraines since law school, long before the development of prescription medications that help alleviate the unbearable pain. I live in dread of these debilitating headaches. They are heralded by a peculiar auditory hallucination, a clicking noise in my left ear only I can hear. In March 2000, if a migraine hit, my only choices were to lie down in a dark room with a cold washcloth across my forehead or tough it out. Lord help me if I got a migraine at work. The same overhead fluorescent lights in my office at the Hughes Justice Complex in Trenton that cannot be switched on on weekends cannot be switched off on weekdays. The best I could manage if a migraine hit at work was to shut my door, clear a space on my desk where I could lay my head, and close my eyes until the headache passed.

Worse, a visual aura might unexpectedly strike during the argument itself. Visual auras plague me far less frequently than migraine headaches, but they are far more frightening. For about fifteen to twenty minutes, a jagged, vibrating lightning bolt of a line only I can see travels slowly across both eyeballs, partially obscuring my field of vision. Imagine a fold in the middle of a page of a book blocking out a portion of the text. This is what my visual auras are like. I can see the pulsating lightning bolt, but not the blocked-out text behind it. If a visual aura were to strike during the argument, I would be unable to see the justice I was addressing.

Then there were the dark moments when my impostor syndrome took hold, convincing me that I was indeed a fraud and I should never have volunteered to argue a case before the Supreme Court of the United States. There's a good reason why most Supreme Court cases are handled by highly experienced Supreme Court advocates with double-Ivy diplomas: *it's the Supreme Court of the United States.* This is no place for amateurs, and I was an amateur.

Flooded with self-doubt, I turned to my husband.

"I can't do this," I told Steven. "It's a huge mistake. I'm going to make a fool of myself."

Steven's loving efforts to console me only made me more aware of my self-imposed predicament.

"I know you can do this, Lisa. *You* know you can do this. But I hate to see you so overwhelmed. If it's too much to take on, there is still time to bow out gracefully."

Bowing out at this point wasn't possible for me, either. Admission of defeat would bring about a different sort of humiliation to bear. I was trapped inside my own head, rapidly cycling between two opposing states of mental paralysis: the inability to move forward and the inability to let go. Fortunately, my little pity parties were short and infrequent. I would soon realize that the time and effort it took to fixate on the negatives were far better spent working on the case. In fact, most of the time I was pretty excited. The odds of me ever going to the United States Supreme Court were zero to none, but I had beaten those odds. Deputy Solicitor General Michael Dreeben said it best: I had won the appellate lottery. It was all I thought about. Driving west to my office in Trenton every day on New Jersey Interstate 195, I passed the exit ramp for Washington Township, New Jersey. The exit sign simply said "Washington." I took the sign as a sign. Most days, I couldn't wait to get to DC. It was scary and thrilling to think it was actually going to happen.

And, of course, I had to look good. What better excuse to buy a new suit and all the accoutrements than arguing in the United States Supreme Court? The suit I purchased was the perfect example of my fashion preference of function over form: classic, solid black, flattering but comfortable, and wrinkle-resistant. As a woman who lived in broken-in jeans, T-shirts, and sneakers, my transition to professional attire in the mid-1980s was challenging. My career began during the era of thick wool, charcoal-gray pinstripe jackets with matching pleated skirts; crisply starched, white button-down collared shirts gussied up with tuxedo ruffles; red clip-on bowties; and unforgiving leather high-heeled pumps. This ensemble was a cross between a man's "power suit" and a parochial schoolgirl's uniform. It was bulky, confining, and, worst of all, itchy. Throw in a pair of control-top pantyhose and it's a wonder that I was able to sit still long enough to get any work done.

Steven and Jordan also bought new clothes for this special occasion. We splurged at Nordstrom's. Jordan felt very grown up picking out his red-and-yellow tie and standing tall as the tailor hemmed his khaki pants and altered the sleeves to his navy-blue, gold-buttoned blazer. I was so happy that Jordan would be watching his mom appear before the nine justices of the United States Supreme Court and even happier that he was mature enough to understand the significance of what I was about to do. My third-grader may not have appreciated the esoteric legal question at the heart of the *Apprendi* litigation, but he knew the matter was important enough to justify taking a few days off from school. The absence note I wrote to his third-grade teacher was unusual, to say the least:

> Dear Mrs. Dolci,
>   Please excuse Jordan from class on Monday March 27, Tuesday March 28, and Wednesday March 29, as he will be in Washington, D.C., to watch his mother argue before the Supreme Court of the United States.
>
> Sincerely,
> Lisa Gochman

—m—

Each of the nine Supreme Court justices wants to know the name of the attorney standing in front of him or her, so arguing counsel must fill out and send back to the Clerk's Office a "Notice of Appearance" form in advance of the scheduled argument date. I was encouraged to see on SCOTUS's "Notice of Appearance" form a blank space in which to write the preferred phonetic pronunciation of my name. I have heard my married name of Gochman verbally mangled as Gockman (rhymes with clock), Gokeman (rhymes with broke), Gookman (rhymes with book), Goochman (rhymes with pooch), and Gouchman (rhymes with couch). I wrote in "rhymes with watch" and hoped for the best.

Supreme Court Rule 28.1 states that "oral argument should emphasize and clarify the written argument in the briefs on the merits" and advises counsel "to assume that all Justices have read the briefs before oral argument."[1] Reading from a prepared text "is not favored."[2] To prepare for my oral argument, I consulted the indispensable tome, *Supreme Court Practice* (better known as *Stern and Gressman*), the bible of United States Supreme Court litigation.[3] It was like reading a pregnancy handbook filled with ominous warnings of everything that could go wrong without adequate preparation and prenatal vitamins. But I soon realized it boiled down to this straightforward advice: know the facts, know the law, and anticipate questions from the individual justices based on how each voted in similar cases. This strategy was no different from preparing for an argument before any appellate court, state or federal. So I focused on knowing the facts, knowing the law, and anticipating questions each justice might ask. I read and reread pertinent United States Supreme Court opinions and then read them again.

I also took note of what *not* to say during argument. Justice Robert H. Jackson offered this tongue-in-cheek advice for attorneys making their debut in the Supreme Court:

> On your first appearance before the Court, do not waste your time and
> ours telling us so. We are likely to discover for ourselves that you are a novice
> but will think none the less of you for it. Every famous lawyer had his first day
> at our bar and perhaps a sad one. It is not ingratiating to tell us you think it is
> an overwhelming honor to appear, for we think of the case as the important
> thing before us, not counsel. . . . Be respectful, of course, but also be self-
> respectful, and neither disparage yourself nor flatter the Justices. We think
> well enough of ourselves already.[4]

Not so long ago, counsels' time before the justices was unlimited, and arguments could last for days. In 1966, attorneys representing the parties and "friends of the court" in *Miranda v. Arizona* argued for more than five hours over three consecutive days.[5] Now, both sides get thirty minutes to present their oral arguments to the Supreme Court.[6] Said Justice Jackson, "Over the years the time allotted for hearing has been shortened, but its importance has not diminished. The significance of the trend is that the shorter the time, the more precious is each minute."[7] Consequently, Jackson advised arguing counsel, "Do not waste time complaining that you do not have enough time."[8]

My actual argument time in *Apprendi* had been whittled down from thirty minutes to twenty minutes when the Supreme Court granted the motion filed by the Office of the Solicitor General "to participate in oral argument and for divided argument" as amicus on behalf of New Jersey.[9] In his motion papers to the court, Solicitor General Seth Waxman noted that many federal criminal statutes authorized the imposition of enhanced sentences on the basis of facts found by the court at sentencing, such as illegal drug type and quantity.[10] The United States government thus had a "strong interest in the proper resolution of the constitutional question presented" in *Apprendi*. The Office of the Solicitor General had also represented the United States government in *Jones* and *Almendarez-Torrez*.[11] "Because of the United States' experience with the issue involved," explained Solicitor General Waxman, "we believe that oral presentation of the federal government's views would be of assistance to the Court."[12]

When I first read the solicitor general's motion papers, I thought, *Wow*, Apprendi *really must be an incredibly important case if the Office of the Solicitor General wants to participate in oral argument*. But then I realized, *Maybe the Office of the Solicitor General just wants to be right there in the courtroom to save the argument in case I screw up royally under the pressure*. I was, after all, a complete unknown to the solicitor general and to the United States Supreme Court. I was pretty sure I could handle oral argument, but what if, when the time came, I couldn't? I was fairly comfortable arguing before the Supreme Court of New Jersey, but arguing before the United States Supreme Court was on a whole new level for me. It's the difference between performing in regional theater and making your Broadway debut, the difference between Trenton Thunder Double-A baseball and the New York Yankees. It didn't matter if I had twenty or thirty minutes of argument time. I had to be prepared for anything the justices threw my way, regardless of how long I stood at the lectern.

I worked diligently on my opening statement, writing and rewriting it, hoping to strike just the right tone. *Guide for Counsel* advises attorneys to "speak in a clear, distinct manner, and try to avoid a monotone delivery."[13] It also reminds counsel that the Supreme Court "is not a jury" and we were to "avoid emotional oration and loud, impassioned pleas . . . without resort to histrionics."[14] My oral presentation needed to land somewhere in the middle:

measured without being tedious, enthusiastic without being theatrical. I high-lighted the words I wanted to emphasize in neon yellow and rehearsed my opening statement out loud over and over, sometimes alone in my office, sometimes in the presence of my colleagues, my husband, or my son, and most often standing in front of my bathroom mirror.

"May it please the Court" is the universal introduction to appellate argu-ments. *Guide for Counsel* directs attorneys appearing in the United States Su-preme Court to begin their arguments with the obligatory phrase "Mr. Chief Justice, and may it please the Court."[15] Steven would immediately chime in with "and even if it doesn't" whenever he heard me rehearsing my argument. He made a valid point. It was entirely possible my argument would not please the justices, but for goodness' sake, Steven, stop planting that idea in my head. Then there was the woman I knew who nervously blurted out during her law school moot court presentation, "May *I* please the Court."

My opening statement needed to cover as much ground as possible before the justices started asking questions, and they could chime in at any time. The Supreme Court of New Jersey, in contrast, offers litigants the option of giving a five-minute, uninterrupted opening statement at oral argument. It's a great idea because it gives me the opportunity to present my case without being knocked off course by questions from any of the seven justices. But about three minutes into my uninterrupted opening statement, I always wonder, *"Why are these people staring at me?"*[16]

I had no idea how much of my opening statement I would realistically get through in the Supreme Court of the United States before the first question cut me off. And what if the justices asked no questions at all? I would need to fill twenty minutes of time without appearing as if I was reading from a prepared text. Alternatively, I could end my argument early. One of the skills of appellate oral advocacy is knowing when to present a full argument to the judges you're standing before and when to sit down and shut up. In most of the criminal cases I handle in the New Jersey state courts, counsel for the defendant argues first and I argue second. Often, the questions posed to my opponent indicate which side of the argument the judges are leaning toward. If I sense that the argument is going my way and there is nothing to be gained by rambling on, I will tell the judges, "I respectfully rely on my written brief," and resume my seat.

This tactic, however, is not suitable for United States Supreme Court oral arguments. As Chief Justice Rehnquist stressed, "oral advocacy is probably more important in the Supreme Court of the United States than in most other appellate courts. . . . The time set for oral argument is the only opportunity that you will have to confront face-to-face the nine Members of the Court who will ponder and decide your case. The opportunity to convince them of the merits of your position is at its high point."[17]

I had just one chance to persuade the United States Supreme Court that New Jersey's Hate Crime Statute was constitutional. There was no higher court to appeal to if I lost.

—⁓—

Three months ahead of the *Apprendi* argument, Steven, Jordan, and I drove down to Washington, DC, for a reconnaissance tour of the Supreme Court building. There we watched an orientation video prepared for visitors to the United States Supreme Court. On the film, Justice Ruth Bader Ginsburg recalled how, when she was a practicing attorney making her debut argument before the court, she realized two minutes into her presentation that she had the justices' full attention while standing at the lectern, so she had better make the most of her time. With the *Apprendi* argument looming closer every day, Justice Ginsburg's words were unnerving. Just me and the nine justices of the Supreme Court of the United States for twenty whole minutes? And at least four of the nine—Stevens, Scalia, Souter, and Ginsburg—had telegraphed through their earlier votes in *Almendarez-Torres* and *Jones* that they would not be unreceptive to my argument in *Apprendi* that motive was a traditional sentencing factor and not an element of the crime of possession of a firearm for an unlawful purpose. For twenty long minutes, it would be me and four justices openly hostile to my position. To think I volunteered to do this.

An attorney in my office, Larry Etzweiler, had argued in the United States Supreme Court thirteen years earlier. I asked him for advice. Larry chuckled and said, "Just have fun."

CHAPTER 11

ON THURSDAY, MARCH 23, 2000, with five days to go before the *Apprendi* argument, I stopped by my office in the Hughes Justice Complex before catching an afternoon Amtrak train from the Trenton Rail Station to Union Station in Washington, DC. I don't remember why I didn't head straight from home to the Trenton train station. Maybe I needed to pick up some papers or do some last-minute research in the attorney general's sixth-floor library. Actually, I do remember: to make sure for the millionth time that everyone knew I was about to argue a case before the United States Supreme Court. I tried not to seem smug by boasting, so I resorted to stealth behavior by walking around, furtively trying to catch everyone's attention.

Most of my colleagues at the Division of Criminal Justice were incredibly supportive and sincerely wished me well. There were a few, I knew, who resented that I was arguing *Apprendi* instead of them. Perhaps they thought I was too inexperienced and incompetent to appear before the United States Supreme Court. And on the day I left for Washington, DC, as I stalked the halls of the Appellate Section, the naysayers still had time to be right. No one yet knew whether I would withstand the intense questioning by the chief justice and the eight associate justices. There was still plenty of time for me to screw up and infinite ways to do so. When I finished my farewell tour, my colleagues Janet Flanagan and Linda Rinaldi walked me to the elevator bank. Janet and Linda watched helplessly as the elevator doors closed behind me and I began my official journey to Washington, DC.

Steven picked me up at the front entrance to the Hughes Justice Complex and drove me to the Trenton train station to catch the 2:20 p.m. Amtrak to Washington, DC. He and Jordan planned to drive down to Washington the following evening in my forest green Honda Accord. I thought I had reserved a seat for myself in business class for the two-and-a-half-hour train ride to Washington so that I could get some work done, but the ticket waiting for me at the counter was for an unreserved seat in the coach section. I tried to upgrade my ticket, but there were no business-class seats left. Anxiety rapidly filled my chest.

The coach car was nearly full, but I managed to find a vacant seat. As Steven helped me load my luggage onto the overhead rack, we felt rumbling beneath our feet.

"Oh, shit, Lisa!" Steven shouted. "The train! It's starting to move! I gotta get off this thing!"

We hurriedly kissed goodbye before Steven heroically leaped off the moving train and onto the platform, sticking the landing. As the Amtrak train pulled away from the Trenton station, I settled into my seat, grabbing some work from my briefcase. The gentle rocking of the car helped me relax.

I love train rides. Once I am safely aboard, there is absolutely nothing to do except quietly read or enjoy the passing scenery. As the southbound Amtrak from Trenton to Washington, DC, crossed the bend in the Schuylkill River in Philadelphia, I had an unobstructed view of historic Boathouse Row, where twelve nineteenth-century stone boathouses line the river just west of the Philadelphia Museum of Art. Relishing the peacefulness of the train, I ordinarily avoid conversations with my fellow passengers. But when my seatmate, an older gentleman, asked why I was traveling to DC, I couldn't help but gush about my upcoming argument in the Supreme Court. I'm sure the poor man was sorry he asked. We eventually fell into a comfortable silence, and I spent the rest of the ride reviewing the three transcripts of the trial court hearings before Judge Rushton Ridgway. Command of the state court record was a critical component of my preparation for the argument.

I had an overstuffed suitcase with me, as well as my black leather briefcase and a bulky (yet classic) black leather Coach bucket bag, a gift from my parents in honor of my argument. The following day, Steven would be bringing with him the two-piece black suit I planned to wear during the argument so that it could hang neatly from the dry-cleaning hook in the rear passenger compartment of our Honda Accord rather than be folded inside a garment bag. It had seemed like a good idea at the time. Sitting on the train, however, I was overcome with dread that my husband would forget to bring my suit. I made a mental note to remind him before he left New Jersey.

Despite Clerk Suter's well-meaning advice in *Guide for Counsel*, I did not pack light. Aside from what I had with me on the train, I had also arranged for my office to ship a large box of photocopied legal research directly to the hotel in DC. My huge circa 1987 suitcase didn't have wheels, so when I arrived in Union Station, I had to drag it behind me as my briefcase and pocketbook slipped off my narrow shoulders. Unable to find anyone to help me carry my luggage up the flight of steps from the train platform and across the vast marble expanse of Union Station's lobby, I was drenched in sweat and close to tears by the time I made it to the taxi stand. The Hyatt Regency on Capitol Hill was less than a mile from the train station, but there was no way I could navigate the crowded sidewalks of Washington, DC, with that heavy suitcase in tow.

As I checked into the Hyatt hotel, I gave the front desk clerk a conspiratorial smile.

"I'm so excited to finally arrive in Washington," I told her. "I'm here to argue a case before the United States Supreme Court this coming Tuesday."

When I reserved the hotel room two months earlier, I had requested a quiet room. I have trouble falling asleep in hotels as guests clomp up and down hallways, elevator doors scrape open and shut, and ice machines noisily dispense cubes into rigid plastic buckets. And I couldn't rely on sleeping pills. What if I overslept on the day of my argument?

"There should be a notation on my reservation that I asked for a room on a high floor, far away from the elevators and ice machine," I politely informed the front desk clerk.

I don't know if the clerk misheard me or if I said something to piss her off or if I was supposed to slip her a twenty-dollar bill, but the hotel room she assigned to me was directly across the street from the red brick District of Columbia Fire Department, Engine No. 3, established 1916, on New Jersey Avenue. On cue, the firehouse bells started clanging in the middle of the night like the train whistle in *My Cousin Vinny*, jolting me awake. The next morning,

I moved to another, much quieter room in the rear of the hotel, far away from the elevators, the ice machine, and the firehouse.

After switching rooms, I left the Hyatt Regency to walk to the National Association of Attorneys General (NAAG) offices near Union Station for my ten o'clock moot court. A moot court is a practice session that attempts to replicate the circumstances counsel will face arguing before the real Supreme Court. NAAG's Center for Supreme Court Advocacy conducts fifteen to twenty-five moot courts each Supreme Court term for states' attorneys and lawyers.[1] Virtually every state's attorney who appears before the United States Supreme Court first participates in a NAAG moot court.

The Supreme Court Institute at Georgetown Law in Washington also offers moot courts for counsel of record in all Supreme Court cases where certiorari has been granted but typically moots only one side of the case on a first-come, first-served basis. When both sides contact Georgetown Law's Supreme Court Institute within twenty-four hours of the time the Supreme Court of the United States grants certiorari, a coin toss decides which side will be mooted: the petitioner is heads, and the respondent is tails.[2] Georgetown's moot courtroom is modeled after the real thing, down to the round, analog clock suspended above the pretend chief justice's head so litigants can practice not looking at it. I had contacted Georgetown Law months earlier to arrange a moot court there, in addition to the one at NAAG, but Apprendi's attorney, Joseph O'Neill, had beaten me to it.

A moot court is as necessary for an attorney appearing before SCOTUS as a dress rehearsal is for an actor appearing on Broadway. The Supreme Court building itself is like an elegant marble theater and the courtroom a magnificent stage set complete with crimson velvet proscenium curtains that part at exactly ten o'clock in the morning on argument days to allow the nine stars of the show to enter magically from backstage. But that is where the comparison ends.

On Broadway, the same production is staged night after night. Actors rehearse the same scripted lines for the same scene for weeks until they are ready to appear before a live audience. When one actor asks a question, the other actor knows far ahead of time precisely how that question will be phrased and what the answer will be, word for word. Appearing before the Supreme Court is closer to improv. There are no lines to memorize. The justices did not provide me with a written list of their questions in advance of the actual argument. I would not know exactly what the justices would ask me until they asked me. And what if a justice threw a question out of left field about my case that I hadn't thought about before, such as, "What is the difference between beer and ale?" I would be left standing very much alone at the lectern doing a mental tap dance as the justice impatiently awaited my answer.

And that is why a moot court or two or three is essential preparation for a United States Supreme Court oral argument. You need other lawyers' knowledge, perspective, and experience to supplement your own. National Association of Attorneys General moot court panelists include Supreme Court practitioners from the Office of the Solicitor General, former United States Supreme Court clerks, and Supreme Court experts in private practice, academia, and the government. Dan Schweitzer, NAAG's Supreme Court director and chief counsel, advised me by email before I arrived in Washington that "because panel members are lawyers with regular exposure to this Court, the questions asked at the moot court closely track those the Justices ask at the oral argument. The panel members are familiar with the concerns and questioning styles of the various Justices; and like the Justices, they will have no reticence about asking any question or hypothetical they can imagine."

Walking from the hotel to NAAG headquarters, however, I wasn't focused on the upcoming moot court. My more immediate concern was my skirt, which was at least one size too big on me and spinning around my waist as I walked. I had to stop on the sidewalk every few steps to fix myself. The stress associated with United States Supreme Court litigation works better than any weight-loss program.

My moot court judges were NAAG Supreme Court Director and Chief Counsel Dan Schweitzer, Assistant Solicitor General Edward DuMont, and two NAAG Supreme Court Fellows, Patrick DeAlmeida and Denise Simpson. The NAAG Supreme Court Fellows Program is like junior year abroad for states' attorneys. Every three to four months, two government attorneys leave their home states for Washington, DC, where they attend oral arguments at the United States Supreme Court, summarize recent SCOTUS decisions and orders for NAAG's newsletter, and write a friend of the court brief in a pending United States Supreme Court matter. (Coincidentally, NAAG Fellow Patrick DeAlmeida was a New Jersey deputy attorney general in the Division of Law and worked in the Hughes Justice Complex in Trenton at the same time I did, although we had not met before.)

During moot courts in preparation for arguments before the Supreme Court of New Jersey, I always stood before the familiar faces of my supervisors and colleagues at the Division of Criminal Justice. Their questioning could be ruthless, but at least I knew who they were. Here at NAAG, I took my place at a portable lectern on one side of a conference table facing four complete strangers. I had to blindly trust that they would whip me into shape for the real thing.

Armed with a rainbow of merits and amici briefs filed by both sides in *Apprendi*, the NAAG moot court panel was as familiar with the legal issues at stake as I was. One of my moot court judges, Edward DuMont, was the assistant solicitor general who had argued *Jones* before SCOTUS on behalf of the United States government exactly one year earlier to the day. *Jones* was the case in which SCOTUS interpreted the federal carjacking statute so that death and serious bodily injury to the victim were elements of the offense to be found by the jury beyond a reasonable doubt, and not sentencing factors to be found by the judge under a lower burden of proof. Ed DuMont was also the assistant solicitor general with whom I would be sharing my thirty-minute argument slot in *Apprendi*.

As soon as the questioning began, I realized that this would not be a repeat of the moot court back home in New Jersey. I came to Washington prepared to answer questions about New Jersey's Hate Crime Statute, but the NAAG judges hit me with far broader hypotheticals testing the outer limits of the Sixth Amendment right to a jury trial. I obviously had a lot more homework to do before the actual argument. Adding insult to injury, the NAAG moot court was videotaped. I was forced to relive the entire session while Dan Schweitzer critiqued my body language like a football coach analyzing a player's mediocre performance on the field.

"You're too animated," Dan told me. "You're shifting your weight from foot to foot. Stop moving around so much while you're listening to the justices' questions and don't gesture with your hands when you're answering a question."

When the pile-on ended, I joined Dan and Patrick DeAlmeida for lunch in the food hall in Union Station. I tend to eat the same foods as a coping mechanism when I am under stress. It's just one less decision for me to make during a demanding day. In the summer of 1984, while studying for the New York State bar exam, I ordered a cup of coffee with cream and a blueberry muffin to go from the West Fourth Street Diner in the West Village every morning on my way to the library. And every afternoon, I took a break from the monotony of contracts and property law by eating an orange-chocolate ice cream cone at a nearby ice cream shop. While in Washington, DC, preparing for the *Apprendi* argument, I ate a lot of tuna salad sandwiches with sliced cucumber on a croissant. (I am a tunaficionado.)

After lunch, I grabbed a taxi to the Department of Justice building on Pennsylvania Avenue to attend Ed DuMont's moot court in the solicitor general's fifth-floor conference room. Unlike the NAAG moot court, for which the state was charged a $1,750 user fee, participation in Ed's moot court was free—sort of. My invitation to sit in on Ed's moot court was in exchange for New Jersey's consent to yield ten minutes of argument time to the solicitor general's office. And only Ed would be mooted. I could ask Ed questions, but no one would ask me anything.

—◊—

The world of law is highly stratified. Many of the brightest students who graduate from the nation's Ivy League law schools become law clerks to the most highly respected federal district court judges across the United States. Many go on from there to more prestigious clerkships with federal appellate court judges. And a select few then clerk for one of the nine justices of the United States Supreme Court, the most coveted clerkship of all. The Office of the Solicitor General employs many of these former United States Supreme Court clerks. They are the *crème de la crème* of the appellate world.

I am not one of them. During the summer between my second and third years of law school, I interned for a federal district court judge who, in a published opinion, advised a plaintiff suing the state of New Jersey for allegedly injecting him in the left eye with radium electric beams that he could "block the broadcast antenna in his brain simply by grounding it. Just as delivery trucks for oil and gasoline are 'grounded' against the accumulation of charges of static electricity, so on the same principle [plaintiff] might have pinned to the back of a trouser leg a short chain of paper clips so that the end would touch the ground and prevent anyone from talking to him inside his brain."[3] Mine was not the most coveted judicial internship.

On Friday afternoon, as I reached the front doors of the main Department of Justice building on Pennsylvania Avenue for Assistant Solicitor General Edward DuMont's moot court, I heard a voice call my name. I turned around to see Attorney General Farmer alight from a black sedan. He had driven down from New Jersey that morning in time to join me at Ed's moot court and to lend moral support. I needed it. There I was, just days before my own United States Supreme Court argument, an unknown state's attorney sitting nervously in the Office of the Solicitor General's conference room surrounded by double–Ivy League assistant solicitors general, waiting for Ed's moot court to begin.

The quiet of the conference room was shattered when Seth Waxman, the solicitor general of the United States, burst through the door and loudly declared, "Well, *this* case is a loser!"

I was dumbfounded. The solicitor general of the United States didn't sugarcoat it or beat around the bush. He came right out and announced that the case I was set to argue in less than four days was "a loser." I hadn't even been introduced to him yet. Maybe Waxman didn't see me sitting there. More frightening, maybe he was right. I always knew there was the possibility of losing *Apprendi*, but, until that moment, I always thought there was the possibility of winning, too.

Further complicating matters, the solicitor general's office's view on the "sentencing factor versus element of the offense" debate was far more expansive than the state's position in *Apprendi*. My narrow argument was that motive, good or bad, was a traditional sentencing factor. Theirs was that pretty much anything Congress or a state legislature defined as a sentencing factor was a sentencing factor and anything Congress or a state legislature defined as an element of the offense was an element of the offense. Advancing this strategy was risky. It had already failed in *Jones* when the Supreme Court held that serious bodily injury was an element of the federal offense of carjacking. But given the multitude of federal statutes authorizing the imposition of enhanced sentences based on facts determined by the judge at sentencing, such as the type and quantity of an illicit drug found in a defendant's possession, Ed had no leeway to deviate from the sweeping position of the Office of the Solicitor General. Maybe that's why Seth Waxman was so sure we would lose.

At the very least, I hoped the federal government would acknowledge that *Jones* was correctly decided. The *Jones* decision would not doom the constitutionality of New Jersey's Hate Crime Statute as long as I could distinguish the traditional sentencing factor of motive from the traditional elements of death and serious bodily injury to the victim. Advocating for anything broader might push SCOTUS to adopt the bright-line rule proposed in footnote 6 of *Jones* that any fact, other than a prior conviction, that increases the maximum penalty for a crime must be proved to the jury beyond a reasonable doubt. The Hate Crime Statute would never survive constitutional scrutiny under this bright-line rule.

Pretending to be a Supreme Court justice, I asked Ed DuMont whether death and serious bodily injury could ever be considered as sentencing factors after *Jones*. I was immediately shut down by my moot court brethren. I could hear them thinking that I lacked the proper academic and professional credentials to sit at their conference table, let alone confront one of their own about one of his cases.

When Ed's moot court ended, Attorney General Farmer and I walked out to the hallway for the postmortem. The attorney general disagreed with Solicitor General Waxman's pessimistic view of the case. He encouraged me to stick with my narrow argument, which we both believed had a far better chance of prevailing before the United States Supreme Court. The court could uphold the constitutionality of New Jersey's Hate Crime Statute on the narrow ground that motive was a traditional sentencing factor without addressing the broader position taken by the Office of the Solicitor General. My responsibility was to defend the constitutionality of New Jersey's Hate Crime Statute, not the constitutionality of any and all federal criminal statutes.

I hailed a taxi back to the Hyatt Regency on Capitol Hill late in the afternoon, bedraggled and utterly drained, as my family started trickling into Washington, DC. My parents and my in-laws flew in from Florida; my sister flew in from California; and my sister-in-law, her husband, and their children, nine-year old Jeffrey and six-year old Alexa, drove down from New Jersey. To my great relief, Steven and Jordan remembered to bring my unwrinkled argument suit with them in the Honda.

Recognizing how much work I had left to do and how much pressure I was under, Steven and Jordan wisely checked into their own hotel room. I needed lots of space to spread out my books and notes and uninterrupted quiet to practice my argument. It was party time in DC for everyone but me, and my parents, especially, clamored for my attention.

"Can you join us for dinner, Lisa?" my mother asked hopefully. "We haven't seen you since Thanksgiving."

But the day's moot courts had left me far too exhausted and apprehensive to be good company. I needed to remain focused on the upcoming argument without further distractions. Steven assumed the role of my consigliere. To get to me, my family had to go through Steven first. I sequestered myself in my hotel room, oblivious to the outside world.

CHAPTER 12

ON SATURDAY, MARCH 25, 2000, while Jordan and Steven played with moon rocks in the Smithsonian's Air and Space Museum on the National Mall, I prepared for my argument, now just three short days away. Clearly, though, I needed to eat if I had lost so much weight that my skirt twirled around my waist like a hula hoop when I walked. That evening, eleven of us drove from the hotel a few miles north to Bethesda, Maryland, to join my cousin Allison and her family at a restaurant for dinner. Afterward, we caravanned back to the Hyatt on Capitol Hill. Our nephew Jeffrey, who, like Jordan, was in third grade, rode back with Steven and me. This was in pre-GPS days, and Jeff took great pleasure in asking, "Are we lost yet? Are we lost yet?" again and again, eliciting peals of laughter from Jordan each time. To a third-grader, there's no such thing as hearing the same joke once too often.

Steven drove up the circular driveway directly in front of the main entrance to the Hyatt Regency and waited with our Honda Accord for the valet service while I brought Jordan and Jeff upstairs to their hotel rooms. I was helping Jordan get ready for bed in his room when my parents knocked on the door. When I opened the hotel room door, my father said grimly, "You have to come with me. Mom will stay with Jordan. Your car was in an accident."

"An accident? How could my car have possibly been in an accident?" Last I knew, it was parked unoccupied in front of the hotel.

As we rang for the elevator, my father assured me that Steven was fine, but, to my great annoyance, he wouldn't offer up any more information. The elevator doors opened, and packed inside was a group of tipsy Shriners, all wearing their signature bright red fezzes, on their way to one of the hotel ballrooms for the annual Shriners convention. My father and I squeezed onto the crowded elevator. I put on quite the show for my captive audience on the ride down as I shouted at my father, *"What the hell happened to my car?"*

What the hell happened was that the valet had failed to do the one job he was hired to do: cautiously drive a guest's vehicle a short distance on New Jersey Avenue, make a quick right on D Street, and make another quick right into the hotel's underground parking garage. Apparently, our valet had watched *Ferris Bueller's Day Off* one too many times and mistook my four-door, mid-size family sedan for a zippy Ferrari 250 GT California Spyder two-door, convertible sports car. The valet raced my Honda Accord down the sidewalk in front of the hotel, completely missing the roadway. He crashed first into a United States Postal Service mailbox and then into a wrought iron garbage can bolted to the concrete, launching both into the air. The valet then careened across the intersection of New Jersey Avenue and D Street, plowing into two parked cars and pushing both up onto the sidewalk where the Japanese American Memorial now stands. Incredibly, the valet did not hit a moving vehicle or a pedestrian in what can be an extremely busy intersection.

Somewhere in the bowels of the United States Post Office building in Washington, DC, a piercing alarm must have sounded, because a Postal Service truck pulled up and workers replaced the beat-up mailbox before the police arrived at the scene of the crash. Neither rain nor sleet nor demolished mailboxes in the dark of night shall stay these couriers from the swift completion of their appointed rounds. Meanwhile, my husband, father, and father-in-law sprang into alpha-male mode, snapping photographs of the extensive front-end damage to my Honda and demanding to speak with the hotel manager. I stood to the side muttering, "I don't need this stress. I don't need this stress," my hands pressed against my cheeks *Home Alone*–style. My Supreme Court argument was less than three days away.

A flatbed tow truck pulled up to whisk away my crumpled Honda Accord. As my vehicle was loaded onto the back of the tow truck, my father asked, "Do you need to get anything out of the car?" Steven and I exchanged "Oh, shit" glances before climbing onto the flatbed of the truck to retrieve the automatic garage door opener from the windshield visor, the registration and insurance documents from the glove compartment, and a case of champagne from the trunk of the car. Steven had purchased the champagne before he left New Jersey for the celebratory luncheon he had arranged at a Capitol Hill restaurant for after my argument. All six bottles were intact.

The hotel's night manager escorted Steven and me to a dingy office behind the front desk in the lobby where he offered to pay for my room. Because I was staying at the Hyatt on New Jersey state business, I couldn't accept this gift, which was bigger than a bagel and more costly than a cup of coffee. But Steven and Jordan were staying in a separate room that we were paying for ourselves. As private citizens, Steven and Jordan took full advantage of the night manager's hospitality by raiding the hotel minibar. Jordan cracked open a cold bottle of Perrier to wash down the Toblerone Swiss milk chocolate bar and peanut M&Ms. He had never tried sparkling water before. Unnerved by the carbonation, Jordan did a spit take, spewing bubbly Perrier in a fizzy arc across the room. Steven, meanwhile, helped himself to the miniature bottles of adult beverages.

That was before the day manager called Steven to say that the night manager misspoke. Apparently, because the Honda was registered in my name only, the hotel wouldn't pay for Steven and Jordan's room, or the mini-bar.

My consolation prize for the totaled Honda was the use of the hotel's chauffeured Lincoln Town Car, the "Hyatt One," for the remainder of my stay. I loved calling down to the front desk to request the Hyatt One and felt like a sparkly Disney princess whenever the driver opened and closed the rear passenger door for me. The kicker came when the front desk clerk handed me the bill at checkout the following Wednesday morning. We had been charged for five nights' parking in the hotel garage.

"You're kidding me, right?" I asked the clerk, jabbing my finger at the parking fee. "We're not paying this bill."

Detecting panic in the front desk clerk's eyes, Steven patiently explained that the valet had totaled our car, and we certainly weren't paying the parking fee. The hapless clerk called his manager, who appeared from the dingy back office. Steven again patiently explained the situation. "Let me see what I can do," the manager smugly told us, as if he were doing us a favor. He tapped a few strokes on the keyboard to bring up another file on the computer monitor. Nodding his head in understanding, the manager agreed to reverse the parking charges for all but Friday night.

"Excuse me?" I asked. "You're charging us for parking on Friday night?"

"Well, I see in your file you did use the valet service of the garage on Friday night," the manager explained without any hint of irony in voice.

Steven is far more easygoing than I am, but even he has his limits.

"Do you understand that *your* valet totaled *our* car?" he asked the hotel manager. "Do you *really* think we are going to pay for the privilege of parking our car in the garage responsible for crashing it into a mailbox on New Jersey Avenue?"

Jordan piped up, "Don't forget the garbage can!"

"And the two parked cars," I added.

The manager relented.

I loved that forest green Honda Accord. One warm spring afternoon in New Jersey, Steven was driving my car, my dad was in the front passenger seat, and my mom, Jordan, and I shared the back seat. We were stopped at a traffic light when two teenagers in a souped-up pickup truck pulled up beside us on the left side of our car. The driver revved his engine, daring Steven to race him. I begged Steven not to take the bait. When the light changed to green, the passenger in the truck showered the inside of our Honda through the open sunroof with an aerosol can before the driver sped off, leaving my father dripping in pink Silly String and Jordan helplessly giggling in the back seat.

—⁂—

Sunday, March 26, 2000. I probably should have been working, but I took a few hours off that morning for a private tour of the White House with my family, arranged by a friend of my in-laws, Fran and Jesse. The Hyatt One dropped off Steven, Jordan, and me at the visitors' entrance. Inside, we peeked into the empty Oval Office from behind a velvet rope and sat on a silk damask couch beneath an oil portrait of First Lady Jacqueline Kennedy. We overheard one Secret Service agent whisper into his radio mouthpiece that "Evergreen," First Lady Hillary Clinton's code name, was "on the move" in the residential quarters. We roamed through the Rose Garden and took turns standing at the podium of the White House Press Briefing Room. We still debate whether taking one of the neatly folded, thick paper towels embossed with the White House seal in gold from the bathrooms is considered theft.

Later that evening, I turned down two equally enticing dinner invitations, one with my parents and my uncle, and another with my husband's Baltimore cousins, to endure one last informal moot court. Dan Schweitzer, Patrick DeAlmeida, and Denise Simpson of the National Association of Attorneys General came to my hotel room and hurled four-part questions and dizzying hypotheticals at me for hours. During this grilling, the immediacy of what I had gotten myself into finally sank in. For months, I had engaged in a theoretical exercise in Supreme Court oral advocacy where March 28, 2000, was always far off in the distant future. Suddenly, the argument was less than a day and a half away. No more moot courts for me. Next up was the genuine thing. My impostor syndrome reared its ugly head.

Later, alone in my room, I called Carol Henderson, the deputy chief of the Division of Criminal Justice's Appellate Section, to confess my inadequacies.

"Oh, Carol," I cried. "What the hell was I thinking? This is the United States Supreme Court, for God's sake! I can't do this! Why did I think I could do this?"

Carol talked me through my existential crisis, reminding me I had lived with the *Apprendi* case since the state appellate brief was first assigned to me four years earlier.

"Lisa, you're going to be fine," Carol assured me. "It's just last-minute nerves. You've argued *Apprendi* twice already in the state courts. No one knows this case better than you." She ticked off the names of other attorneys from our office who had argued before SCOTUS in recent years.

"If they can do it," Carol said, "you certainly can. I've watched you argue many times in the Supreme Court of New Jersey, and I have complete confidence in your oral advocacy skills."

Obviously, Carol had never heard me blurt out "gooing chum."

Carol might well have been lying, but what else could she say? Even if she agreed with me that, why, yes, I *was* stupid for thinking I was competent enough to appear before the United States Supreme Court, it was far too late to tell me that now. All I could hope for at this point was to get a decent night's sleep. There was much more work to be done tomorrow.

Guide for Counsel encourages attorneys to attend a courtroom session before their scheduled argument day.[1] At ten o'clock in the morning, March 27, 2000, with exactly twenty-four hours to go before the *Apprendi* argument, I was seated in the section reserved for members of the bar in the United States Supreme Court courtroom to acclimate myself to the setting and procedure during two unrelated oral arguments.

The courtroom is the inner sanctum of the highest temple of justice in the United States, the symmetry and grand proportions of its neoclassical architecture befitting ancient Greek and Roman temples. Nearly square at eighty-two feet by ninety-one feet, the chamber is flanked by twenty-four white marble Ionic columns standing thirty feet high, each capped with a distinctive spiral design. The shaft of each column is so wide that if I wrapped my arms around one, my fingertips would not touch. Bas-relief marble friezes depicting allegorical and historical figures line the upper third of all four walls of the courtroom. The coffered ceiling is adorned with three-dimensional red, blue, and gold rosettes bordered by a Greek key motif.

At the far end of this stately and imposing courtroom were the justices in their high-back black leather chairs seated nine across behind their raised Honduran mahogany bench.[2] Seeing them in person, hearing their voices— it was almost too much for me. I was gripped, not with fear but with awe. I had watched arguments in the United States Supreme Court before, so this wasn't my first time in the audience, but this *was* my first time in the audience knowing that, the next morning, it would be me standing at the altar of the appellate gods.

I tried to focus on the two civil cases on the day's calendar, but I knew nothing about them, and I found the arguments difficult to follow. The first case, *Robin Free v. Abbot Laboratories*, entailed federal jurisdiction and class action lawsuits.[3] The second case, *Donald E. Nelson v. Adams USA, Inc.*, addressed the scope of due process afforded to parties named in amended and supplemental pleadings under the Federal Rules of Procedure.[4] Justice Ginsburg would later spice up her majority opinion in *Nelson v. Adams* by quoting author Lewis Carroll to drive home the point that, even in fictitious Wonderland, parties being sued for civil damages are entitled to notice and due process of law to defend themselves in court. Ginsburg wrote,

"'Herald, read the accusation!' said the King. On this the White Rabbit blew three blasts on the trumpet, and then unrolled the parchment scroll, and read as follows:

'The Queen of Hearts, she made some tarts,
All on a summer day;
The Knave of Hearts, he stole those tarts,
And took them quite away.'

'Consider your verdict,' the King said to the jury.
'Not yet, not yet!' the Rabbit interrupted. 'There's a great deal to come before that!'"[5]

But there were no recitations of nursery rhymes or quotes from Lewis Carroll during the oral argument itself, which was a shame, because it would have perked things up for the audience.

Why, then, do lawyers, students, and tourists alike rise in the dark, early hours of the morning to claim their place in line on the marble steps of the Supreme Court building, waiting outside in the cold March winds to sit through a technical argument on debate regarding an arcane point of federal law? Because SCOTUS has a long-standing rule prohibiting both still and television cameras inside the courtroom. The justices do not give press conferences to explain the significance of an argument they just heard or a decision they just handed down. Oral arguments are the "only publicly visible part of the Supreme Court's decision process," and they are visible only to the people physically inside the courtroom during the argument.[6] The only way to see all nine justices in action is to attend an oral argument. You literally have to be there.

When the second argument ended at noon and the justices recessed for lunch, I left the courtroom praying I was prepared enough, skilled enough, poised enough to appear in this storied hall of justice. Tomorrow I would be on full display before the justices and the spectators.

I grabbed another tuna salad sandwich with sliced cucumber on a croissant from the food court in Union Station on my way to NAAG's headquarters, where I spent the final afternoon before my argument squirreled away in one of the offices reserved for attorneys general and their staff visiting from out of town. In the quiet of the borrowed office, I reread key Supreme Court cases, including *Almendarez-Torres* (a prior conviction is a sentencing factor) and

Jones (serious bodily injury to the victim is an element of the offense); honed my opening statement; and organized the black three-ring binder of notes I planned to take with me to the lectern. I chose a plain black binder because *Guide for Counsel* advises that "turning pages in a notebook appears more professional than flipping pages of a legal pad."[7]

At five o'clock that evening, NAAG Supreme Court Director and Chief Counsel Dan Schweitzer gently suggested it was time for me to return to my hotel and take the rest of the evening off. By then, I was preternaturally calm. The crushing self-doubt that had enveloped me the night before had dissipated. Back in my hotel room at the Hyatt Regency on Capitol Hill, I serenely rehearsed my argument before an imaginary court until it was time for bed. I knew I was ready.

Bring it on.

CHAPTER 13

THE LOCAL FORECAST FOR ARGUMENT day called for a strong line of thunderstorms as a cold front approached. "Dammit," I grumbled at the weatherman. The Supreme Court of the United States does not offer indoor parking or a covered entryway to protect visitors or arguing counsel from the elements. On top of everything else, now I had to worry about wrestling with an umbrella in the wind and rain. "Drowned rat" was not the image I was aiming for at my one and only Supreme Court argument. I recoiled at the thought of cold, wet pantyhose clinging to my legs. But when I threw open the blackout curtains in my hotel room on the morning of Tuesday, March 28, 2000, it was all bright blue skies and, as my mother had predicted, pink cherry blossoms.

I had slept peacefully the night before, largely due to the captivating memoir *A Walk in the Woods* that I read before falling sleep. *A Walk in the Woods* is the true adventure of author Bill Bryson's attempt to hike all twenty-one hundred miles of the Appalachian Trail from its southern terminus in Springer Mountain in Georgia to its northern terminus in Mount Katahdin in Maine with his equally out-of-shape, middle-aged friend. I, too, am unathletic, but having spent many summers at sleepaway camp in the eastern white pine forests of Maine, it was easy to imagine myself ambling alongside Bill and his companion as they moseyed through the tranquil woods. To me, the book was the perfect metaphor for my impending challenge: how ordinary people can accomplish extraordinary things through hard work, good luck, and comfortable shoes. Thankfully, I hadn't yet gotten to the part of the story where Bill and his friend both gave up and went home early.

I showered and blow-dried my shoulder-length hair perfectly straight, which was no small feat in the primeval age before portable flat irons. My fluffy tresses have a will of their own. They are too curly to be straight, too straight to be curly, and always ultrasensitive to the barest hint of moisture in the air. Washington, DC, was built on swampland and has a well-deserved reputation for insufferable humidity. I was painfully aware that my hair might frizz up the second I left the air-conditioned cocoon of the hotel lobby.

My hair had to be perfect from all angles. Appellate courtrooms are universally designed so that the judges sit across the back wall facing the spectators' gallery. Appellate attorneys stand at a lectern facing the judges with their backs to the audience. In the United States Supreme Court courtroom, news reporters and sketch artists sit to the left of arguing counsel. Visiting dignitaries and the justices' guests and law clerks sit to counsel's right. I would be on view for a full 360 degrees. It was theater-in-the-round. There was no plan B.

The Notice to Counsel sent to me by the Clerk's Office prior to the argument date advised that "appropriate attire for counsel is conservative business dress." In its early years, SCOTUS required all attorneys, who were almost always men, to wear formal morning clothes during their appearances before the court. Arguing counsel would stand at the lectern decked out in black-and-gray-striped trousers, a gray ascot, a gray waistcoat, and a gray cutaway morning coat.[1] By the 1950s, the court had adopted a more laissez-faire approach to courtroom attire. But, as Justice Robert Jackson then observed,

> The tradition remains that appearance before the Court is no ordinary occasion. Government lawyers and many others, particularly older ones, adhere to the custom of formal morning dress. The Clerk's Office advises that either this or a dark business suit is appropriate. But the informality which permeates all official life has penetrated the Court. It lays down no rule for its [lawyers].
>
> No toleration, however, can repeal the teaching of Polonius that, "The apparel oft proclaims the man." You will not be stopped from arguing if you wear a race-track suit or sport a rainbow necktie. You will just create a first impression that you have strayed in at the wrong bar.[2]

In 2000, the United States solicitor general still required his attorneys to appear in formal morning dress. I imagined a large walk-in closet at the Department of Justice on Pennsylvania Avenue where identical gray morning coats and striped trousers hung in size order from extra-small to extra-extra-large from which assistant solicitors general could select their outfits for their arguments.

As a representative of the state of New Jersey and not the federal government, I was not required to wear formal morning attire for my argument. Instead, I put on my single-button black suit jacket and matching skirt with a straw yellow, jewel neck, long-sleeved silk blouse and my late grandmother's pearl necklace. A robust topic of debate among the women in my office before I left for Washington was the pantyhose color I should wear, sheer black or nude. Sheer black pantyhose with a black skirt was all the rage that year, because the uniformity of color supposedly created the illusion that the wearer was taller than she really was. At barely five feet two inches in height, I needed all the illusion I could get. Not that any of the justices would see my legs, which would remain hidden from their view whether I sat at counsel table or stood at the lectern. But the Supreme Court is a major tourist attraction, and I wanted to make New Jersey proud, if not by my dazzling advocacy skills then at least by my au courant fashion sense. I bowed to peer pressure and chose sheer black pantyhose. Then I put on my brand-new black leather pumps with patent leather cap toes and prayed I would not topple off the midsized heels. Before I left home, I had sandpapered the soles of my new shoes to minimize the chances of sliding on the highly polished marble floors of the courthouse and falling on my ass.

At 8:00 a.m., hotel room service delivered scrambled eggs, dry whole wheat toast, orange juice, and coffee with cream to my room. I had placed the order the night before, not knowing whether I would be able to stomach any food at all. I hoped to at least keep down the toast. Although I am not a big breakfast eater, I knew I had to eat something so I didn't keel over from low blood sugar midway through the argument. But I woke up uncharacteristically famished and ate it all. Ready and raring to go, I walked to Steven and Jordan's hotel room and knocked on their door.

"Good morning!" I chirped as Jordan opened the door. "Did you sleep well last night? I slept great! Can you believe today is the day?" I spun around to give my husband and son the full 360-degree view of my awesomeness. "Don't you love this suit? And look at my perfect hair!" Steven and Jordan eyed me suspiciously. I'm not a morning person and am rarely chipper at any time of the day.

Right then I realized that neither Steven nor Jordan was ready to go. Swiftly transitioning from giddy Supreme Court advocate to exasperated mom, I demanded, "Why aren't either of you dressed? Jordan, did you shower yet? Steven, did you order food? We won't have time to stop for breakfast on the way to the courthouse, you know." But there, tucked into a far corner of their room, was a room service table with starched white linens and stainless-steel covers resting atop untouched ceramic plates.

"Ooh, what did you order?" I asked. "I already ate, but I'm still hungry."

Steven was incredulous. "You ate breakfast?"

"Yes, scrambled eggs."

Steven and Jordan gagged in unison, both too anxious about my impending argument to think about eating coagulated egg protein. As they finished getting dressed, I poured myself a cup of hot coffee and sampled the assorted muffins and pastries in the Hyatt's "Rise 'n' Shine" breakfast basket.

Steven and Jordan looked so handsome, Steven in his new black suit and Jordan in his navy blue blazer, white oxford shirt, khaki pants, and red-and-yellow tie. (At nine years old, Jordan resembled Harry Potter with his straight dark hair and round-rimmed glasses, and he was a runner-up the following year in the *Asbury Park Press*'s Harry Potter Look-Alike Contest.) I was as proud of Steven and Jordan as they were of me. We descended to the lobby in the hotel's interior glass elevator. I had reserved the Hyatt One for the ride to the Supreme Court, and the shiny black Lincoln Town Car was waiting for us outside the revolving doors of the lobby. Our driver, Tom, held the rear passenger door open and I climbed into the back seat, careful not to snag my sheer black pantyhose. Steven and Jordan climbed in after me. The car crash three nights earlier was legendary among the hotel staff, and Tom asked us about it. As we headed south on New Jersey Avenue toward the Supreme Court, Jordan pointed out the various inanimate objects the valet had knocked over with my beloved Honda Accord.

Visitors to the Supreme Court in 2000 entered the main entrance to the building up a flight of forty-four marble steps and through imposing seventeen-foot-high, thirteen-ton, bronze double doors ornamented with sculpted panels depicting the "Evolution of Justice." Arguing attorneys, in contrast, there for the most important event in their legal careers, entered through a nondescript, ground level, human-scale side door on Maryland Avenue.

During the short ride from the hotel, Jordan boasted to our driver that his mom was on her way to argue before the Supreme Court. Tom was genuinely impressed; he had never chauffeured a Supreme Court advocate before. He blithely ignored my request to be dropped off at the attorneys' entrance on the Maryland Avenue side of the building.

"No, no, no," Tom good-naturedly insisted. "This is a special day for you. You see all those people waiting in line to get inside the courthouse? I'm parking directly out front of so all those people will see you exiting a chauffeured Town Car. Make sure you wait for me to open the door before you get out."

Tom flipped a possibly illegal U-turn on First Street and parked the Town Car at the curb directly in front of the courthouse. He walked around to the rear passenger door, held it open with his right hand, and extended his left hand to help me exit the car. As I stepped onto the sidewalk, I looked up at the gleaming white marble Supreme Court building backdropped against a brilliant blue sky. It was picture-perfect. I had imagined this scene many times over the past nine months, but the vision in my head didn't hold a candle to the real thing. Tom shook my hand, wished me good luck, and drove off in the Hyatt One.

Steven, Jordan, and I walked past the visitors' line extending down the marble steps and onto the street-level plaza. Waiting in the long queue were Bob Luther, the Cumberland County assistant prosecutor who had served Charles C. Apprendi Jr. with the fateful motion for an extended prison term under New Jersey's Hate Crime Statute, and Bob's wife, Roseanne. Closer to the front of the line were Steven's sister, Karen, and her husband, Mitchell, who had arrived at the courthouse at seven o'clock in the morning and *still* had twenty people waiting ahead of them. For more than two hours, Karen and Mitch stood on the cold marble steps chatting with lawyers, students, and journalists fluent in *Apprendi*-ese. These brave souls shivered in the general admission line outside the courthouse in the early morning to grab a seat inside, just to attend the *Apprendi* argument.

Supreme Court courtroom seating is extremely limited, and spectators are seated on a first-come, first-served basis. Two lines start early in the morning before the building opens. One line is for visitors who want to attend an entire one-hour argument. The other "three-minute line" is for visitors content to pop in for a very limited time and witness the action from the back of the courtroom.

Arguing counsel are allotted six reserved seats in the public section of the courtroom for family and friends, unless, like me, you are splitting your argument time, in which case you get only four reserved seats. Four seats were woefully inadequate for my large group of family and friends who planned to attend. Attorney General John Farmer, Deputy Solicitor General Michael Dreeben, and Assistant Solicitor General Edward DuMont, all of whom would be sitting with me at counsel table, had generously offered their reserved seats to me, so I was up to sixteen. (Four times four is sixteen. *It's always going to be sixteen.*)

I had arranged with Dale Bosley, the marshal of the court, for another reserved seat. In yet another seating coup, my college classmate Michael Remez, the Washington correspondent for the *Hartford Courant*, sat in one of the thirty-six seats in the courtroom section reserved for members of the Supreme Court press corps. (Some of the seats in the press section have obstructed views, Mike later told me. Mike and other reporters were left to figure out which justice was speaking by identifying the sound of his or her voice.) I was left several tickets short, which was why Bob, Roseanne, Karen, and Mitch had agreed to wake up extra early on Tuesday morning to wait outside in the cold.

As Steven, Jordan, and I walked toward the court's Maryland Avenue entrance, a tall gentleman approached me. "Are you Lisa Gochman?" he asked. It was Brian Levin, a national authority on hate crimes and the author of one of the kelly green friend of the court briefs filed on behalf of the state of New Jersey. Professor Levin had flown in from California that morning just to watch the *Apprendi* argument.

After passing through the metal detector at the Maryland Avenue entrance to the United States Supreme Courthouse, Steven and Jordan wished me luck and gave me one last hug before they headed to the ground-floor-level cafeteria. I reported to the first-floor Lawyers' Lounge, the Supreme Court's equivalent of the celebrity greenroom where movie stars wait backstage for their turn to engage in witty banter with the talk show host.

All attorneys scheduled for oral argument must arrive at the Lawyers' Lounge by 9:15 a.m. for a short orientation by the clerk of the court and his staff. Floor-to-ceiling windows in the Lawyers' Lounge overlook a large courtyard, multitier brass Federalist-style chandeliers hang from the high ceiling, and heavy gold brocade curtains drape the windows. As soon as I crossed the threshold into this stately room, my enthusiasm evaporated. The tension in this room of Supreme Court rookies was so palpable, a military-grade machete would have been inadequate to hack through it.

I spotted General Farmer across the Lawyers' Lounge and walked over to him.

"Good morning, General," I said, trying hard to appear nonchalant. "This is it. Today is the day."

"You're going to be great, Lisa. I'm really looking forward to this." Easy for him to say. He wasn't arguing the case. I had been looking forward to this, too, but in that moment the high-pitched voice in the back of my head, the one that could cut glass, was shrieking, *What the hell are you doing here? Get out! Get out while you still can!* Slipping unnoticed through a side door, however, was off the table.

Joseph O'Neill joined Attorney General Farmer and me. Although Joe and I were inextricably bound together by the *Apprendi* litigation, we hadn't seen one another in person since the oral argument before the Supreme Court of New Jersey in Trenton eighteen months earlier. But we were both too jittery to engage in anything but nonsensical chitchat as we prepared for the firing squad that is the United States Supreme Court bench. I half-expected someone to offer me a blindfold and a cigarette, and I was beginning to regret the extra cup of coffee I drank earlier in Steven and Jordan's hotel room. Elsewhere in the building was an office reserved exclusively for attorneys from the Office of the Solicitor General, who are neither required nor expected to attend the orientation. I pictured Edward DuMont and his colleagues standing around the water cooler dressed in their formal cutaway coats, casually dissecting the previous night's episode of *Everybody Loves Raymond*.

Supreme Court Clerk William Suter entered the Lawyers' Lounge and we took our seats. After welcoming us to the court, Clerk Suter reviewed some of the rules and protocol of oral argument.

"Do not begin your argument until you are recognized by the chief justice," Suter instructed us. "Do not introduce yourself or cocounsel at the time of argument. Begin your argument with 'Mr. Chief Justice, and may it please the Court.'" No ad-libbing permitted. "Please address the members of the court by their proper titles, 'Chief Justice' or 'Justice,' but definitely not as 'Judge.'" So far, so good.

Here's where it got tricky: arguing counsel were expected to keep track of their own time limitations and were not to ask the court how much argument time was remaining. But, wait, *Guide for Counsel* expressly warned me *not* to look at my watch or at the clock located high on the wall behind the justices.[3] How was I supposed to keep track of my time? My sole temporal clue would be a small white light appearing on the lectern when five minutes of argument time remained and a small red light appearing when time expired. And when that red light did appear, Clerk Suter sternly warned us, we were to conclude our arguments promptly.

Denise McNerney, the assistant clerk for merits cases and my personal angel who had been so helpful as I drafted the merits brief, addressed us next. Until now, McNerney had been a disembodied voice on the other end of the telephone. It was nice to finally meet her in person.

"If any of you are in need," McNerney said soothingly, "I have cough drops, aspirin, Band-Aids, and a sewing kit you can use." I had brought my own emergency supplies stashed in the outside pocket of my briefcase, including tissues, lip balm, and a bottle of clear nail polish to dab on my sheer black pantyhose if they started to run. But McNerney also had with her an indispensable item I hadn't thought to pack: smelling salts. I was comforted to know that fainting in the United States Supreme Court was not unprecedented.

Three months earlier, when Steven, Jordan, and I took our reconnaissance tour of the Supreme Court building, I had not known who would be arguing *Apprendi*, and the possibility still existed that it could be me. As we walked down the Great Hall, our footsteps echoing on the Madre cream marble floor, I mentally mapped out where the public bathrooms were located so I would know where to throw up before the argument in March. I needn't have worried. Inside the Lawyers' Lounge is a private bathroom reserved for arguing counsel.

Thankfully, I neither fainted nor threw up. Clerk Suter's orientation grounded me and renewed my focus. I was as calm, present, and prepared as I was ever going to be. And I was having a good hair day to boot.

Clerk Suter handed me an off-white, four-inch-by-four-inch cardstock square with my name, the docket number of the *Apprendi* argument, and the date printed at the top. Below, in much smaller print, were reminders of some of the rules arguing counsel were expected to follow.

October Term 1999

Issued to: .....Lisa S. Gochman...

Counsel in No. 99-478................... Date ....3/28/00......

1. Display this card to the attendant seated at the entrance to the Bar Section.
2. Remain seated at the reserved table behind Counsel's table *throughout* the argument of the case immediately preceding your case.
3. When your turn comes to argue, proceed immediately to the rostrum without waiting to be called. **Do not begin argument until you have been recognized by the Chief Justice,** then open with "Mr. Chief Justice, and may it please the Court ——." Do not introduce yourself or co-counsel to the Court. Address a member of the Court as "Chief Justice" or "Justice"—*not* "judge."
4. Keep account of your remaining time during argument. *Do not* make inquiry of the Chief Justice.
5. If you desire lunch, you will be escorted from the Clerk's desk at 12:00 o'clock. (Only card-holding counsel are authorized this courtesy.)
6. This card entitles you to use the Supreme Court Library on this date.

CLER0017-8-99

Identification card for arguing counsel.

This was my identification card granting me access to counsel table in the very front of the courtroom. It was Willie Wonka's Golden Ticket and a first row center orchestra seat to a Bruce Springsteen concert rolled into one.

Arguing counsel were also given an off-white, four-inch-by-two-inch cardstock rectangle with the seating chart of the major players in the courtroom. The justices sat side by side on a slightly curved, raised bench, towering above everyone else. Chief Justice Rehnquist sat in the middle chair, flanked on either side by the eight associate justices in order of seniority. The most senior

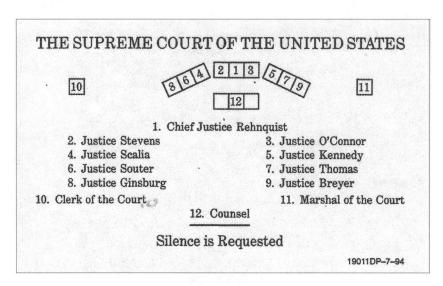

Seating chart for Supreme Court Justices.

associate justice, John Paul Stevens, sat to the chief justice's immediate right; the second most senior associate justice, Sandra Day O'Connor, sat to the chief justice's immediate left; and so on. The two most junior justices, Ruth Bader Ginsburg and Steven G. Breyer, sat on either end. The card listed the justices' last names only. Perhaps the justices were afraid that in our heightened state of nervousness we attorneys might accidently yell out "Sandy" or "Bill." I recall thinking at that moment that if you were about to appear before SCOTUS for oral argument and didn't know the names of the justices or where they sat, you had no business being there at all.

At the close of Clerk Suter's orientation, we filed out of the Lawyers' Lounge and headed toward the courtroom directly across the hall. I displayed my identification card to the officer manning the metal detector at the entrance to the courtroom. My mother and my cousin Allison were waiting in line, and I flashed them a wide "Hey, look at me!" smile as I cut in front of them. Inside the courtroom, I showed my identification card to security personnel stationed at the brass railing separating the audience from the well of the courtroom where the justices sat. A guard allowed me to pass through the swinging half-gate to reach my seat at counsel table. I was Dorothy Gale about to present the broomstick to the Great and Powerful Oz.

Counsel on both sides of the case share one rectangular table. When I visited the Supreme Court courtroom three months earlier, the court was not in session, and counsel table was empty. I hadn't realized then how cramped the seating arrangements would be once all seven attorneys in the *Apprendi* case took their chairs. In the New Jersey appellate courtrooms where *Apprendi* was argued, Joe O'Neill sat at one table on the left side of the room, and I sat at a separate table on the right, like sparring boxers assigned to opposite corners of the ring. We presented our respective arguments at a freestanding podium close to the judges.

In Washington, there is barely a buffer zone between adversaries. Joe sat directly to my left and we were separated by only a two-foot-wide wooden lectern positioned on top of the table. My opponent's proximity to me was disconcerting. When Joe stood for his argument at the lectern, he would be looming over my chair. If Joe wildly hand-gestured during his presentation, he might smack me on the head.

And I couldn't scoot over to give myself more elbow room. To my immediate right was Attorney General Farmer, there to lend moral support and to experience a Supreme Court argument from the best seat in the house. The justices would not be asking any questions of the general, so he was free to sit back, relax, and enjoy the spectacle. Seated to the attorney general's immediate right was Assistant Solicitor General Edward DuMont, who was sharing ten minutes of New Jersey's half-hour argument time on behalf of the federal government. I had first seen DuMont that morning when he joined me at counsel table, dressed in his formal attire. DuMont's gray cutaway morning coat and striped trousers stood out among the sea of twenty-first-century business suits. It was like being on a movie set of the Supreme Court with DuMont dressed in full period costume. Deputy Solicitor General Dreeben was also on my side of counsel table, sitting to DuMont's immediate right in his role as DuMont's supervisor.

On Joe O'Neill's side of counsel table were his law firm associate Charles Coant as well as Jeffrey Green of the DC law firm Sidley Austin, who had assisted Joe in writing his daffodil yellow reply brief to the court. Coant and Green were there solely for Joe's moral support; Joe would have petitioner's entire thirty-minute portion of the *Apprendi* argument to himself. It wasn't lost on me that, of the seven attorneys crowded around counsel table in the high-stakes United States Supreme Court, I was the only woman.

Carefully placed on counsel table in front of each of the seven high-back black leather chairs were two pristine, ten-inch-long, white goose-feather quill pens crossing each other in an X. As *Guide for Counsel* explained, "The quill pens at your argument table are gifts to you—a souvenir of your having argued before the highest Court in the land. Take them with you. They are handcrafted and usable as writing quills."

It would have been fun to scribble notes to Attorney General Farmer with our quill pens during the argument, but there weren't any inkwells. Sharpened pencils and plain white notepads were provided instead. If I needed a specific Supreme Court decision during the argument, I could write down the volume number of the reporter it appeared in and hand the notepaper to a page, who would fetch the reporter for me. *A page!* It was so old-school and refined.

The perks didn't end with the quill pens. Also waiting for us on counsel table were tall drinking glasses made of actual glass filled with cold water and ice cubes. I was unaccustomed to such five-star service in a courtroom. It's DIY in New Jersey. The best you get in Trenton is a stainless steel carafe of tepid water and a flimsy plastic cup that collapses at the slightest pressure of your fingertips. Once, with just seconds to spare before the justices of the Supreme Court of New Jersey were due to enter the courtroom to hear one of my criminal appeals, I poured myself a cup of water. Miscalculating the level of liquid in the opaque carafe, I tipped it too far and sloshed water all over counsel table. I sheepishly asked the court clerk for a paper towel to mop up the spill, but it was too late. The New Jersey justices were taking their seats, forcing me to the far end of counsel table, away from the expanding puddle.

Managing to keep my klutziness in check in the United States Supreme Court, I spread out my black binder, my dog-eared copy of New Jersey's Code of Criminal Justice, a stack of SCOTUS decisions, and a yellow legal pad across counsel table without incident. The justices hear two cases during the morning session, and a few weeks earlier I had received written notice that the *Apprendi* argument would be scheduled first. This was fortunate for me, because I could arrange all my paraphernalia at counsel table to my liking in advance of the argument. The attorneys whose argument was scheduled second at eleven o'clock in the matter of *Sims v. Apfel* (which would determine whether a Social Security claimant had exhausted her administrative remedies) would not have the luxury of setting up in advance.[4] They would sit at the backup counsel table directly behind mine during the first argument.

Seated (*left to right*): Justice Antonin Scalia, Justice John Paul Stevens, Chief Justice William H. Rehnquist, Justice Sandra Day O'Connor, Justice Anthony M. Kennedy. Standing (*left to right*): Justice Ruth Bader Ginsburg, Justice David Souter, Justice Clarence Thomas, Justice Stephen G. Breyer.

As soon as the *Apprendi* argument ended, the attorneys in *Sims v. Apfel* were required to move up immediately to the front table, carrying all their law books, papers, briefcases, and quill pens with them, and launch right into their argument without time to set up. Worse, one unlucky attorney in the second case might be left standing at the lectern if the Supreme Court recessed for lunch at high noon in the middle of the argument. With just one hour until the court reconvened at one o'clock, Supreme Court escorts "arrange speedy service" for arguing counsel in the ground-floor cafeteria—that is, if arguing counsel has any appetite.[5]

—⚏—

It was nearly ten o'clock, and the courtroom was buzzing with anticipation. I glanced around the room, drinking it all in. I was amazed at the hundreds of spectators sitting behind me. This was the big leagues, and I had never argued in front of such a large crowd before.

Promptly at 10:00 a.m., Supreme Court Marshal Dale Bosley cried out the traditional "Oyez" (pronounced "Oh, yay!") to bring the courtroom to order:

> The Honorable, the Chief Justice and the Associate Justices of the Supreme Court of the United States. Oyez! Oyez! Oyez! All persons having business before the Honorable, the Supreme Court of the United States, are admonished to draw near and give their attention, for the Court is now sitting. God save the United States and this Honorable Court!

The room fell silent as the chief justice and eight associate justices, all wearing voluminous black silk judicial robes, simultaneously appeared from behind the heavy, crimson velvet curtains and took their seats. At least I think they simultaneously appeared. I was leaning down to grab a pen out of my black leather briefcase and missed the ritual. And as I lifted my head, pen in hand, there it was—the large, round analog clock hanging from the pediment high above the chief justice's head, the hour hand on the X and the minute hand on the XII—the clock that *Guide for Counsel* had expressly warned me *not to look at!*

Directly above the courtroom on the top floor of the Supreme Court building is a basketball court. Dubbed the "Highest Court in the Land," the basketball court is reserved for the nine justices and staff of the Supreme Court. Near the entrance to the gym, a sign warns, "Playing basketball and weightlifting are prohibited while the court is in session."[6] Chief Justice Rehnquist played basketball there. Associate Justice Sandra Day O'Connor, appointed in 1981 as the first woman justice, "understood that male dominance of the building extended to the fifth floor . . . and reserved the gym for a morning aerobics class, encouraging other women in the building to attend."[7] And on the crystalline blue morning of March 28, 2000, as the justices took their seats in the "Second Highest Court in the Land" to hear argument in *Charles C. Apprendi, Jr. v. New Jersey*, Docket No. 99-478, there was a slim possibility that, beneath their flowy black silk judicial robes, Rehnquist and O'Connor were wearing their gym shorts and sneakers.

CHAPTER 14

CHIEF JUSTICE REHNQUIST BRUSQUELY CALLED the first order of business: the announcement of the court's written opinions issued that morning. Traditionally, the justice who wrote the opinion on behalf of the court's majority reads a five-minute synopsis of the decision from the bench. On this day, SCOTUS issued its opinions in *Garner v. Jones,* a matter addressing an amendment to a Georgia statute extending the period between a state prisoner's parole hearing dates, and *Florida v. J.L.,* a Fourth Amendment search-and-seizure case addressing the reliability of anonymous tips to the police.[1] Justice Anthony M. Kennedy wrote the majority opinion in *Garner;* Justice Ruth Bader Ginsberg wrote the majority opinion in *J.L.* As a prosecutor, I have since cited Justice Ginsburg's majority opinion in the *J.L.* decision in several search-and-seizure briefs. Whenever I do, I marvel at my good fortune to have been inside the Supreme Court courtroom to hear the Notorious RBG personally explain the facts and legal holding of *J.L.* for the very first time. As I listened to Justice Ginsberg summarize her majority opinion, I picked up my water glass to take a sip. Hearing the ice cubes clink gently against the inside wall of the glass, I realized my hand was shaking slightly from nerves.

The next order of business was moving attorneys for admission to practice before the bar of the United States Supreme Court. My sister, Jill, an intellectual property lawyer practicing in California, had arranged ahead of time for me to sponsor her admission to the United States Supreme Court bar in person. We thought it would be a nice surprise for our parents to watch Jill's admission ceremony. As a bonus, her admission to the bar would ensure she had a reserved seat in the courtroom during my argument.

Earlier that morning in the Lawyers' Lounge, Clerk Suter had handed me a preprinted sheet with my name in bold letters directly below the seal of the Supreme Court instructing me on precisely what to do and what to say during the admission ceremony:

SUPREME COURT OF THE UNITED STATES

Lisa Gochman

TO MOVANT: Do not use the title of an applicant except for an active or retired state or federal judge, or a member of the U.S. Senate or House of Representatives. It is acceptable to use the following terms, as appropriate: son, daughter, husband, wife, sister, brother, aunt, uncle, son-in-law, daughter-in-law, father, or mother. It is inappropriate to make comments about an applicant such as referring to former service as a law clerk.

PROCEED TO THE ROSTRUM WHEN YOUR NAME IS CALLED BY THE CLERK. WAIT FOR THE CHIEF JUSTICE TO ANNOUNCE YOUR NAME BEFORE MAKING THE FOLLOWING STATEMENT:

"MR. CHIEF JUSTICE AND MAY IT PLEASE THE COURT, I MOVE THE ADMISSION OF JILL SARNOFF RIOLA OF THE BAR OF THE STATE OF CALIFORNIA. ⌐MY SISTER

I AM SATISFIED SHE POSSESSES THE NECESSARY QUALIFICATIONS."

RETURN TO YOUR SEAT AFTER THE CHIEF JUSTICE GRANTS YOUR MOTION.

Movant statement.

I handwrote "my sister" in red ink before her name to remind me to identify her sororal relationship to me when I read aloud the required paragraph during the admission ceremony. Clerk Suter saw me jotting something down on the instruction sheet and hurried over to make sure I wasn't adding a highly inappropriate qualifier, such as "former law clerk."

Admission to the United States Supreme Court bar is actually fairly simple. Any attorney who is a member in good standing for three years of the bar in the highest court of any state can apply to practice before the United States Supreme Court bar by filing a two-page application form along with the names and signatures of two current bar members and a check for $200.[2] Admission may be accomplished on the papers alone, saving applicants the time and expense of traveling to Washington, DC. You can be a lifelong member of the bar of the Supreme Court of the United States without ever setting foot inside the courthouse.

But nothing beats the in-person admission ceremony with all its splendor and ritual in the majestic United States Supreme Court courtroom. Law schools regularly schedule group admissions for their alumni. The American Bar Association and other federal and state bar associations host similar admission programs for their members. Small groups of up to twelve attorneys are admitted on oral argument days; larger groups of up to fifty attorneys are admitted on non-oral argument days. Membership has a special perk unavailable to the general public: only members of the Supreme Court bar are permitted entry into the oak-paneled third-floor library with its two-story arches and miles of shelves holding close to half a million books.[3]

As per the written instructions Clerk Suter had handed me in the Lawyers' Lounge, I proceeded to the lectern when Chief Justice Rehnquist called my name (rhymes with "watch") and read out loud from the prepared statement. It was a great opportunity for me to test out my voice before the real show began.

"Mr. Chief Justice, and may it please the court. I move for the admission of my sister, Jill Sarnoff Riola, of the bar of the state of California. I am satisfied she possesses the necessary qualifications."

Jill rose from her seat in the bar section for Clerk Suter to administer the oath. Raising her right hand, Jill dutifully repeated, "I, Jill Sarnoff Riola, do solemnly swear that as an attorney and as a counselor of this court I will conduct myself uprightly and according to the law, and that I will support the Constitution of the United States." Chief Justice Rehnquist personally welcomed my sister to the Supreme Court bar. My mother later told me that the high back of the leather chair I sat in at counsel table rose above my head. From her seat in the spectators' gallery behind counsel table, my mother had not spotted me in the courtroom me until I stood up to move for Jill's admission.

—ɷ—

Finally, it was time for the main event. Hearing the chief's booming voice announce, "We will hear argument now in number 99-478, *Charles C. Apprendi Jr. versus New Jersey*," was electrifying. Charles Apprendi's attorney Joseph O'Neill and I had squared off back home twice before, first in the Superior Court of New Jersey, Appellate Division, and then in the Supreme Court of New Jersey. But this! As Beetlejuice says, "It's showtime!"

Counsel for petitioner always goes first. Joseph O'Neill rose from his seat, took one step to his right to the lectern, and waited for the chief justice to recognize him by name. Joe then began his opening statement with a voice so calm and steady you'd never guess this was his first United States Supreme Court argument.

"Mr. Chief Justice, and may it please the court," Joe began. "This case is about the erosion of the jury by the New Jersey legislature."[4]

Joe's opening line was impressive. Using a bare minimum of words, Joe crystallized the fundamental constitutional problem that he believed the Hate Crime Statute caused (the erosion of the jury as the trier of fact) and identified the source of the problem (the New Jersey State Legislature). Joe was appealing to the justices' soft spot for jury trials while tacitly reminding them that SCOTUS owed no deference to a state legislative body.

Joe continued, "The statute at issue in this case violates the Fourteenth and Sixth Amendments by permitting the judge to consider or assess a defendant's mental state by a preponderance of the evidence and sentence that person to a term of up to double the time permitted upon conviction of the predicate crime. Here, petitioner pled guilty to three crimes, but was sentenced on four."

I did not agree with Joe that his client Charles Apprendi was sentenced on four crimes. Apprendi pleaded guilty to three crimes (two counts of second-degree possession of a firearm for an unlawful purpose and one count of third-degree unlawful possession of an antipersonnel bomb) and was sentenced for those three crimes. His complaint was that the length of his sentence on one of the second-degree crimes (count eighteen) was equal to a sentence reserved for first-degree crimes. That's a longer sentence, not a separate sentence. But it was a small point. And no matter what Joe said, I could not interrupt the proceedings to voice my opposition. This was not a trial where counsel can bring the momentum to a screeching halt by jumping up and yelling, "Objection!" If Joe said something I needed to correct or explore further with the court, I had to wait patiently until it was my turn. I could not raise my hand to be called on by the justices. I had to sit very still, be very quiet, and wear my professional poker face throughout Joe's thirty-minute argument.

Joe went on. "In *Jones v. the United States*, this court constructed a proposed test for the constitutionality of the statute as to determine whether the statute creates a separate element of a crime or a sentencing factor." (*Uh, oh. Here comes the dreaded bright-line rule.*)

Reciting footnote 6 of *Jones*, Joe intoned, "Any fact, other than prior conviction, which increases the maximum sentence, implicates constitutional protections of beyond a reasonable doubt, notice by—"

Joe was cut off mid-bright-line rule by the first of eighty-nine rapid-fire questions asked by the justices during his thirty-minute period. Nina Totenberg, the Supreme Court correspondent for National Public Radio, describes oral argument before the United States Supreme Court as "often something of a dignified free-for-all."[5] That's one way to put it. What I was witnessing was a major league baseball game with Joe up at bat against nine Cy Young Award winning pitchers simultaneously hurling ninety-five-mile-per-hour fastballs straight down the center of home plate. The justices would lure Joe in with deceptively straightforward questions about the constitutional parameters of one hypothetical sentencing statute or another, only to ferociously spit him back out. So much for the myth that United States Supreme Court justices go easy on attorneys appearing before them for the first time.

I was hunched over counsel table taking notes on a yellow legal pad with my red pen when the justices started ripping into Joe. Confident that I knew the answers to the questions the justices were asking him, I relaxed a little and leaned back in my chair, listening intently. I wasn't shaken by the justices' overt hostility toward my adversary, reading it instead as an encouraging sign that Joe had the losing argument.

Silly, silly me.

CHAPTER 15

"MS. GOCHMAN, WE'LL HEAR FROM YOU."

Actually, Chief Justice Rehnquist called me "Mister" but quickly corrected himself. No matter. I was happy he had pronounced my last name correctly (rhymes with "watch"). I stepped to the lectern, straightened my jacket, and picked up my black three-ring binder and red pen. Inside the binder were photocopies of my opening statement, my merits brief, and the major Supreme Court opinions addressing the "sentencing factor versus element of the offense" debate at issue in *Apprendi*, neatly separated by color-coded tabs. The red pen was just something to keep a death grip on so I didn't haphazardly wave my hands around during the argument. Flipping open the cover of the binder to the first page of my opening statement, I felt each one of the nine justices of the Supreme Court of the United States watching me intently, waiting for me to begin.

All the preparation during the previous four years, all the hard work, all the late nights, led up to this one moment (well, twenty minutes) in time. I had missed most of my son's third-grade school year as I wrote the *Apprendi* merits brief, compiled the joint appendix, and prepared for oral argument. Aside from drilling him on his multiplication tables as I drove him to and from elementary school ("Jordan, four times four is sixteen! *It's always going to be sixteen!*"), I barely saw my son at all. And when I did, he was seat-belted in the back of my Honda Accord (may it rest in peace), and all I got to see of Jordan was his adorable face in my rearview mirror. The next twenty minutes would tell whether the sacrifice was worth it.

Here I stood in the exact spot where Thurgood Marshall denounced "separate but equal" segregated public schools in *Brown v. Board of Education of Topeka*, where Abe Fortes argued in *Gideon v. Wainwright* that indigent criminal defendants have a Sixth Amendment right to counsel at trial, and where Ruth Bader Ginsburg fought for gender equality in the six cases she argued before SCOTUS between 1973 and 1979.[1] But I was so swept up in the powerful rip current of the *Apprendi* argument that when my turn finally arrived, I wasn't thinking about whether I was worthy enough to be there. After the shellacking Joe O'Neill got, I was sure mine was the winning argument. That belief, accurate or not, boosted my courage. My lawyer persona easily vanquished my impostor syndrome. I faced the justices, ready to engage in the most important oral argument of my career with the most illustrious jurists in the nation. All distractions in the courtroom receded into the background, including that damn clock.

I looked up at the justices and settled my focus on Chief Justice Rehnquist, seated in the middle of the bench. Then I began my opening statement, hoping to convince the court that, like a prior criminal conviction (*Almendarez-Torres*) and unlike serious bodily injury to a carjacking victim (*Jones*), motive was a traditional sentencing factor for the judge, not the jury, to consider. My words needed to convey the long-standing principles of federalism and comity that state legislatures, not the federal courts, bear the primary authority to define and enforce the criminal laws for their citizens. The New Jersey Legislature was free to define motive as a sentencing factor without trampling on a criminal defendant's constitutional rights.

My more immediate challenge, however, was reading from my prepared statement without looking like I was reading from my prepared statement.

"Mr. Chief Justice, and may it please the court. The New Jersey Legislature has made clear, and the New Jersey Supreme Court has confirmed, that the extended term provision of the Hate Crime Statute, which addresses motive, is a sentencing factor, and not an element of the predicate offense. Motive, as this court recognized over one hundred years ago, may be probative of guilt, but it is not essential to a conviction unless the legislature chooses to include it as an element of a particular offense."[2]

This was as far as I got before being interrupted by the first of fifty-nine questions, an average of three questions per minute during my allotted twenty-minute argument. Apprendi's attorney Joseph O'Neill was asked more questions, but Joe also had ten minutes more argument time than I did. Not that I'm counting.

The first question came from Justice Antonin "Pit Bull" Scalia: "So I suppose that means that the New Jersey legislature could provide for first degree murder is murder with malice aforethought, and could provide the death penalty for that crime, and could leave it up to a judge to decide whether there was malice aforethought, and to decide that just by a preponderance of the evidence?"

Yay! I knew the answer!

"Respectfully, malice aforethought is not the same as motive," I replied. "Malice aforethought is that, yes, you intended to commit this crime, but even with malice aforethought, the prosecution does not need to prove the defendant's motive, *why* did he want to commit the crime. He may have wanted to kill somebody because he owed him money, because he made some sort of unwarranted advances. But malice aforethought has always been deemed intention, and part of mens rea, and it's different from motive. Motive goes to the underlying reason. In this case for example, the defense, by its plea of guilty, satisfied the elements of New Jersey's possession of a weapon for an unlawful purpose."

Chief Justice Rehnquist followed up my spot-on (albeit wordy) response to Justice Scalia with a softball question: "Traditionally, as I understand the common law, there was no inquiry into motive," Justice Rehnquist said. "It was just intent."

"That's correct," I said.

"The motive didn't make any difference."

"That's correct."

Easy-peasy! I had this! Oral argument was a cakewalk!

And that is when the ambush began. The hostility flung at my adversary suddenly was directed squarely at me. Now I was the frilly piñata dangling before the proverbial hot bench for the justices' amusement. Justices Stevens and Souter were openly skeptical of New Jersey's position that motive was a traditional sentencing factor, but Justice Scalia was downright belligerent. I may be way off base, but I think Justice Scalia's antagonism toward me was grounded in the fact that early in the argument I had exposed a gaping hole in his legal reasoning. Scalia's position in *Apprendi* was diametrically opposed to the position he had taken ten years earlier when he joined the majority opinion in a death penalty case called *Walton v. Arizona*.[3]

In 1986, an Arizona jury found defendant Jeffrey Alan Walton guilty of capital murder for the armed robbery and execution-style shooting of Thomas Powell, a young, off-duty marine.[4] The medical examiner determined that Powell had been blinded and rendered unconscious by the bullet to his head but was not immediately killed. Powell regained consciousness and struggled alone in the Arizona desert for a week before dying from dehydration, starvation, and pneumonia.[5]

Under Arizona state law at the time, after the jury found Walton guilty of capital murder, it was up to the trial judge to impose a sentence of life in prison or the death penalty, depending on whether the judge found one or more statutory aggravating sentencing factors to exist. A Pima County, Arizona, prosecutor argued to the judge that Walton deserved the death penalty based on two statutory aggravating sentencing factors applicable to Walton's crime: one, the murder was committed "in an especially heinous, cruel or depraved manner" and, two, Walton's motive for murdering his victim was the monetary gain from the armed robbery.[6] The judge agreed that both aggravating sentencing factors presented by the state applied and sentenced Walton to death.[7] The Arizona Supreme Court affirmed Walton's convictions and death sentence.

SCOTUS granted Walton's certiorari petition to consider his argument that the Sixth Amendment to the United States Constitution required that every finding of fact increasing a capital defendant's sentence from life imprisonment to death must be made by a jury, not a judge. In an opinion issued in June 1990, the United States Supreme Court rejected Walton's claim. The *Walton* court held that statutory aggravating factors, including motive, which elevate a capital murder defendant's sentence from life imprisonment to death were not elements of the crime of capital murder for the jury's consideration but were sentencing factors for the judge to find.[8]

New Jersey's Hate Crime Statute similarly authorized the trial judge to make a specific finding of motive to increase a defendant's sentence beyond the statutory maximum. But a visibly peeved Justice Scalia was now attempting to craft a meaningful distinction between Arizona's death penalty statute and New Jersey's Hate Crime Statute where there was none.

"What about an espionage prosecution?" Justice Scalia asked me. "Someone has stolen highly secret papers from the Defense Department. It is treason punishable by death if the reason they were taken was to give them over to a foreign power that is hostile to the United States."

"If Congress chose to make that motive an element of that particular crime, then yes, that would have to go to the jury."

"No, if—Congress—no, I—Congress chooses *not* to make it an element. Congress just says, anyone who takes papers from the Defense Department that are classified secret is guilty of an offense, ten years in prison. However, if the purpose of taking them is to give them over to a foreign power hostile to the United States, the death penalty, and the latter question will be decided by a judge on the basis of whether it's more likely than not. You know, it's a close question, but on balance I think it's more likely than not that he should get the death penalty. That would be okay?"

"Under this Court's capital punishment jurisprudence" of *Walton v. Arizona*, I explained, "that would be permissible so long as the jury finds beyond a reasonable doubt the elements of the predicate offense. It then goes to the judge to determine the aggravating factors, including—"

Justice Scalia interrupted my response. "That doesn't shock you, that outcome, at all? I mean, that seems to you in accord with our traditions of jury trial and proof beyond a reasonable doubt?"

I pointed out that under *Walton*, sentencing judges were constitutionally authorized to consider a defendant's motive in imposing capital punishment. "That's in accord with this court's jurisprudence on death penalty cases," I told Justice Scalia.

In his quiet, passive-aggressive voice, Justice Scalia chastised me that "death penalty cases are cases apart. I mean, death penalty cases are not in accord with our jurisprudence on anything else, and to—you know, to decide this case on the basis of death penalty cases would be extraordinary."

I responded, in what I hoped sounded like a neutral tone, "Well, respectfully, Your Honor, if a judge can increase a defendant's sentence from life imprisonment to death based on aggravating factors, and that's constitutional under the Sixth and Fourteenth Amendments, then certainly it would be constitutional to increase the petitioner's sentence by a mere two years on a noncapital offense. We're dealing with the same constitutional amendments and the same clauses."

Nailed it! Perfect answer! I flipped Justice Scalia's argument on its head to support my opposing argument that the Hate Crime Statute gave Charles Apprendi the same constitutional safeguards afforded to capital murder defendants. If a trial judge can make factual findings that increase a defendant's sentence from life imprisonment to death, then a trial judge can make factual findings that increase a defendant's prison sentence by two years. There I was, a Supreme Court virgin, exposing Justice Scalia's position on death penalty jurisprudence as incompatible with his position on Sixth Amendment jurisprudence.

Victorious, I forged ahead, emphasizing that, more than one hundred years earlier, the United States Supreme Court had held that motive is never an essential element of the crime of murder.[9]

Justice Souter was not impressed. Motive, he countered, "has never had the significance that it has under the New Jersey statute. The motive, so far as I know, has never traditionally been the difference between ten and twenty years and if, therefore, the motive is not part of the definition of the crime and it does not go to the permissible sentence, the law in effect sort of shrugged and said, so what, it's not that important to anything that is essential in the constitutional structure."

I referred Justice Souter back to the court's capital punishment cases. "There are several types of motive that are used in capital sentencing schemes," I told him. I was about to list a few examples of the types of motive that sentencing judges have considered in imposing the death penalty in various states (monetary gain, racial animus, avoiding apprehension) but was interrupted when Justice Souter asked, "May I interrupt your answer?" Justice Souter did not wait for my assent, however, before interrupting my answer.

"Am I correct that this tradition of shrugging at the motive grows out of a tradition in which the motive does not determine the maximum sentence? Is that historically true?" Souter asked.

No, this was not historically true. I reiterated that "under death penalty schemes motive can be used to increase the sentence to death." My response to Justice Souter clearly irritated Justice Scalia, who was now sneering at me.

"You said traditionally," Justice Scalia scoffed. "Death penalty schemes are a creation of the last twenty years. I don't consider that much of a tradition." (*Let me get this straight, Justice Scalia. It's okay for a judge to increase a defendant's sentence from life in prison to death, the most severe enhancement of all, but it's not okay for the same judge to increase a defendant's sentence in prison by two years?*)

I was given a moment of relative calm by Justice O'Connor. Often a justice will ask a question during oral argument not to trip up the attorney standing before her but to broadcast to her colleagues her position on the matter. Justice O'Connor did just that when she escorted me down memory lane in her home state of Arizona.

"Ms. Gochman, now, in my day as a sentencing judge it was not uncommon to have statutes making a crime, let's say of robbery, punishable for anything from one year to life. Let the judge decide. And within that range, it was not uncommon for judges to consider such things as the motive of the crime, or the lack of remorse, if that was the case, by the defendant, or, if you had a defendant that just appeared to be absolutely without remorse, and intending to create as much trouble as he could for Black citizens, the judge could take that into consideration and impose the life sentence rather than the one year. Now that was traditional, wasn't it, for a long time around the country."

"Yes," I replied.

Midway through this discourse on Arizona sentencing law, I found myself thinking, *This is so cool! Justice O'Connor is asking me a question!* I had barely started my first semester in law school when Sandra Day O'Connor was sworn in on September 15, 1981, as the United States Supreme Court's first female associate justice, shattering the highest glass ceiling in the legal world. The year after Justice O'Connor's appointment, I was seated in a large lecture hall listening to a constitutional law professor dissect one of O'Connor's earliest Supreme Court majority opinions when a classmate leaned over and scribbled in the margin of my textbook "I Am Woman, Hear Me Roar." I laughed then, never imagining I would be standing before Justice O'Connor in real life—yet here she was, speaking directly to me from the bench of the United States Supreme Court. From his seat in the spectators' gallery, my husband noticed Justice O'Connor smiling at me as she spoke. Based on her prior votes in *Almendarez-Torres* and *Jones*, I was sure I had Justice O'Connor on my side.

This was an extraordinary moment. There was no way to know until my segment of the argument began how I would handle myself before the justices. Would I be unfazed by the fact that I was arguing in the United States Supreme Court? Or would I be so cowed by my situation that I would just stand there trembling? I didn't know. I had never done this before. Sometimes nerves seize you and don't let go. But somehow, some way, I was composed and present and treasuring my interaction with my idol, Justice Sandra Day O'Connor.

"And what we see today," Justice O'Connor continued, "is a series of sentencing schemes that have imposed greater restrictions on the sentencing judge, giving them narrower options, is that correct?"

"That's correct." (*I love this woman.*)

"And within that, the legislative branch has tried to say, 'well, if there really is a lack of remorse or a bad purpose here, you can increase the sentence.' Is that what's happening?"

"That's correct." (*I love this woman so much!*)

Referring to the extended-term sentencing hearing held before Judge Ridgway in the Cumberland County courthouse, I responded, "In this particular instance the defendant has probably been given more due process than was given under a more discretionary scheme."

I thought the tide had turned in my direction, but the reprieve was short-lived. Justice Scalia resumed his badgering, not bothering to hide his contempt for me.

"Well, let me ask this about the traditional old days," Justice Scalia said, his voice dripping with disdain. "Did the defendant in the traditional old days have an entitlement not to get more than one year if he was shown to be really remorseful?"

"I'm not sure, Your Honor," I candidly admitted. "I don't know if that sentencing scheme fit within a particular crime or—"

"Gee," Justice Scalia said mockingly. "You were very familiar with the traditional scheme when Justice O'Connor described it, and all of a sudden it's not clear. It's a traditional statute for this crime, one year to life. Now, if the defendant showed enormous remorse, would he be entitled to get only one year, or only twenty, or only thirty? He had no entitlement whatever, did he?"

"That's correct," I answered, fervently hoping this wasn't a trick question.

Justice Scalia continued, "If he did the crime, he knew he got life, and if he got any less than life it was a matter of grace and good luck, and if he got a hanging judge, too bad. You did the crime. That's the risk you took. Wasn't that the system?"

Justice Scalia barreled ahead, not waiting for my reply. "Now, there are no risks here. Here there is an entitlement to get a lesser sentence. Isn't there an absolute entitlement unless you are found to have this state of mind?"

"Not if it's a sentencing factor," I responded, "because it's not a state of mind. State of mind goes to the underlying—"

Yet another interruption by Justice Scalia: "You're saying he's not entitled even if—"

Fed up with Justice Scalia's bullying, Chief Justice Rehnquist cut in and ordered Scalia to "Let her answer" the question. Justice Scalia shot back, "She's answering the wrong question, Chief Justice." I reflexively thought to myself, "*Fuck you, Justice Scalia*," then prayed I hadn't said it out loud. This instantly regrettable expletive would have lived on and on, forever and ever, in the Motion Picture, Sound, and Video Branch of the National Archives in College Park, Maryland, which holds the official tapes for all United States Supreme Court oral arguments.[10]

Rather than allow me to answer his last question, Justice Scalia asked yet another one about a criminal defendant's entitlement in sentencing. Justice Scalia and I argued back and forth for a while, but it was an academic exercise in futility. Justice Scalia wasn't going to agree with anything I said, and he gave up his assault.

Sensing a lull in the action, Justice Ruth Bader Ginsburg swooped in, bringing civility back into the argument. Justice Ginsburg politely prefaced her question to me with "May I ask you, Ms. Gochman?" (*You may, Justice Ginsburg, you may!*)

Justice Ginsburg's courtesy toward me did not suggest that she agreed with my position in *Apprendi*. Heading into the argument, I knew that, based on her past votes in the *Almendarez-Torres* and *Jones* opinions and barring a miracle, she would not find New Jersey's Hate Crime Statute constitutional. But I appreciated the sharp contrast between Justice Ginsburg's professional demeanor and Justice Scalia's scorched-earth approach in questioning an attorney who was advocating a position diametrically opposed to theirs.

Justice Ginsburg asked me why the phrase "with a purpose to" appearing in New Jersey's burglary statute referred to a criminal's intent but the identical phrase "with a purpose to" appearing in New Jersey's Hate Crime Statute referred to a criminal's motive. This was a very fair question. Words have meaning, and state legislators are supposed to be familiar with the laws they enact so that terms and phrases used in one statute carry the same meaning when they appear in a different statute.[11] I explained that the phrase "with a purpose to" in the burglary statute referred to the crime the burglar intended to commit once inside the house (robbery, for instance). But the prosecution did not have to prove *why* the burglar wanted to commit the robbery. The "why" was motive, and I offered several examples of a burglar's motive for breaking into a home and stealing money:

"Did he want to commit a robbery because he had a claim of right to that money? Did he want to commit a robbery because he wanted to feed his drug habit? Did he want to commit a robbery because he wanted to feed his hungry family?"

I was in the middle of answering Justice Ginsburg's question when the red light on the lectern lit up, signaling the end to the longest twenty minutes of my life. Chief Justice Rehnquist cut me off midsentence.

"Thank you, Ms. Gochman," the chief justice said.

"Thank you," I replied and resumed my seat at counsel table.

With that I became the 518th woman to argue before the United States Supreme Court.[12] Some of my 517 esteemed sisters argued more than once, so by March 28, 2000, women had appeared before the Supreme Court a total of 934 times.[13] That may seem like a lot, but it averages out to just seven to eight women per year in the 120-year span between 1880 and 2000. By March 2000, at the turn of the twenty-first century, the Supreme Court was still very much an old boys' club. Of the 183 advocates who argued before the Supreme Court during the October 1999 term, only 27, including me, were women. I am a very proud member of a highly selective sorority.

As I sank back down into the leather chair, Attorney General Farmer leaned over to me at counsel table and whispered, "Great job." I was so glad he thought so. General Farmer had ceded the oral argument to me, and I never wanted to give him any cause to regret his decision. But it wasn't yet time for us to celebrate. The chief justice was calling Assistant Solicitor General Edward DuMont to the lectern.

CHAPTER 16

"MR. DUMONT, WE'LL HEAR FROM YOU."[1]

Now it was the Office of the Solicitor General's turn in its role as amicus to support New Jersey's Hate Crime Statute. Looking dashing in his morning coat (which he called his "institutional armor"), Assistant Solicitor General Edward DuMont took his place at the lectern for his ten-minute segment of the *Apprendi* argument. Ed was granted far more uninterrupted time to present his opening statement than Joe O'Neill or me. Perhaps the justices were showing deference toward Ed, a highly respected Supreme Court advocate who had argued more than a dozen times before the court, including in *Jones*. Or perhaps the justices were just too tuckered out from swatting Joe and me around like piñatas for the last fifty minutes or too woozy from watching us spin.

"Thank you, Mr. Chief Justice, and may it please the court," Ed DuMont began. I was lost in a postargument stupor and didn't hear a thing Ed said for the first few seconds. I reminded myself that the argument was still going on and I'd better pay attention. I hoped Ed would concentrate on New Jersey's Hate Crime Statute and not veer off into a discussion about unrelated federal statutes that, in my mind, unconstitutionally treated elements of the offense, such as type and quantity of illegal drugs, as sentencing factors.

"In this case," Ed told the justices, "what New Jersey did was to convict Charles Apprendi of a very traditional, conventional crime, possession of a weapon for an unlawful purpose. It's a crime with a long common law tradition. It seeks to punish him more severely than it otherwise would for that crime for an equally conventional reason, that he acted with a particularly bad purpose." (*Sounds good.*)

Ed continued, "Now, that sentencing policy decision does not, in our view, become unconstitutional simply because the state specified the bad motive factor in a statute and required the judge to find it by a preponderance of the evidence before he was permitted to go over a certain level in the sentence." (*Yes, Ed. Thank you for sticking to motive.*)

"Now, we all agree, I think," Ed said, "that the legislature normally may define the elements of a crime and fix the minimum and maximum punishments for that crime." (*I agree, Ed. I agree.*)

"What the legislature does in these cases is to make a subsidiary decision that a particular factor is not sufficiently central to guilt or innocence, or perhaps it would be so cumbersome or unfair to present at trial that it should not be sent to the jury as an element of the offense, but that it is important enough, in the legislature's view, to the proper punishment for the offense that the judge should be constrained in his sentencing decisions in that finding this factor by a preponderance—not by reasonable doubt, but by a preponderance—should be necessary before the judge may go over a certain level in sentencing." (*Huh? Sorry, Ed, you lost me there.*)

Right then, the unimaginable happened. Justice Clarence Thomas asked a question. Justice Thomas rarely asks questions from the bench. Speaking before the Supreme Court Historical Society in 2019, Thomas explained that, as a self-proclaimed introvert, he prefers quiet learning over the back-and-forth of interactive questioning during oral argument. "I like the court the way it was when I came on board" twenty-eight years earlier, Thomas said. "Fewer questions, more opportunity for the lawyers to talk, more opportunity for the justices to have a conversation with the lawyers."[2] And when Justice Thomas does ask a question from the bench, it is the stuff of newspaper headlines.[3] Even Ed DuMont, a seasoned Supreme Court advocate, was startled at hearing Justice Thomas's voice.

The hush in the courtroom grew hushier as Justice Thomas spoke.

"Mr. DuMont, that's just the problem."

Justice Thomas's voice is powerful; it is deep and sonorous. Justice Clarence Thomas is the James Earl Jones of the United States Supreme Court.

"You agree that if it's an element of the offense it goes to the jury."

"Yes," Ed replied.

"You agree that if it's an enhancement it can go to the judge as a sentencing factor. The difficulty I have is that nowhere have we defined what the distinction is between an element of the offense and an enhancement factor, and if you could do that in your few minutes it would be very helpful."

Here was Justice Thomas, the swing vote I desperately needed if the *Apprendi* court's anticipated 5-4 split was going to weigh in my favor, dredging up the dreaded bright-line rule proposed in footnote 6 of the *Jones* decision issued one year earlier. This proposed rule stated, "Any fact (other than prior conviction) that increases the maximum penalty for a crime must be charged in an indictment, submitted to a jury and proven beyond a reasonable doubt."[4] I had argued in my merits brief against this bright-line rule, asking the court instead to apply the case-by-case approach it had followed in *Almendarez-Torres* and *Jones*.

Under the case-by-case approach, SCOTUS could consider the constitutionality of New Jersey's Hate Crime Statute without tackling other state or federal penalty-enhancing statutes. In turn, SCOTUS could make the narrow finding that motive, much like a prior conviction, was a traditional sentencing factor that a judge could consider to increase the defendant's prison term above the maximum statutory sentence for the crime committed. Under the bright-line rule suggested in *Jones*, on the other hand, New Jersey's Hate Crime Statute and a host of state and federal criminal statutes authorizing judges to make factual findings that subject a defendant to enhanced punishment would fall on the unconstitutional side of the line.

Now, during the *Apprendi* argument, Justice Thomas was asking Ed Du-Mont where the federal government drew the line between an element of a criminal offense (determined by juries under the "reasonable doubt" standard) and a sentencing factor (determined by judges under the much less onerous "preponderance of the evidence" standard). Ed acknowledged that the justice's request was "a tall order." As the attorney who had represented the United States in *Jones*, Ed was well aware of the multitude of federal criminal statutes that might be declared unconstitutional under a bright-line rule. He argued to Justice Thomas that state legislatures and Congress were perfectly capable of defining the elements of a crime without depriving defendants of their right to a jury trial, making a bright-line rule unnecessary. (*Hear! Hear!*)

Justices Stevens, Scalia, and Souter picked up where Justice Thomas left off, trying to pin Ed down on precisely where the constitutional line between a sentencing factor and an element of the offense should be drawn. Ed held firm in attempting to dissuade the justices from adopting a bright-line rule: "What we know is, the Constitution presumes that legislatures act within the constitutional bounds of their power, and there ought to be a high burden on one who suggests that they have not, and our suggestion is that the bright-line rule suggested here, although it has an attractive superficial clarity, will cut out a wide variety of appropriate legislative conduct like the conduct here, and there's no justification for doing that in order to prevent the outlier case."

"Why isn't *Apprendi* an outlier case?" Justice Stevens demanded. "There's no precedent for this particular statute, is there?"

Ed replied, "It's not an outlier case because all New Jersey did was decide that something bad, a particularly bad purpose which is traditional—"

"Ups the sentence by ten years," Justice Stevens said sharply, finishing Ed's sentence for him.

Just then, the red light on the lectern lit up. Ed DuMont's time had expired. He thanked the court and sat down at counsel table. At 11:09 a.m., exactly one hour after it began, Chief Justice Rehnquist concluded the *Apprendi* argument by announcing, "The case is submitted."

—ɷ—

CHAPTER 17

THE SEVEN ATTORNEYS AT COUNSEL table in *Apprendi* were quickly ushered out of the courtroom through a side gate leading to a narrow windowed hallway off-limits to the general public. To say that relief washed over me is an understatement. I can tell when I've had a good appellate argument and when I've had a bad appellate argument (hey, it happens), and I'd just had a great appellate argument. I had remained focused and knew the answers to the justices' questions, even if the justices didn't agree with what I said. Because the interrogation by the justices was so unrelenting, I never did find an opportunity to circle back to my prepared statement. I could only hope that I had hit all my salient points as my head swiveled left to right and back again while responding to the barrage of questions from the bench.

Because the Supreme Court of the United States does not permit television or still cameras inside the courtroom to broadcast or record oral arguments, my husband had commissioned an artist to draw me as I argued before the justices. I wear eyeglasses, and the sketch the artist drew made me look like Little Orphan Annie with large, white ovals where my pupils should be, giving me a deer-in-the-headlights appearance. But I didn't feel that way. Justice Scalia was merciless, but I withstood the pressure. I never wavered from my position despite Justice Scalia's best efforts to lead me astray. I did dodge a rather large-caliber bullet, though, when Justice Scalia challenged my position for the umpteenth time that motive was not the same as intent. I responded, "Two answers to that, Your Honor," and rattled off my first answer. Thankfully,

Justice Scalia interrupted me yet *again* before I could give my second answer, because, frankly, I couldn't remember what my second answer was going to be.

And it could have so easily gone so wrong in so many other ways. None of the worst-case scenarios I had imagined might befall me occurred as I argued in the United States Supreme Court, in full view of the nine justices, the attorney general of New Jersey, the Office of the Solicitor General, the Supreme Court press corps, my family, my friends, and hundreds of total strangers filling the gallery seats. I didn't spill ice water all over counsel table; I didn't topple off my high heels during my presentation; my red pen didn't leak; my sheer black pantyhose didn't run; I didn't sneeze, hiccup, faint, cry, or throw up; I didn't get a migraine headache or a visual aura; I didn't trip over my words; I didn't curse out loud; and I didn't call Justice O'Connor "Sandy." And not once did I look up at the clock above the chief justice's head during my twenty-minute argument. Ironically, there wasn't time to do so.

Back in the Lawyers' Lounge immediately following the *Apprendi* argument was Charles Apprendi's attorney Joseph O'Neill, O'Neill's law associate Charles Coant, Jeffrey Green of the law firm of Sidley Austin, New Jersey Attorney General Farmer, and me, each of us guessing how the individual justices might vote. Members of the Office of the Solicitor General—the same double-Ivy Leaguers who just days earlier during Edward DuMont's moot court at the Justice Department had conveyed the attitude of "Move aside, little girl, and let the real lawyers handle this"—congratulated me on fielding tough questions from a hostile bench.

The second argument, *Sims v. Apfel*, was under way inside the courtroom, and security personnel reprimanded us for talking too loudly. Attorney General Farmer and I gathered our belongings and quietly left the building through the massive bronze doors. Outside, Chuck Davis, the press secretary for the New Jersey Office of the Attorney General, had escaped the notice of the Supreme Court police force and was sneaking a cigarette behind one of the sixteen enormous, fluted Corinthian marble columns at the top of the steps. Chuck told us there were no reporters waiting for interviews on the plaza below.

As Attorney General Farmer and I descended the well-worn marble stairs, I wondered whether sandpapering the soles of my new shoes was enough to prevent me from sliding down. My arms were filled with papers and books,

Left to right: New Jersey Attorney General John J. Farmer Jr.; Deputy Attorney General Lisa Sarnoff Gochman; Lisa's son, Jordan Gochman.

and my briefcase was slung precariously off one shoulder, weighted down with more papers and books. Although I am more apt to trip up a staircase than down, I am naturally prone to falling. Walking down these steps without slipping was a delicate balancing act requiring my full attention.

My family and friends waiting on the plaza below began clapping when they spotted Attorney General Farmer and me at the top of the stairs. Tourists standing in line to enter the Supreme Court to watch the second argument turned toward the general and me and joined in the applause, although there was no possibility that any person in that line had any idea who we were. My son scampered up the stairs to greet us, which ordinarily isn't permitted, but the Supreme Court police officers didn't stop him. We posed for photographs with Attorney General Farmer.

That smile on my face is one of genuine happiness.

The long line of visitors on the steps waiting to enter the courthouse hid the phalanx of national news reporters from CNN and other media outlets gathered on the plaza below, their microphone stands set up and television cameras ready to roll. When he saw the large gathering of journalists that his press secretary Chuck Davis had confidently told us weren't there, Attorney General Farmer turned to me and joked, "I'm going to have to talk to Chuck about this."

As the chief law enforcement officer for the state of New Jersey, Attorney General Farmer had every right to speak to the national press corps himself, but he told me I had handled myself so expertly before the court that he would once again yield the spotlight. I stepped up to the microphones. The Supreme Court reporters were primarily interested in the hate crime aspect of *Apprendi*. Sentencing law doesn't pull in high ratings. Why was it so important for the judge, not the jury, the reporters wanted to know, to decide whether Apprendi's crime was racially motivated? I explained that evidence of racial bias is highly prejudicial, and defendants usually fight tooth and nail to keep such inflammatory evidence from the jury. New Jersey's Hate Crime Statute ensured that juries would not be swayed by the defendant's racist views.

Then I was off with my entourage to La Colline, a brasserie a few blocks away on D Street, for a private après-argument luncheon Steven had arranged. As we walked past the Maryland Avenue side of the Supreme Court building, my friend Diane's husband, Ben, spotted a four-star Navy admiral walking in front of a group of other high-ranking naval officers, all without their regulation hats. Ben, an ex-Navy man, bellowed, *"Hey, Admiral! Where's your cover?"* The admiral yelled back to Ben, *"Don't need one!"* Ben countered, *"Betcha when I was a swabbie you would have busted me down to E-zero if I said that to you!"*

Holy crap! I had just survived a metaphoric firing squad inside the courthouse, and now Ben was taunting a commander of the United States Naval Forces on the streets of Washington, DC, in broad daylight. The admiral laughed, and he and Ben cheerfully waved each other goodbye. Ben later explained to me that "E-zero" is an inside Navy joke because the enlisted ranks don't go any lower than E-one.

—⚊—

La Colline is French for "the hill," a fitting name for a French restaurant located on Capitol Hill. Nineteen years after the *Apprendi* argument, I asked Jordan if he recalled the name of the restaurant. He did not, but he did remember eating tricolor tortellini. Our specially prepared menu for the après-argument lunch offered our guests a choice of four appetizers, three entrées,

Cup of Split Pea Soup
Onion Soup Gratinee
La Colline Spring Mix Salad
Caesar Salad "Maison

Pan Seared Filet of Norwegian Salmon
Served on Lentils du Puy
Wilted Spinach, Fried Leeks & Sauce Genevoise

Breast of Chicken Saute w/ Fresh Garden Herbs

Tri Color Tortellini w/ Tomato Sauce

Criollo
Chocolate Purse Filled w/ El Rey Chocolate Mousse
Served w/ Vanilla Bean Sauce

Warm Apple Tart w/ Vanilla Ice Cream

Menu from La Colline.

and two desserts. Each of my guests received a commemorative menu specially printed for the occasion.

Unlike Jordan, I do not recall what I ate that early spring afternoon. I was too busy enjoying a bottle of Dom Perignon that Steven had rescued from the trunk of my crumpled Honda Accord after the Hyatt Regency parking valet crashed the car.

The luncheon in my honor at La Colline was one of the most wonderful and significant celebrations of my life. This was a gathering of the people I loved most and who most loved me, who rooted for me, supported me, and had traveled hundreds of miles just to sit in the spectators' gallery inside the United States Supreme Court courtroom to watch the back of my head and listen to my voice for twenty minutes. It was like a wedding reception just for the bride.

After lunch, I returned to my hotel room and called Anne Paskow, the chief of the Appellate Section in the Division of Criminal Justice in Trenton, to tell her about the argument. Anne had already heard positive reports from Attorney General Farmer. I mentioned to Anne that I was going to discard much of my legal research rather than box it up and lug it back to New Jersey.

"Don't get rid of anything," Anne cautioned. "What if the Supreme Court orders a rehearing?"

(*Oh, dear God. No.*)

—⟶⟵—

The weather that afternoon turned foul as the predicted line of thunderstorms finally pushed through the Washington, DC, area, but it didn't stop the celebration. Dinner that evening was at B. Smith's restaurant in Union Station with Steven, Jordan, my parents, and my in-laws. Steven and I had dined at B. Smith's in New York City's theater district several times. Her individual sweet potato pies, garnished with a single pecan and fresh whipped cream, were heavenly, and we ordered them at the same time we ordered our entrées to be sure the restaurant didn't run out before dessert.

But first, toasts to me! My beverage of choice back then was Scotch on the rocks. I was finishing my second drink when I heard the telltale clicking in my left ear. Sure enough, the most god-awful migraine headache hit me like a freight train, brought on by a precipitous drop in barometric pressure and adrenaline, and amplified by a couple of glasses of alcohol. My body and brain were telling me, "So sorry, lady, we did our best to keep you pain-free as long as possible, but now that the *Apprendi* argument is over, we just can't hang on one second longer." I was grateful to have made it through the argument without a throbbing headache or a visual aura but annoyed that the postargument festivities were marred by a migraine. This was my party, though, and I vowed to tough it out rather than return to the hotel early. But I couldn't bear to look at the sweet potato pie.

CHAPTER 18

"OH, LEE-SAH! I HAVE PRESENTS for you!"

Steven was cradling a stack of newspapers purchased in the Hyatt Regency's gift shop. He walked over to the table in the lobby restaurant where Jordan and I were debating between chocolate chip pancakes and strawberry waffles for breakfast. I ditched my menu to scan the *New York Times*, the *Washington Post*, and *USA Today* for coverage of the *Apprendi* argument the day before.

Arguing *Apprendi* before the United States Supreme Court is, without question, the highlight of my legal career. A close runner-up was seeing my name in print the next morning in the very first section of the *New York Times* in an article covering the *Apprendi* argument written by Linda Greenhouse, the *Times* Supreme Court reporter.[1] I'm a lifelong reader of the *New York Times*. I grew up in a New York City bedroom community, so the *Times* was my hometown newspaper. I have solved the *Times* crossword puzzle in ink almost every day since high school. And I'm a huge fan of Linda Greenhouse. I was so excited to know that not only had Greenhouse attended the *Apprendi* argument, but she also wrote a full-length article about it. Her reporting was straightforward and fact based, and I was mentioned only briefly, but still, I was mentioned in a *New York Times* first-section article by Linda Greenhouse.

Other Supreme Court journalists focused on the nonstop interrogation of Joe O'Neill and me by the justices, confirming my suspicions that the justices were testier than usual during the *Apprendi* argument. Tony Mauro observed in the *Legal Times* that "the Supreme Court was in a surly mood last week, giving the advocates in *Apprendi v. New Jersey* a hard time all around."[2] Justices Breyer, Scalia, and Ginsburg "hit O'Neill with hypotheticals and tough, contradictory questions," Mauro wrote.[3] "Gochman was given an equally hard time by the justices, who seemed suddenly to be sympathetic toward Apprendi."[4]

Another reporter noted that when Joe O'Neill paused at the lectern for seven long seconds to get his bearings, Chief Justice Rehnquist teased him, "You can argue all by yourself, without any questions," provoking laughter from the packed courtroom.[5] The word *laughter* appears in parentheses in the official transcript of the *Apprendi* argument. *Guide for Counsel* warns that "attempts at humor usually fall flat," but this advice is directed at arguing counsel.[6] Chief Justice Rehnquist, however, was on a roll. When Joe enthusiastically agreed with Justice Scalia's rejoinder to a question posed by Justice Breyer, the chief justice asked Joe, "Shall we charge Justice Scalia's question to your time?" The word *laughter* appears in parentheses in the official transcript there, too.

I was also the subject of a hilarious *Slate* "Supreme Court Dispatches" article by Supreme Court reporter Dahlia Lithwick entitled "Clarence Thomas Speaks!" Highlights of the *Apprendi* argument, Lithwick wrote, included "Justice Scalia's leveling of counsel with questioning that would daunt Torquemada."[7] As for me,

> Lisa Gochman is the deputy attorney general in New Jersey, and she defends the hate-crime statute by insisting that hate is not a component of the criminal's *mens rea*, or intent, but rather of his motive, which is not a jury question.
>
> Justice O'Connor drags Gochman down memory lane to her own day as a sentencing judge, when judges had the discretion to give sentences ranging from "one year to life." Gochman concedes. Scalia asks her about this "traditional sentencing scheme" with which she now says she is not familiar. Scalia sneers that she seemed "very familiar with it when Justice O'Connor was asking about it," and then asks whether defendants have an absolute entitlement to a lesser sentence. She tries to answer, and he cuts her off. Rehnquist tells him to "let her answer." (Talk about the Doberman telling the pit bull not to bite.)
>
> "She's answering the wrong question, chief judge," Scalia retorts, then starts in on her again. I wouldn't be surprised to hear that Gochman had to

be carried out of court today. *Had she been Scalia's daughter, brought home in a squad car with a hickey at 3:00 a.m., she would not have had a tougher twenty minutes.*[8]

I love this last line so much. It's so irreverent and inappropriate to the solemnity of the occasion, yet it perfectly captured the tenor of the argument.

—⚬—

By midmorning on Wednesday, my family and friends had all returned home. Steven, Jordan, and I stayed in Washington, DC, for a well-deserved day of sightseeing, just the three of us. The thunderstorms the night before had ushered in a bitter cold front. We bundled up and walked two and a half miles from Capitol Hill to the Jefferson Memorial to see the cherry blossoms in bloom. I thought strolling beneath the pink-petaled archways created by the interwoven branches of hundreds of cherry trees was spectacular. Steven was freezing and thought otherwise. He leaned down and whispered in Jordan's ear, "Yeah, right, nice flowers. Let's get out of here already." Steven would have gotten away with this snarky remark had Jordan not started giggling.

We trudged headlong into the chilly March winds to the National Archives Museum on the Constitution Avenue side of the National Mall. In retrospect, we should have called for the Hyatt One Town Car to drive us through DC. It was, after all, my last day as a chauffeur-driven princess.

The National Archives building houses the original founding documents of the United States of America. Inside a large rotunda, the Declaration of Independence, the United States Constitution, and the Bill of Rights are publicly displayed inside airtight, temperature-controlled cases. I wanted to show Jordan the Bill of Rights. Since 1791, the Sixth Amendment to the Bill of Rights has guaranteed criminal defendants the right to trial by an impartial jury. This faded piece of parchment was the genesis of the *Apprendi* argument. It was amazing to think that the Bill of Rights was more than two hundred years old, yet the justices of the Supreme Court of the United States were still fighting over its meaning.

Next stop was the Supreme Court gift store. "Can you believe I argued here?" I asked Steven and Jordan as we passed through the metal detectors to enter the building. I hadn't yet processed my new reality that the *Apprendi* argument was over. For four long years, I had invested so much sweat equity into the *Apprendi* litigation. And it wasn't simply that the work itself was done. I had fulfilled my dream of arguing in the United States Supreme Court. And now I was returning to this great hall of justice, triumphant and ready to shop.

We walked downstairs to the basement (more grandly known as the Lower Great Hall) and turned left at the larger-than-life seated bronze statue of Chief Justice John Marshall. Inside the small gift shop, one of Justice O'Connor's law clerks approached me. She told me that Justice O'Connor thought I did a great job during the *Apprendi* argument the day before. (*Oh my goodness! My idol, Sandra Day O'Connor, the first woman associate justice of the Supreme Court of the United States, thought I did a great job! She just said so! Okay, it was secondhand hearsay through her law clerk, but I'm sure the law clerk was trustworthy and wouldn't just go up to some random woman in the gift shop the day after a Supreme Court argument and tell her Justice O'Connor thought she did a great job if Justice O'Connor never told her that, would she?*) I was floating on air.

Here are the souvenirs I bought in the Supreme Court gift shop: a pencil with a two-headed eraser that makes the pencil look like a gavel; a bookmark with a lenticular image showing the outside facade of the Supreme Court building when viewed from one angle and the interior of the Supreme Court courtroom when viewed from a slightly different angle; a cobalt blue glass vase and a clear glass paperweight, both etched with the seal of the Supreme Court; and a poster-sized, black-and-white photograph of the exterior of the Supreme Court building in the winter. I also purchased an intricately carved miniature United States Supreme Court building encased in a snow globe. When I shake the snow globe, tiny squares of iridescent confetti settle on the tiny roof of the tiny Supreme Courthouse.

In a corner of the gift shop, my son presented me with a cobalt blue glass inkwell with a pewter lid in honor of my argument.

"This is for you, Mom," Jordan said proudly. "You can keep your quill pens in it."

And I do. I have never used the goose feather quills as writing instruments, and they are in perfect condition. I keep one of my quill pens in the prized cobalt blue inkwell Jordan bought for me at the Supreme Court gift shop. The other is mounted in a shadow box alongside Attorney General Farmer's copy of New Jersey's ruby red merits brief. He had returned the brief to me with this gracious handwritten note on the cover: "Lisa—Excellent brief! This is a difficult issue, but you've argued it cogently and with graceful prose. I look forward to meeting your family next month, John." Attorney General Farmer gave me his pair of quill pens, too, which I proudly display in the cobalt blue glass vase etched with the seal of the United States Supreme Court. John J. Farmer Jr., the man who would go on to serve as senior counsel on the 9/11 Commission, who would be appointed dean of Rutgers School of Law–Newark, and who is now director of Rutger's Eagleton Institute of Politics, is a true mensch.

The rarest of all United States Supreme Court souvenirs are, sadly, unavailable for purchase in the Supreme Court gift shop or any retail store. Law professor Ross Davies of George Mason University's Antonin Scalia School of Law creates limited edition bobblehead dolls of the justices.[9] These rare and highly sought-after bobbleheads are distributed only to subscribers of the *Green Bag*, the law school's quarterly law journal. So few bobblehead dolls are produced that even *Green Bag* subscribers are not guaranteed to receive one. The prototypes of the more than two dozen bobblehead justices produced by the *Green Bag* are safely archived at Yale University's Law Library.[10]

The Justice Sandra Day O'Connor bobblehead doll was issued in 2004, four years after my argument in *Apprendi*. The *Green Bag* website has an "Annotated Bobblehead Justice Sandra Day O'Connor" page explaining the unique features of the doll.[11] Justice O'Connor stands about eight inches tall in her black robe and white ruffled jabot, wearing tiny replicas of the low-heeled beige shoes she wore when she was sworn in as the first female United States Supreme Court associate justice on September 21, 1981. A brown-and-white Hereford cow lies by her side, a reference to her childhood on the Lazy B Ranch in Arizona. And the cow's head nods, as it, too, is a bobblehead. A double bobblehead!

Justice O'Connor holds volume number 530 of the official United States Supreme Court Reporter in recognition of her majority opinion in *Troxel v. Granville*, a case on parental visitation rights decided during the same term as *Apprendi*.[12] Volume 530 of the official United States Supreme Court Reporter is also where the *Apprendi* opinion is published. I needed this bobblehead doll so badly. I contacted the law school to start a subscription to the *Green Bag* but was bluntly informed that one had to have an existing subscription to receive the Justice Sandra Day O'Connor bobblehead doll. I was desperate.

I offered to allow the *Green Bag* to publish a poem I had written about the *Apprendi* argument in exchange for the bobblehead doll, but bartering was not permitted. Rats.

In June 2014, an original Justice Sandra Day O'Connor double bobblehead doll sold on eBay for $810. If I were fortunate enough to own one, I would never, *ever* part with mine.

CHAPTER 19

MY BRUISED AND BATTERED HONDA Accord stayed behind in an auto body repair shop in DC while Steven, Jordan, and I drove home to New Jersey in a rented Toyota Camry. I don't know why the valet driver crashed my beloved car. We battled with the auto insurance company for weeks until the District of Columbia Police Department report was issued. That very day, the insurance company reversed course and agreed to pay us the full replacement cost of the Honda. I've never read the police report, but I suspect the valet driver was drunk or high or suffered a medical episode. Whatever the cause, it was evident the Hyatt Regency on Capitol Hill was fully liable for the damage caused by one of its contractors. And I got a brand-new Honda Accord.

Back home in New Jersey, there was nothing to do but wait for the Supreme Court of the United States to issue its decision. After more than four years of living and breathing *Apprendi*, it was completely out of my hands. I was adrift at sea. Mountains of laundry and new work assignments kept me busy, but my thoughts always turned back to Washington, DC, where the nine justices were deciding whether New Jersey's Hate Crime Statute was constitutional. For cases argued on Mondays, the justices meet in private conference two days later on Wednesday afternoons to discuss the arguments and cast preliminary votes.[1] For cases, like *Apprendi*, argued on Tuesdays or Wednesdays, the justices meet in private conference on Friday afternoons.[2] Speaking to the Faculty of Law of the University of Guanajuato, Mexico, in 2001, Chief Justice Rehnquist described the court's postargument process:

At the appointed time the nine members of the Court meet in the conference room. We all shake hands with one another when we come in and we have whatever materials we want with us. . . . There is no one in the room except the nine of us. If our conference is interrupted by a knock on the door indicating that there is a message for one of the Justices, the most junior Justice answers the door and delivers it. Justice Stephen G. Breyer . . . has been the junior Justice for seven years, and I suspect he is a little tired of answering the door.[3]

After the preliminary votes are cast, opinion-writing assignments are made. When among the majority, the chief justice assigns himself or another justice to write the majority opinion. When the chief justice finds himself among the minority, the most senior justice in the majority writes the opinion or assigns it to another justice in the majority. Neither the preliminary votes among the justices nor the assignment of the majority opinion is made public. Not even arguing counsel are notified. I would have to wait until the *Apprendi* decision was finalized and issued to the public to find out how each justice voted.

At 10:00 a.m. every Monday through Wednesday for the next twelve weeks, I waited anxiously by the phone for Andrea Hampton at the National Association of Attorneys General to let me know whether *Apprendi* was one of the opinions issued that morning. The weeks crawled by without word.

The National Association of Criminal Defense Lawyers named the *Apprendi* case one of the most important to be argued during SCOTUS's 1999 term, but I didn't think *Apprendi* qualified for such lofty status.[4] Wasn't *Apprendi* just a minor sentencing law case? If the court accepted my argument that motive was a traditional sentencing factor, its decision would merely affirm the precedent set in *Almendarez-Torres* that traditional sentencing factors, such as prior convictions, are not elements of the underlying offense. If the court rejected my argument, it could do so on the very narrow ground that motive was not a traditional sentencing factor and strike down New Jersey's Hate Crime Statute as unconstitutional without invalidating other state and federal laws or making any sweeping changes to current Supreme Court precedent. Either way, *Apprendi* would just be the next case in line after *Almendarez-Torres* and *Jones* as the "sentencing factor versus element of the offense" debate inched inexorably forward.

That SCOTUS would stick to its narrow case-by-case approach in *Apprendi* became more likely on June 5, 2000, two months after the *Apprendi* argument, when SCOTUS issued its opinion in *Castillo v. United States*.[5] Defendant Jaime Castillo was a member of the Branch-Davidian religious sect involved in a violent confrontation in 1993 with federal agents from the Bureau of Alcohol, Tobacco, and Firearms near Waco, Texas. Following a trial for conspiracy to murder federal officers, a jury found that Castillo had knowingly used or carried a firearm during the commission of a crime of violence. A federal statute authorized the sentencing judge, rather than the jury, to determine the type of firearm Castillo had used or carried during the violent crime. The type of firearm, in turn, determined Castillo's maximum prison sentence on the weapons offense: handguns carried a five-year maximum term; short-barreled rifles and shotguns carried a ten-year maximum term; and machine guns and other destructive devices carried a thirty-year maximum term.[6] The trial judge found that Castillo had possessed machine guns and hand grenades and sentenced him under the federal statute to a mandatory maximum sentence of thirty years in federal prison.[7]

The issue before SCOTUS in *Castillo* was whether the type of firearm a criminal possessed during the commission of a violent crime was a sentencing factor or an element of the underlying crime. Once again, the Supreme Court employed the multipronged *McMillan* test to reach its conclusion, as it had done in *Almendarez-Torres* and *Jones*. SCOTUS considered five separate factors: one, the overall structure of the federal firearms statute strongly favored the "new crime" interpretation; two, the type of firearm used in the commission of an offense was not a traditional sentencing factor; three, asking the jury to determine the type of firearm used would not unduly prejudice the defendant; four, the legislative history of the statute suggested that Congress had intended to create new substantive crimes based on the weapon used; and, five, the length and severity of the added mandatory sentence "assumes a preference for traditional jury determination of so important a factual matter."[8] Writing for a unanimous court, Justice Stephen Breyer found that the federal firearms statute created three separate substantive crimes based on the type of firearm used during the commission of the underlying offense. Only a jury, not a judge, could determine whether the firearm was a handgun, a short-barreled rifle, or a machine gun.[9]

I was equally dejected and elated by the *Castillo* decision. On the negative side of the equation was the fifth *Castillo* factor—namely, the length and severity of the added mandatory maximum sentence. Like the federal firearms statute in *Castillo*, New Jersey's Hate Crime Statute bumped up Charles Apprendi's prison term for his conviction into a higher sentencing range. I cringed recalling Justice Souter's lecture to me at the *Apprendi* oral argument in March that "motive has never had the significance that it has under the New Jersey statute. The motive, so far as I know, has never traditionally been the difference between ten and twenty years." This was the crux of Charles Apprendi's argument, and the nine justices of SCOTUS had just unanimously agreed in *Castillo* that an increase in the maximum sentence "weighs in favor of treating such offense-related words as referring to an element" of the offense.[10] This part of the court's opinion in *Castillo* was problematic for New Jersey's Hate Crime Statute.

On the positive side of the equation, however, the *Castillo* court did not adopt the bright-line rule suggested in footnote 6 of *Jones*. The court instead applied a multipronged approach. Several factors the *Castillo* court considered supported the constitutionality of the Hate Crime Statute. First, by placing the Hate Crime Statute within the sentencing provisions of the state's Code of Criminal Justice, the New Jersey Legislature indicated that the commission of a hate crime was a sentencing factor. Second, unlike the type of firearm used in a crime, motive was a traditional sentencing factor under the century-old United States Supreme Court jurisprudence of *Pointer v. United States*.[11] Third, evidence that the accused was racist was highly inflammatory, and New Jersey's Hate Crime Statute ensured that the jury never heard this prejudicial information. There was still a realistic possibility that the Hate Crime Statute would survive constitutional scrutiny following *Castillo*.

A New Jersey court rule urges litigants with active cases to file a supplemental letter alerting the state court in which the case is pending to recently issued legal decisions and newly enacted legislation relevant to the pending case.[12] I had sent such a supplemental letter to the Supreme Court of New Jersey after filing the state's brief in *Apprendi* but prior to the argument in Trenton to explain how the then recent SCOTUS decision in *Almendarez-Torres* supported the constitutionality of the Hate Crime Statute. SCOTUS has a parallel rule permitting supplemental briefs, but the rule applies only "up to the time the case is called for oral argument."[13] After oral argument, the clerk will not accept any brief for filing without permission of the court.

I was leaning toward filing a motion with SCOTUS seeking permission for the state to submit a supplemental brief offering the justices New Jersey's view on the *Castillo* decision. This course of action would afford me one last opportunity to frame the "sentencing factor versus element of the offense" debate favorably to the state. There were, however, substantial logistical hurdles and financial costs to consider, including drafting, typesetting, printing, and filing forty formal booklet briefs (with their requisite adhesive bandage tan covers) with the Clerk's Office in a considerably short amount of time.[14] If I were to file a supplemental brief with SCOTUS addressing the relevance of its *Castillo* decision to the pending *Apprendi* case, I had to do so immediately. There were just a few weeks left in the court's 1999 term, and the *Apprendi* decision could be handed down any day now.

I called my go-to adviser on all things United States Supreme Court, Michael Dreeben, the deputy solicitor general for SCOTUS's criminal docket, for his sage advice. The Office of the Solicitor General had represented the federal government in the *Castillo* argument, and both Deputy Solicitor General Dreeben and Assistant Solicitor Edward DuMont had contributed to the government's brief in *Castillo*. Dreeben counseled me against filing a supplemental letter to SCOTUS.

"The United States Supreme Court is familiar with its own decisions," Dreeben told me. "The justices don't need to hear from either of us at this point."

Once again, all I could do was wait. With just three weeks left before the Supreme Court broke for its summer recess, the justices were no longer hearing oral arguments and had turned their full attention to writing their majority, concurring, and dissenting opinions in the seventeen cases still pending. The very last week of June is traditionally reserved for the court's "blockbuster" decisions, the ones so significant that they deserve special notice or the ones where the court is so deeply divided that multiple justices write in-depth concurring and dissenting opinions.

I had expected the *Apprendi* decision to come down long before the last week of June. I knew *Apprendi* was important, but I remained unconvinced that it merited blockbuster status, even if the justices adopted a bright-line rule and used *Apprendi* as the vehicle to put the "sentencing factor versus element of the offense" debate to rest once and for all. Most of the cases yet to be decided by the court were of far more interest to the general public than *Apprendi*. For example, *Hill v. Colorado* would set the limitations of First Amendment rights on protesters outside abortion clinics.[15] *Stenberg v. Carhart* would determine the constitutionality of a Nebraska law banning partial-birth abortions.[16] *Dickerson v. United States* would resolve whether Congress could legislatively overrule the *Miranda v. Arizona* decision and its well-known warnings to arrestees that "anything you say can be held against you in a court of law."[17] *Santa Fe Independent School District v. Doe* would address whether student-led prayer at public school football games was constitutional.[18] *Boy Scouts of America v. Dale*, which, like *Apprendi*, originated in the New Jersey state courts, would decide whether the Boy Scouts of America could revoke the adult membership of Eagle Scout James Dale after the youth organization learned that Dale was a homosexual and gay rights activist.[19]

On the Monday morning of the second-to-last week of June 2000, Steven, Jordan, and I boarded a plane at the Atlantic City, New Jersey, airport for a long-planned, five-day Walt Disney World vacation in Florida. I love Disney World. I love riding the Doom Buggies at the Haunted Mansion and the pirate ships soaring over London's gaslit streets on Peter Pan's Flight. I love the colorful fireworks painting the sky above Cinderella's Castle and the unpredictable, stomach-churning drops of Twilight Zone Tower of Terror. I love slurping pineapple Dole Whips as they melt in the hot Florida sun, and, most of all, I love nibbling on gingerbread Mickey cookies with their semisweet-chocolate-dipped mouse ears. On any other day, I would have been as joyful as my nine-year-old to be flying to the Most Magical Place on Earth.

Instead, I was a mess on the entire flight to Florida, stuck on a plane without cellular phone service to contact Andrea Hampton at the National Association of Attorneys General. As soon as we landed at the Orlando International Airport, I searched for a relatively secluded spot in the terminal and called NAAG. Hampton told me there was no *Apprendi* decision forthcoming from SCOTUS that day. Nor did the court issue its *Apprendi* decision the next day or the day after that. *Charles C. Apprendi, Jr., v. New Jersey* would be among the blockbuster opinions for the court's 1999 term after all. A few days cavorting through the Magic Kingdom and racing down water slides at Blizzard Beach with my family was a much-needed distraction for my *Apprendi*-addled brain.

—⁘—

The final week of SCOTUS's term is a heady time for court watchers. It is the only week in the court's nine-month term when it is known for sure which opinions will be released. For arguing counsel anxiously waiting for their decisions, the anticipation is unbearable.

On Monday, June 26, 2000, during the final week of the 1999 court term, the Supreme Court convened in open session with all nine justices sitting on the bench. Chief Justice Rehnquist proclaimed in his serious voice, "The opinion of the court in number 99-478, *Apprendi v. New Jersey*, will be announced by Justice Stevens." As the justice with the most seniority among the majority members in the *Apprendi* decision, Justice Stevens could assign the task of writing the opinion to another justice or keep it for himself. He kept it for himself.

Unlike the New Jersey appellate courts, SCOTUS does not notify the parties in advance when decisions on their cases are about to be issued. Of course, it was the last week of June, and the *Apprendi* opinion had not yet been released, so it was all but inevitable that the decision would come down that week. But it did not occur to me to travel to Washington, DC, and stake out a seat in the bar section of the courtroom to learn the outcome of *Apprendi* live and in person. It was just as well.

Had I been in the courtroom that Monday morning in late June, I would have figured out as soon as I heard Chief Justice Rehnquist say Justice Stevens's name that I had lost *Apprendi*. Stevens was a fierce proponent of the Sixth Amendment right to trial by an impartial jury. His voting record in *McMillan, Walton, Almendarez-Torres, Jones,* and most recently, *Castillo,* was consistent with his belief that "using a sentencing factor to increase either a mandatory minimum sentence or the permissible maximum sentence violates the rule requiring proof beyond a reasonable doubt of every fact necessary to support a finding of guilt."[20] I'm glad I wasn't inside the courtroom to hear Justice Stevens spell out exactly why I had lost in *Apprendi*. I would have been the woman in the bar section sobbing.

—⁘—

Unencumbered by the "doctrine of constitutional doubt" that had re-stricted the court's reach in *Jones*, the United States Supreme Court went full bore and struck down the New Jersey Legislature's Hate Crime Statute as unconstitutional. The court abandoned the multipronged approach it applied just three weeks earlier in *Castillo* and adopted the bright-line rule proposed in footnote 6 of *Jones* that I had so strenuously argued against. New Jersey's Hate Crime Statute fell with a thud on the unconstitutional side of the bright line drawn by the court.

Justice Stevens gave his synopsis of the *Apprendi* case from the bench:

> The case comes to us from the Supreme Court of New Jersey. It originated in a town called Vineland, New Jersey, where the defendant one evening, late at night, I should say about two o'clock in the morning, after he consumed a good deal of alcohol, fired several bullets at a house that was occupied by an African-American family. He was picked up by the police about an hour later and acknowledged the shooting and was therefore indicted for the crime of unlawful possession of a weapon, which is a second degree offense in New Jersey that carries a sentence of from five to ten years, and he pleaded guilty to that offense.
>
> But there is a separate statute in New Jersey that's called a hate crime law, and it provides for an extended term of imprisonment if a crime is committed with the purpose to intimidate an individual or group because of race, color, or gender, or handicap, religion, sexual orientation, or ethnicity, and if the extended term is authorized by a finding of that kind, the sentence, instead of being from five to ten years, is from ten to twenty years.
>
> Under the extended-term statute, the New Jersey Legislature has provided that the finding should be made by a judge based on a preponderance of the evidence rather than by a jury based on proof beyond a reasonable doubt as is customary for elements of a crime.
>
> Back in 1970, in a case called *In re Winship*, we held that the Due Process Clause protects the accused against conviction upon proof beyond a reasonable doubt of every fact necessary to constitute the crime with which he is charged.
>
> Now, in this case, the judge did find the unlawful bias and therefore imposed the sentence in excess, what would otherwise be the maximum of ten years, he imposed a twelve-year sentence for this crime, and the question is whether the finding that authorized that sentence had to be made by a jury on the higher standard of proof or was it permissible on the preponderance of the evidence.

The New Jersey Supreme Court upheld the sentence and we granted certiorari to review that holding and today we reverse that judgment. We conclude that the fact that has the importance in the sentencing scheme that it raises the maximum sentence from ten to twenty years, is one that has to be found by the jury and on the standard of proof beyond a reasonable doubt.

Justice Scalia has filed a concurring opinion. He ends with the sentence, "The guarantee that in all criminal prosecutions the accused shall enjoy the right to trial by an impartial jury has no intelligible content unless it means that all the facts which must exist in order to subject the defendant to a legally prescribed punishment must be found by the jury." That is the essence of the holding of the majority.

In addition to Justice Scalia's concurring opinion, Justice Thomas has filed a concurring opinion which is joined by Justice Scalia, which carefully reviews the history of that provision.

Justice O'Connor has filed a dissenting opinion in which the Chief Justice, Justice Kennedy and Justice Breyer joined, and Justice Breyer has filed a dissenting opinion in which the Chief Justice joined.[21]

Apprendi was a 5-4 decision. I had lost by a single vote. The voting blocs were identical to those in *Almendarez-Torres* and *Jones*: Rehnquist, O'Connor, Kennedy, and Breyer versus Stevens, Scalia, Souter, and Ginsburg. Justice Thomas, the swing vote in *Almendarez-Torres* and *Jones*, joined Stevens, Scalia, Souter, and Ginsburg to form the five-justice majority in *Apprendi*.[22]

Andrea Hampton of the National Association of Attorneys General had the unenviable job of calling me with the disappointing news that I had lost. At least Trenton, New Jersey, was in the same time zone as Washington, DC. *Guide for Counsel* notes that, "due to time zone differences, counsel might not be notified until several hours after the media have had access to an opinion."[23] The last thing I would have wanted that day was a newspaper or television reporter asking me to describe how it felt to lose my one and only case in the United States Supreme Court when I didn't yet know I had lost. Blinking back tears, I walked down the seemingly endless hallway to Anne Paskow's office to give her the news. On the way, I passed my colleagues standing in their office doorways, eager to learn if today was decision day. I couldn't make eye contact with anyone.

"I lost," I mumbled with my head down, and slinked past their offices. I was utterly crushed.

CHAPTER 20

ANDREA HAMPTON FAXED ME A copy of the *Apprendi* opinion, which in June 2000 was the fastest way to get my hands on the decision. The first-generation fax machine at the Division of Criminal Justice slowly, slowly, slowly churned out page after page of shiny thermal paper that refused to lie flat. I took the thick stack of curling paper back to my office and shut my door, a box of tissues close by. I had always known that losing *Apprendi* was a possibility, but I hadn't expected the depth of despair I felt. My emotions were too raw to read the opinion right away. At the same time that Joseph O'Neill was visiting his client Charles Apprendi to share his good news that the Supreme Court had ruled in his favor, I was calling my husband to share my sorry news that the Supreme Court had ruled against me. Then I contacted a long list of people associated with the *Apprendi* litigation, including New Jersey Attorney General John Farmer and Cumberland County First Assistant Prosecutor Robert Luther, to let them know the result. My office phone started ringing as news reporters around the country sought comment on New Jersey's loss in *Apprendi*. My personal reaction was not fit to print. But I was a professional and gave the standard "the state of New Jersey is disappointed in the result" response.

When the initial hoopla died down, I forced myself to read the entire ninety-nine page decision. *Apprendi* is a long and tedious opinion. It is dense and esoteric and recounts in excruciating detail the historical and constitutional foundations for the rights to due process and to jury trials. Slogging through it was all the more painful because I represented the losing party. It's hard to remain objective when the Supreme Court of the United States is smacking down all your arguments one by one.

Writing for the majority of five members of the court (Stevens, Scalia, Thomas, Souter, and Ginsburg), Justice Stevens identified the issue "starkly presented" to the United States Supreme Court as "whether Charles Apprendi had a constitutional right to have a jury find racial bias on the basis of proof beyond a reasonable doubt."[1] The answer, Justice Stevens explained, was foreshadowed by the *Jones* decision where the court had held that serious bodily injury to the victim was an element of the federal crime of carjacking because that factual finding exposed Jones to an extended prison term.[2] The court did not care whether a fact was traditionally considered to be a sentencing factor. What mattered was the result of a finding that the fact exists. If a finding that a fact exists bumps up the defendant's custodial sentence into the next higher sentencing range, it's an element of the offense. If it's an element of the offense, only a jury finding under the "beyond a reasonable doubt" standard or a defendant's guilty plea to this fact is constitutionally sufficient before the trial court may impose an extended term.

Gone in one fell swoop was the multipronged approach used in *McMillan, Almendarez-Torrez, Jones,* and, most recently, *Castillo.* In its place was the bright-line rule suggested in footnote 6 of *Jones.* What one year earlier had been nonbinding dicta was now the precedential "*Apprendi* rule." The *Apprendi* rule states, "Other than the fact of a prior conviction, any fact that increases the penalty for a crime beyond the prescribed statutory maximum must be submitted to a jury, and proved beyond a reasonable doubt."[3] New Jersey's Hate Crime Statute might have survived a multipronged analysis under *McMillan, Almendarez-Torres, Jones,* and *Castillo,* but it never stood a chance under the new *Apprendi* rule.

The sole exception to this bright-line rule is a defendant's criminal history. Prior convictions are exempt, Justice Stevens explained, because prior guilty pleas and jury verdicts are entered pursuant to court proceedings with substantial procedural safeguards of their own, "mitigating the due process and Sixth Amendment concerns otherwise implicated in allowing a judge to determine a 'fact' increasing punishment beyond the maximum of the statutory range."[4] The majority ruling in *Apprendi* thus left intact the holding of *Almendarez-Torres* that prior convictions are sentencing factors, despite

Justice Stevens's musings that "it is arguable that *Almendarez-Torres* was incorrectly decided."[5]

Justice Scalia joined Justice Stevens's majority opinion but wrote a separate concurring opinion reiterating his adherence to the jurisprudence of original intent. The United States Constitution, Justice Scalia wrote, does not "mean what we think it ought to mean . . . it means what it says. And the guarantee that 'in all criminal prosecutions, the accused shall enjoy the right to trial, by an impartial jury,' has no intelligible content unless it means that all the facts which must exist in order to subject the defendant to a legally prescribed punishment *must* be found by the jury."[6]

Justice Thomas, like his conservative colleague Antonin Scalia, also joined Stevens's majority opinion in *Apprendi* and also wrote his own concurring opinion. Thomas was the justice who made national news by asking his first question in years during the *Apprendi* oral argument. And Justice Thomas didn't ask just any question. *Slate* reporter Dahlia Lithwick best describes this unforgettable moment in Supreme Court history:

> Edward DuMont from the solicitor general's office offers up his own defense of the New Jersey statute. . . . He's upstaged when his first question comes from Justice Thomas, who asks him to define a distinction between an element of the crime—a jury question—and a sentencing enhancement—a question for the judge. Since this is the central issue in the case, Thomas is either asking the obvious threshold question or subtly reframing the entire issue. I'm too shocked to tell. When Thomas finishes speaking, he leans back in his chair and looks somewhat shocked himself.
>
> All around me, the sketch artists are clamoring to amend their drawings to show Thomas' mouth open. It will be their biggest sketch of the year.[7]

The real shocker for me was Thomas's position in *Apprendi*, which was far more radical than that of the other four members of the *Apprendi* majority in drawing a constitutional line in the sand. Thomas stated in his concurring opinion that "the Constitution requires a broader rule than the court adopts."[8] According to Justice Thomas, *any* factor increasing a sentence above the statutory maximum, including a prior conviction, is an element of the crime that only a jury may find.[9]

I did not see that one coming.

Walking into the United States Supreme Court for the *Apprendi* argument on that sunny Tuesday morning in March 2000, I was realistic enough to know that, based on their prior votes in *Almendarez-Torres* and *Jones*, it would be nearly impossible to persuade Justices Stevens, Scalia, Ginsburg, and Souter to cross over to the "sentencing factor" side of the debate. But I was also fairly confident that I had Chief Justice Rehnquist and Justices O'Connor, Kennedy, and Breyer with me on the "sentencing factor" side based on their prior votes in *Almendarez-Torres* and *Jones*. I only needed one more vote. A 5-4 majority is razor-thin, but it still counts as a win in the Supreme Court of the United States.

My best strategy for winning *Apprendi* was to persuade Justice Thomas, the swing vote in *Almendarez-Torres* and *Jones*, that motive was a traditional sentencing factor. Thomas had joined the *Almendarez-Torres* majority, which held that a defendant's prior conviction is a traditional sentencing factor. He had also joined the *Jones* majority, which held that serious bodily injury and death to the victim are elements of the crime of carjacking. These two holdings were consistent with each other and consistent with New Jersey's position that motive was a traditional sentencing factor. Justice Thomas's votes in *Almendarez-Torres* and *Jones* signaled to me that he was not committed to the bright-line rule proposed in footnote 6 of *Jones*.

I could not have been more wrong. As it turned out, I never had Justice Thomas on my side at all. In his concurring opinion in *Apprendi*, Justice Thomas admitted that he voted the wrong way in *Almendarez-Torres*:

> One of the chief errors of *Almendarez-Torres*—an error to which I
> succumbed—was to attempt to discern whether a particular fact is
> traditionally (or typically) a basis for a sentencing court to increase an
> offender's sentence. For the reasons I have given, it should be clear that this
> approach just defines away the real issue. What matters is the way by which
> a fact enters into the sentence. If a fact is by law the basis for imposing or
> increasing punishment—for establishing or increasing the prosecution's
> entitlement—it is an element.[10]

At least I did not know on argument day that the outcome of *Apprendi* was preordained. How demoralizing it must be to labor over a case in the United States Supreme Court for months, knowing from the start that you will not win. As it is, arguing a case in the United States Supreme Court is a zero-sum game: one side will win; the other side will lose. Sometimes you're the wind-shield; sometimes you're the bug. Even the most seasoned Supreme Court advocates lose. Legend has it that when Chief Justice John Roberts was an attorney appearing before the court, he was asked by his disappointed client to explain why he had lost the case 9-0. Roberts answered "Because there were only nine justices." At least I had four justices who voted in my favor.

—⚭—

Chief Justice Rehnquist was the most senior justice among the four members of the court who disagreed with Justice Stevens's majority opinion. Rehnquist had the choice to assign the task of writing the dissenting opinion to another justice in the minority or keep it for himself.[11] He assigned the principal dissent-ing opinion to my idol, Justice O'Connor. In her dissent, O'Connor foresaw that the new bright-line rule of *Apprendi* would "surely be remembered as a water-shed change in constitutional law."[12] "In one bold stroke," O'Connor wrote, "the Court today casts aside our traditional cautious approach and instead embraces a universal and seemingly bright-line rule limiting the power of Congress and state legislatures to define criminal offenses and the sentences that follow from convictions thereunder."[13]

O'Connor echoed my answer to Justice Scalia during oral argument that Scalia's position in *Apprendi* was inconsistent with the court's prior opinion in the capital murder case of *Walton v. Arizona.* Justice O'Connor wrote, "If a State can remove from the jury a factual determination that makes the dif-ference between life and death as *Walton* holds that it can, it is inconceivable why a State cannot do the same with respect to a factual determination that results in only a ten-year increase in the maximum sentence to which a de-fendant is exposed."[14]

Although it was nice to have four of the nine justices on my side, in the grander scheme of things it was meaningless. The impact of a 5-4 decision is the same as that of a 9-0 decision. I had lost. I was devastated and more than a little embarrassed to lose the most important oral argument of my career. When I walked out of the Supreme Court in Washington, DC, on March 28, 2000, I was sure I had the winning argument. I had done my best work, but it wasn't good enough. The attorney general of New Jersey had entrusted me with every aspect of the *Apprendi* litigation, but I had let him down. I had let down the Fowlkes family, too, and the citizens of New Jersey. It particularly pained me to break the news to my family and friends, who had offered me unconditional love and support throughout the long and arduous process.[15]

My wounded pride was, of course, beside the point. It was the victims of Charles Apprendi's racist shooting rampages—Michael Fowlkes Sr., Mattie Harrell Fowlkes, and their three children, Phillip, Dawn, and Michael Jr.—who suffered the real-life impact of my loss in the Supreme Court. Mattie Harrell told the *New York Times* that the high court's ruling in *Apprendi* resurrected the tremendous emotional and psychological pain her family had suffered through in 1994.

"It tore the whole family up," Harrell said. "We will never be the same. Today is a slap in the face as far as being a minority goes."[16]

Mattie and Michael Fowlkes were divorced by then. Mattie and her three children remained in their dream house in Vineland.

"I'm a very religious person," said Mattie Harrell. "I'm not going to live my life in fear. The only person who can move me is God."[17]

—⁂—

It's called a judicial "opinion" but it's not as if the justices had debated a theoretical point of Sixth Amendment law and then wrote ninety-nine pages about it just for fun. Under the new bright-line rule of law that bore his name, Charles Apprendi's twelve-year prison sentence was no longer constitutional. At the close of the majority opinion in *Apprendi*, Justice Stevens wrote: "It is so ordered."[18]

Apprendi was entitled to be brought back before the New Jersey courts for resentencing in a reasonable amount of time. In a separate one-page order issued on the same date as the *Apprendi* opinion, SCOTUS remanded the matter to the New Jersey courts "for further proceedings not inconsistent with the opinion of this Court." Like most cases on review from a state court, SCOTUS's mandate in *Apprendi* was stayed for twenty-five days.[19] This short postponement gave the losing party, the state of New Jersey, time to file a petition for rehearing with the court.[20] Filing a petition for rehearing would further stay the court's mandate.[21]

There was never any serious discussion in my office, however, about filing a petition for a rehearing. No matter how disappointed we were with the result, there was no legitimate basis available to us to challenge the final decision. The Supreme Court of the United States had spoken, and we had lost. Filing a petition for a rehearing would get us nowhere. I jettisoned the hundreds of pages of research I had lugged home from Washington, DC, into the recycling bin.

On July 21, 2000, the twenty-fifth day after the *Apprendi* opinion was issued, SCOTUS's mandate was finalized, formally bringing Charles C. Apprendi Jr.'s case before the Supreme Court of the United States to a close. Jurisdiction was kicked back to the New Jersey state courts. Wasting no time, Apprendi and his attorney Joseph O'Neill returned to Judge Rushton Ridgway's courtroom in Bridgeton, New Jersey, that very same day for resentencing on count eighteen of the indictment charging second-degree possession of a firearm for an unlawful purpose.

In New Jersey, when resentencing is ordered after a defendant's successful appeal, the trial court views that defendant as he stands before the court on resentencing day.[22] And on July 21, 2000, with New Jersey's Hate Crime Statute officially dead in the water, the trial judge could no longer rely on his prior factual finding that Apprendi's crime was racially motivated to impose a prison term above the ordinary statutory maximum of ten years. Before Judge Ridgway could reinstate Apprendi's original twelve-year sentence, the prosecution would first have to prove Apprendi's biased motive to a jury beyond a reasonable doubt.

But Cumberland County Prosecutor Arthur J. Marchand believed that the double jeopardy clause of the Fifth Amendment prohibited his office from retrying Apprendi on the charge of second-degree possession of a firearm for an unlawful purpose.[23] Without a jury finding of racial bias, Judge Ridgway no longer had any constitutional authority to bump up Apprendi's sentence into the statutory sentencing range for a first-degree crime. Instead of facing up to twenty years in a New Jersey state prison, Charles Apprendi now faced up to ten years.

Judge Ridgway reduced Apprendi's maximum custodial sentence to seven years. By this time, Apprendi had been released from state prison and was serving the remainder of his custodial term in a halfway house in Camden, New Jersey. Prosecutor Marchand joined Apprendi's application to the New Jersey Parole Board to further reduce Apprendi's custodial sentence to time served.[24]

—⁂—

Attorney General John J. Farmer Jr. vowed to continue prosecuting bias crime cases aggressively in New Jersey. Governor Christine Todd Whitman and the New Jersey Legislature worked quickly to amend the unconstitutional Hate Crime Statute by shifting the authority to determine a defendant's racial motive from the judge to the jury. The following year, in 2001, the New Jersey Legislature repealed the Hate Crime Statute and replaced it with the substantive crime of bias intimidation.[25] Now, whenever a criminal is charged with a hate crime in New Jersey, the state must prove to a jury beyond a reasonable doubt that the underlying offense (homicide, aggravated assault, kidnapping, etc.) was committed with a purpose to intimidate an individual or group of individuals *or* knowing that an individual or group of individuals would be intimidated *and* the crime was committed against the victim because of race, color, religion, gender, disability, sexual orientation, gender identity or expression, national origin, or ethnicity.[26]

The crime of bias intimidation is graded one degree higher than the underlying offense. The new bias intimidation statute yields the same result as the old Hate Crime Statute by punishing the defendant more harshly for his or her bad motive. But unlike the original Hate Crime Statute challenged in *Apprendi*, bad motive is now an element of the offense that the jury must find beyond a reasonable doubt before enhanced punishment may be imposed.

Nationwide, "from a practical standpoint, the *Apprendi* decision [was] apt to have little effect on most hate crimes, because in most states it was already the jury's job, rather than the judge's, to determine motive."[27] But *Apprendi* wasn't about hate crimes anymore. *Apprendi* was *way* bigger than that.

CHAPTER 21

HAD I WON IN THE United States Supreme Court, *Apprendi v. New Jersey* would have maintained the status quo of Supreme Court jurisprudence by confirming the principle that motive is a traditional sentencing factor regardless of its impact on the length of the prison term imposed. The *Apprendi* decision would have been a mere footnote in sentencing history. But I didn't win. And if you're going to lose in the Supreme Court of the United States, lose big. Erwin Chemerinsky, a renowned expert in constitutional law and the dean of the University of California at Berkeley School of Law, called *Apprendi* "one of the most important U.S. Supreme Court decisions in years.... Every lawyer who practices criminal law and every judge who hears criminal cases must deal with *Apprendi* on a regular basis. Rarely has any case had such an immediate and dramatic impact on the practice of law."[1]

Apprendi is what is known as a "sleeper" decision because it attracted relatively little attention the day it was argued or the day it was decided. Court watchers were far more interested in a different case, *Dickerson v. United States*, decided on the same day as *Apprendi*.[2] In *Dickerson*, the Supreme Court of the United States considered whether a federal statute effectively overruled *Miranda v. Arizona*, the 1966 decision requiring police officers to apprise suspects of their constitutional rights before statements made during custodial interrogation may be admitted into evidence at trial.[3] So important was the issue in *Dickerson* that the solicitor general himself, Seth Waxman, argued the case on behalf of the federal government. So important was the decision in

Dickerson that the chief justice himself, William Rehnquist, wrote the majority opinion upholding *Miranda*.

But it was *Apprendi*, not *Dickerson*, that took off like a rocket. The authors of the delightfully titled law review article "*Apprendi*citis" wrote, "In all likelihood, the court's 1999 term will be remembered not for reaffirming a suspect's *Miranda* rights, but rather . . . for ushering in a revolution in sentencing reform."[4]

The *Apprendi* decision upended sentencing law nationwide. True, *Apprendi v. New Jersey* is hardly a household name, but it developed into a major tornado of a case, spinning off more than forty thousand published state and federal court opinions. Criminal statutes across the country were declared unconstitutional in *Apprendi*'s wake as untold numbers of criminal defendants in state and federal courts brought successful *Apprendi* challenges to reduce the length of their prison sentences. As much as it's impossible to predict which petitions SCOTUS will grant, it's even harder to predict which opinions handed down by the court will have far-reaching implications drastically altering the course of United States criminal jurisprudence.

Justice John Paul Stevens's majority opinion in *Apprendi* is his legacy after serving thirty-five years on the Supreme Court bench. In his 2019 autobiography, *The Making of a Justice: Reflections on My First 94 Years*, Justice Stevens named *Apprendi v. New Jersey* as "what may well be the most significant majority opinion I authored as a justice."[5] Paul Clement, the solicitor general of the United States from June 2005 to June 2008, ranks *Apprendi* among the top three Stevens opinions.[6] The *American Bar Association Journal* places *Apprendi* at the top of its list of Justice Stevens's ten most influential opinions.[7]

Not to be outdone, Justice Scalia took credit for the sea change in sentencing law brought about by *Apprendi*. Justice Scalia boasted that "he had felt the winds blowing his way" in the "sentencing factor versus element of the offense" debate beginning with his dissenting vote in the 1998 *Almendarez-Torres* case. "I led the charge" toward implementing the bright-line rule in *Apprendi*, Scalia bragged in an interview with his biographer, author Joan Biskupic.[8] Justice Stevens, who wrote the majority opinion in *Apprendi*, "grinned when he heard of Scalia's 'led the charge' remark."[9] But Stevens "did not want to quibble with Scalia's view of who was in charge. 'If that's the way he assesses it, that's okay,' Stevens said. 'I'm happy to have him think he led the charge.'"[10]

Back in New Jersey, whenever a judge gives me a hard time during an oral argument, I think to myself, *I've lost in better courtrooms than this!*

—⁓—

During my tête-à-tête with Justice Scalia at the *Apprendi* argument, I had relied on the 1990 Supreme Court decision in *Walton v. Arizona* to support my argument that New Jersey's Hate Crime Statute was constitutional.[11] The Hate Crime Statute and Arizona's death penalty statute, I argued, both allowed sentencing judges to find specific facts that increase the defendant's sentence above the statutory maximum term. The increase under the Hate Crime Statute was from ten to twenty years; the increase under Arizona's death penalty statute was from life in prison to death. In response to one of the billions of questions Justice Scalia asked me during oral argument, I stressed that the sentencing procedure authorized by the Hate Crime Statute gave Charles Apprendi the same constitutional safeguards afforded to capital murder defendants:

"Your Honor, if a judge can increase a defendant's sentence from life imprisonment to death based on aggravating factors, and that's constitutional under the Sixth and Fourteenth Amendments, then certainly it would be constitutional to increase the petitioner's sentence by a mere two years on a non-capital offense. It's the same—we're dealing with the same constitutional amendments and the same clauses."

The *Apprendi* majority opinion dismissed my argument out of hand. Citing *Walton*, Justice Stevens wrote that "this Court has previously considered and rejected the argument that the principles guiding our decision today [in *Apprendi*] render invalid state capital sentencing schemes requiring judges, after a jury verdict holding a defendant guilty of a capital crime, to find specific aggravating factors before imposing a sentence of death.... Capital cases are not controlling."[12]

Two years later, I would be proved right, but it was a hollow victory. On June 24, 2002, SCOTUS issued its opinion in *Ring v. Arizona,* a case that forced the justices to confront the glaring constitutional discrepancy between the holdings of *Apprendi* and *Walton.*[13]

Deadlocked on the charge of the premeditated murder of the driver of a Wells Fargo armored van, an Arizona jury found defendant Timothy Stuart

Ring guilty of felony murder. At the subsequent capital sentencing hearing, Ring's codefendant, who was by then cooperating with the prosecution, told the judge it was Ring who fatally shot the victim, a damning allegation the prosecution never presented to the jury. The trial court sentenced Ring to death on the basis of the codefendant's testimony at the sentencing hearing.[14] The issue presented to SCOTUS in *Ring* was whether Arizona's death penalty statute—the exact same death penalty statute found constitutional in 1990 in *Walton v. Arizona*—was now unconstitutional under *Apprendi*'s bright-line rule that "other than the fact of a prior conviction, any fact that increases the penalty for a crime beyond the prescribed statutory maximum must be submitted to a jury, and proved beyond a reasonable doubt."[15]

On behalf of the 7-2 majority in *Ring*, Justice Ruth Bader Ginsburg wrote that Arizona's death penalty statute and New Jersey's Hate Crime Statute were on equal footing because both laws authorized judges to make findings of fact that increased the defendant's sentence above the statutory maximum for the crime. Despite this similarity between the two statutes, however, the precedential holdings of the two cases were polar opposites. The *Walton* court allowed judges to make factual findings resulting in an increase in the statutory maximum sentence; the *Apprendi* court prohibited judges from doing so. "We hold that *Walton* and *Apprendi* are irreconcilable," Justice Ginsburg wrote in *Ring*. "Our Sixth Amendment jurisprudence cannot be home to both."[16] Following the *Apprendi* decision, the *Ring* majority concluded, only juries may make findings of aggravating sentencing factors that elevate a capital murder defendant's sentence from life in prison to death.

The *Ring* court overruled its prior decision in *Walton* in which it held ten years earlier that it *was* constitutional for judges to make findings regarding a defendant's motive under Arizona's death penalty statute. Justice Ginsberg noted the court's rare break from precedent: "Although the doctrine of *stare decisis* is of fundamental importance to the rule of law . . . our precedents are not sacrosanct. We have overruled prior decisions where the necessity and propriety of doing so has been established. We are satisfied that this is such a case."[17]

Stare decisis is Latin for "the idea that today's Court should stand by yesterday's decisions."[18] Under this doctrine, courts defer to their prior decisions in order to promote "evenhanded, predictable, and consistent development of legal principles, foster reliance on judicial decisions, and contribute to the actual and perceived integrity of the judicial process."[19] I had relied on the precedent established in *Walton* to argue in *Apprendi* that judges could make factual findings increasing a defendant's sentence above the ordinary maximum term. The *Ring* court turned the tables, ditched the ten-year-old precedent of *Walton*, and applied the more recent rule adopted just two years earlier in *Apprendi* to declare Arizona's death penalty statute unconstitutional. (Luckily for death row inmate Jeffrey Alan Walton, his death sentence, which SCOTUS upheld in 1990, had not been carried out by the state of Arizona by the time *Ring* was decided a decade later. Three months following the *Ring* decision, Walton's death sentence was reduced to life in prison without the possibility of parole for the first twenty-five years.[20])

Six justices (Stevens, Scalia, Kennedy, Souter, Thomas, and Breyer) joined Justice Ginsburg's majority opinion in *Ring*. Justice Kennedy wrote in a concurring opinion that he agreed that "*Apprendi* and *Walton* cannot stand together as the law."[21] Although he believed "*Apprendi* was wrongly decided," Justice Kennedy concluded that "*Apprendi* is now the law, and its holding must be implemented in a principled way. . . . No principled reading of *Apprendi* would allow *Walton* to stand."[22]

Justice Scalia wrote his own concurring opinion in *Ring* to clarify his belief that the jury trial guarantee of the Sixth Amendment requires a jury to find beyond a reasonable doubt all facts that determine the degree of the crime. The Sixth Amendment, Scalia said, did not permit sentencing judges to make findings of facts that expose the defendant to greater punishment.[23]

Justice Scalia grudgingly conceded in his concurring opinion in *Ring* that by voting with the majority he had to abandon the position he had so vociferously clung to during the *Apprendi* argument two years earlier. Back then, Justice Scalia thought it was perfectly reasonable under the jury trial clause of the Sixth Amendment for a judge to sentence a person to death (*Walton*), but it was unreasonable under the exact same clause of the exact same amendment of the exact same federal Constitution for a judge to increase a prison sentence by two years (*Apprendi*). The question presented in *Ring*—whether the *Walton* decision survived *Apprendi*—required Scalia to make a choice. He could align himself with *Walton*, or he could align himself with *Apprendi*, but he could not align himself with both. Forced to choose between the two, Justice Scalia aligned himself with *Apprendi*.[24]

I hate to say I told you so, Justice Scalia, but I told you so. And so did Justice O'Connor in her dissenting opinion in *Apprendi* when she pointed out that the Supreme Court's prior decision in *Walton* was irreconcilable with the new bright-line rule of *Apprendi* that "other than the fact of a prior conviction, any fact that increases the penalty for a crime beyond the prescribed statutory maximum must be submitted to a jury, and proved beyond a reasonable doubt."[25] O'Connor would later write in her dissenting opinion in *Ring* (joined by Chief Justice Rehnquist) that, although she agreed with the *Ring* majority that the reasoning in *Apprendi* was incompatible with the reasoning in *Walton*, "in choosing which to overrule, I would choose *Apprendi*, not *Walton*."[26] The *Apprendi* decision, Justice O'Connor believed, "was a serious mistake."[27]

—⁓—

Justice Breyer, too, wrote a separate concurring opinion to *Ring*. Like Justices O'Connor and Kennedy, Justice Breyer reiterated his position that *Apprendi* was wrongly decided. Breyer nonetheless joined the *Ring* majority, he explained, because he believed that jury sentencing in capital cases was required by the Eighth Amendment's ban on cruel and unusual punishment.[28] Justice Breyer did not at all address the Sixth Amendment right to trial by an impartial jury.

Justice Scalia could not resist taking a jab at Justice Breyer's half-hearted choice to join the *Ring* majority. Scalia wrote in his concurring opinion to *Ring* that, despite their ideological differences on the issue, he was "as always, pleased to travel in Justice Breyer's company."[29] But was he? In his very next breath, Justice Scalia chided Justice Breyer for relying on the Eighth Amendment rather than the Sixth Amendment to find that Arizona's death penalty statute was unconstitutional: "There is really no way in which Justice Breyer can travel with the happy band that reaches today's result unless he says yes to *Apprendi*," Justice Scalia wrote. "Concisely put, Justice Breyer is on the wrong flight; he should either get off before the doors close, or buy a ticket to *Apprendi*-land."[30]

I want to go to *Apprendi*-land.

Apprendi-land is a theme park filled with exhilarating thrill rides painted in the garish colors of the various Supreme Court booklet covers. *Apprendi*-land's premier attraction is the Agitator, a Halloween orange steel roller coaster mimicking the twists and turns of United States Supreme Court litigation by throwing riders violently side to side while careening up and down impossibly steep hills at warp speed. Then there is the ruby red perimeter train chugging in a continuous loop around *Apprendi*-land, and it never stops. The only way off the circling train is by leaping onto the station platform feet first, as my husband heroically did in Trenton. Bumper cars engineered to look like friend of the court dark green Honda Accords crash uncontrollably into United States Postal Service mailboxes and wrought iron garbage cans. And, of course, there's the Haunted Supreme Court House where an audio-animatronic Justice Antonin Scalia jumps out of nowhere and screams in your face.

CHAPTER 22

AFTER MUCH REFLECTION, I CAN'T think of anything I could have included in my merits brief or added during oral argument that would have made any difference in the justices' votes in *Apprendi v. New Jersey*. Joe O'Neill and I could have spent our allotted time singing the "Alphabet Song" in two-part harmony or clutching the lectern for dear life while mumbling "homina, homina, homina" and it wouldn't have changed any minds. In his concurring opinion in *Apprendi*, Justice Thomas confessed he had voted the wrong way in *Almendarez-Torres*, effectively shutting down all possibility that the 5-4 split in Apprendi's favor was anything but predetermined. The remaining eight justices stayed fully committed to the positions they had previously staked out in *Almendarez-Torres* and *Jones*. Other than Thomas, not one justice switched sides in *Apprendi*. Joe and I were merely passengers on the *Apprendi*-land roller coaster as it hurtled along the track.

Each state and federal lower court decision striking down one sentencing law after another as unconstitutional in *Apprendi's* wake nonetheless felt to me like a kick in the gut. Every attorney who cited the United States Supreme Court's *Apprendi* opinion, every judge who applied its bright-line rule to a defendant's motion for resentencing, each of them read arguing counsels' names listed at the beginning of the decision. "Joseph D. O'Neill" was the undeniable hero in *Apprendi*, the underdog champion of criminal defendants in pursuit of their constitutional right to impartial jury trials. "Lisa Sarnoff Gochman" was the poor schlemiel personally responsible for criminal sentencing statutes falling like dominoes across the United States.

I am worse than a pessimist. A pessimist's glass is half-empty, but I don't even have a glass. I obsess over mistakes made decades ago, relive embarrassing moments in my head in an endless blooper reel, and second-guess everything I've ever said to everyone I've ever met. In my world, every silver lining has a cloud. Fulfilling my dream to argue before the Supreme Court of the United States was my silver lining; losing *Apprendi* was my cloud.

But then, in January 2002, eighteen months after *Apprendi* was decided, Supreme Court Director and Chief Counsel Dan Schweitzer of the National Association of Attorneys General invited me to write an amicus brief in support of the United States government in the matter of *Harris v. United States*, an *Apprendi* offshoot.[1] Dan was clearly unaware that I was an incompetent fraud responsible for New Jersey's loss in *Apprendi*. But my impostor syndrome retreated into remission as I delved into the question squarely presented in *Harris*: whether the bright-line rule of *Apprendi* applied to mandatory minimum sentences (the number of years a defendant must serve in prison before he or she becomes eligible for parole).

Defendant William Harris was found guilty in federal district court of selling illegal drugs out of his North Carolina pawnshop to an undercover law enforcement agent on two consecutive days. Both times, Harris was carrying a semiautomatic handgun at his side in an unconcealed hip holster. During one of the undercover buys, Harris removed the gun from its holster and told the agent that it "was an outlawed firearm because it had a high-capacity magazine" and that his homemade bullets could pierce a police officer's armored jacket.[2]

The federal criminal statute Harris violated required the sentencing judge to impose a mandatory minimum sentence depending on the existence of certain facts: if the judge found that Harris carried the firearm during the drug trafficking crime, a mandatory minimum term of not less than five years was required; if the judge found that Harris brandished the firearm during the crime, a mandatory minimum term of not less than seven years was required; and, if the judge found Harris discharged the firearm during the crime, a mandatory minimum term of not less than ten years was required.[3] At the sentencing hearing, the district court judge found by a preponderance of the evidence that Harris had brandished the semiautomatic pistol during one of the drug sales. The judge imposed a mandatory minimum sentence of seven years in federal prison.[4]

Harris asked SCOTUS to extend the new bright-line rule established in *Apprendi* to mandatory minimum sentences, arguing that the jury had to find guilt beyond a reasonable doubt that Harris had brandished the firearm before the seven-year mandatory minimum sentence could be imposed. Essentially, Harris was asking SCOTUS to overrule *McMillan v. Pennsylvania*, the 1986 case allowing judges to make the factual finding of visible possession of a firearm that resulted in the imposition of a five-year mandatory minimum sentence. Although Justice Stevens was careful in *Apprendi* to explain that its holding did not overrule *McMillan*, Stevens did not rule out the possibility of reconsidering *McMillan* at some future date in light of the new *Apprendi* bright-line rule.[5]

As a party to the appeal, the Office of the Solicitor General represented the United States government. Although the solicitor general was fully capable of defending the constitutionality of the federal firearms statute, given the vast number of state statutes authorizing judge-imposed mandatory minimum sentences on all sorts of crimes, an amicus brief would inform SCOTUS of the turmoil states would be thrown into if these statutes were suddenly invalidated. My pre-*Apprendi* prediction that the sky would fall if New Jersey's Hate Crime Statute was declared unconstitutional had gone unheeded; not one state offered to file an amicus brief in support of New Jersey during the *Apprendi* litigation. Now, in the post-*Apprendi* sentencing landscape, states' attorneys were lining up in support of the federal government's argument in *Harris* that *Apprendi*'s bright-line rule did not apply to mandatory minimum sentences. The attorneys general of twenty-five states and territories signed onto New Jersey's Kelly green amicus brief filed with the Supreme Court Clerk's Office on February 22, 2002.

My colleague Debra Owens and I traveled to Washington, DC, to watch the *Harris* argument, held at ten o'clock on the morning of Monday, March 25, 2002. We sat in the front row of the bar section of the courtroom. This time, I made sure to watch the justices emerge from behind the crimson curtains. As she took her seat on the bench, Justice O'Connor made eye contact with me and nodded in acknowledgment. She must have recognized my name on the cover of the amicus brief in *Harris* and remembered me from the *Apprendi* argument two years earlier. I'll take that over a Sandra Day O'Connor bobblehead doll any day.

I did not argue as amicus in *Harris*. I was happy to witness Deputy Solicitor General Michael Dreeben's exceptional performance from the safety of my seat in the audience. His presentation in *Harris* was a master class in Supreme Court oral advocacy. (Dreeben had argued over one hundred times before SCOTUS, amassing more than two hundred white goose feather quill pens. He told me he gave away most of his quill pens, his children used some to practice calligraphy, and a few are stored in his attic.) When he was called on by Chief Justice Rehnquist to begin his argument in *Harris*, Dreeben calmly stepped up to the lectern without a single note or law book for reference. The tone of the argument was conversational, not combative, in vivid contrast to the verbal beating Joseph O'Neill and I had endured two years earlier. The justices were deferential to Dreeben, barely interrupting him and genuinely interested in hearing his views on mandatory minimum sentences.

And we won. In a late June 2002 opinion, the four dissenting justices in *Apprendi* (Rehnquist, O'Connor, Kennedy, and Breyer), now joined by Justice Scalia, agreed in *Harris* that *Apprendi*'s bright-line rule did not apply to mandatory minimum sentences.[6] "If the facts judges consider when exercising their discretion within the statutory range are not elements," wrote the *Harris* court, "they do not become as much merely because legislatures require the judge to impose a minimum sentence when those facts are found—a sentence the judge could have imposed absent the finding."[7] Although Justice Scalia did not write a separate concurring opinion expressing his own thoughts on the topic, by joining the majority opinion in *Harris*, he signaled his unwillingness to permit mandatory minimum sentences to board the plane to *Apprendi*-land. Even Scalia had his limits on the Sixth Amendment right to a jury trial.

And then we lost. Thirteen years after *Harris*, Justice Thomas, writing for the court, concluded in *Alleyne v. United States* that the holding of *Harris* was incompatible with the holding of *Apprendi*.[8] The *Alleyne* majority abandoned the precedent of both *McMillan* and *Harris*, finding that "mandatory minimum sentences increase the penalty for a crime. It follows, then, that any fact that increases the mandatory minimum is an 'element' that must be submitted to the jury. Accordingly, *Harris* is overruled."[9] Win some, lose some.

—✳—

In the two decades since I argued *Apprendi*, the United States Supreme Court has issued more than twenty written decisions based on the *Apprendi* opinion and considered countless state and federal inmates' certiorari petitions raising alleged *Apprendi* error. The court has applied the *Apprendi* rule to Arizona's and Florida's death penalty statutes, the federal sentencing guidelines, mandatory minimum sentences, and the imposition of criminal fines, to name but a few examples.[10] *United States v. Haymond*, issued on June 25, 2019, almost exactly nineteen years to the day *Apprendi* was decided, reaffirmed the precedential *Apprendi* rule that, with the exception of prior convictions, "any fact that increases the penalty for a crime beyond the prescribed statutory maximum must be submitted to the jury, and proved beyond a reasonable doubt."[11]

By the opening of the Supreme Court's 2022 term, only one of the nine justices who had participated in the *Apprendi* argument in March 2000—Clarence Thomas—remains on the bench. Chief Justice Rehnquist died in September 2005, Justice O'Connor retired in January 2006, Justice Souter retired in June 2009, Justice Scalia died in February 2016, Justice Kennedy retired in July 2018, Justice Stevens died in July 2019, and Justice Ginsburg died in September 2020. At the end of January 2022, Justice Breyer announced he would be retiring from the Supreme Court bench after nearly twenty-eight years when the court recessed for the summer. With Justice Breyer's retirement, there are eight justices on the bench who did not participate in the *Apprendi* argument. Despite the change in personnel, in the two decades since *Apprendi* was decided, SCOTUS has never given any indication that a new alignment of five or more justices is ready to dismantle the *Apprendi* rule.

Despite my initial distress at having lost in the United States Supreme Court, I have wholeheartedly come to accept that *Apprendi v. New Jersey* was correctly decided. The weakness in my position that motive has always been a traditional sentencing factor was exposed by Justice Souter's observation at the *Apprendi* oral argument that "motive has never had the significance that it has under the New Jersey statute." Bad motive within the meaning of New Jersey's Hate Crime Statute behaved like an element of the underlying offense by bumping up the statutory sentencing range reserved for second-degree crimes (five to ten years in prison) into the range reserved for first-degree crimes (ten to twenty years in prison). To paraphrase Justice Scalia, it doesn't matter whether you call a fact essential to the crime a sentencing factor, an element of the offense, or Mary Jane.[12] If that fact exposes a defendant to a higher degree of crime and, in turn, enhanced punishment, it must be admitted to by the defendant at his plea hearing or found by a jury to exist beyond a reasonable doubt.[13]

The *Apprendi* decision also furthers consistency in prosecutions throughout the United States. Congress and state legislatures remain free to define their own criminal laws, but within the constitutional limits set by the *Apprendi* court to ensure those laws are carried out uniformly under the federal Constitution. Before *Apprendi*, the type and quantity of illicit drugs in a defendant's possession were treated as elements of the possessory offense in New Jersey but treated as sentencing factors in the federal system. After *Apprendi*, whenever the type and quantity of any controlled dangerous substance serves to increase the sentence above the mandatory maximum prison term for the underlying possessory offense, the government must prove both the type of drugs and the quantity of those drugs to a jury beyond a reasonable doubt, regardless of whether the matter is prosecuted in state or federal court. The same holds true for death or serious bodily injury to a victim and any other fact bumping up a defendant's sentencing exposure into a higher sentencing range. The defense bar owes Joseph C. O'Neill, Esquire, a huge debt of gratitude for recognizing the constitutional issues embedded in New Jersey's Hate Crime Statute and doggedly pursuing the case all the way up to the Supreme Court of the United States.

Truthfully, though, there is no downside for the state or federal government following the *Apprendi* decision. Prosecutors may continue to seek convictions for hate crimes, just as they did before. Judges may continue to find a defendant's motive, bad or good, to be an applicable sentencing factor, just as they did before, as long as the maximum sentence imposed falls within the statutory range for the crime charged.

The real-world effect of the *Apprendi* bright-line rule disfavors defendants who are accused of hate crimes. Prior to the *Apprendi* decision, highly prejudicial evidence of the accused's bad motive spurring him or her to violence against another person simply because of the color of the victim's skin was scrupulously shielded from the jury as too prejudicial to the defendant. After *Apprendi*, whenever racial bias is an element of the crime, the prosecution has a constitutional duty to submit this evidence to the jury for its consideration. Had the Cumberland County Prosecutor's Office tried Charles C. Apprendi Jr. under New Jersey's bias intimidation law, the jury would have heard testimony at trial that Apprendi had purposely fired his rifle into the home of the Fowlkes family because he was "sending them a message" that Black people were unwelcome in his neighborhood. As New Jersey Supreme Court Justice Daniel O'Hern cautioned Apprendi in his majority opinion upholding the constitutionality of New Jersey's Hate Crime Statute, be careful what you wish for.

—ᴡᴡ—

The "*Apprendi* doctrine" is firmly ensconced in the lexicon of criminal law in the United States. I continue to practice criminal appellate litigation and still come across *Apprendi* issues more than twenty years later. The *Apprendi* doctrine is also taught in law schools. In the spring of Jordan's junior year in high school, we toured colleges in Massachusetts. While browsing in the Boston University bookstore, we checked out the textbooks in the law school aisle. And there, inside a constitutional law textbook, was an entire section devoted to the analysis of *Apprendi v. New Jersey* and its progeny. An undergraduate employee came over to investigate the squealing. I pointed to the textbook and told her I had argued *Apprendi* in the United States Supreme Court, but she did not share in my delight. Her reaction was more "Yeah, lady, whatever." I get that often. Not everyone is interested in my excellent adventures in Washington, DC.

But some people are. Stu Rees, an entertainment lawyer in California, and his wife, Maddy, draw single-panel, law-themed cartoons. One of their more popular illustrations is based on the *Apprendi* case.

This cartoon popped up one day as I was searching the keyword *Apprendi* online. My periodic internet searches for *Apprendi* ordinarily turn up dry academic treatments of the case: newspaper articles objectively recounting the various court proceedings, criminal defense attorneys' blogs explaining the holding and practical effect of the *Apprendi* decision, and scholarly law reviews analyzing the more obscure aspects of the opinion. It was fun to find an amusing *Apprendi* cartoon among these search results. It reminds me not to take myself too seriously.

In the two decades since I argued *Apprendi*, not a single criminal appeal handled by the New Jersey Division of Criminal Justice or the twenty-one

Reprinted with permission. © Stu Rees.

county prosecutors' offices in the state has made its way up to the United States Supreme Court. I always hoped one of my colleagues would argue before SCOTUS so I could relive my experience vicariously through him or her. As for me, I never want to appear before the United States Supreme Court again. I had a wonderful time on the morning on March 28, 2000, and it could only go downhill from there. With age, the dam stopping every thought in my brain from tumbling out of my mouth unchecked becomes more porous and unstable. I'm now in my mid-sixties with no guarantee that my once-reliable filter will preempt an audible "Fuck you" the next time around.

———※———

The twentieth anniversary of the *Apprendi* argument was on March 28, 2020, but I couldn't imagine that anyone outside of my immediate family cared, other than Joseph O'Neill and his client Charles Apprendi. Or so I thought. In October 2020, the University of North Carolina School of Law hosted a symposium titled "*Apprendi* at 20." Nine legal experts in the field of sentencing law offered their perspectives on *Apprendi*'s cataclysmic impact on jury trials, guilty pleas, and sentencing during the past two decades. The following June, the school's *Law Review* devoted an entire volume—all six articles plus the introduction and closing essay—to a retrospective of the *Apprendi* decision.[14]

The twentieth anniversary of my argument was a great excuse to gather with my family in Washington, DC, for a long weekend. My now-grown-up son, Jordan, and his wife, Ashley, booked flights from Orlando, Florida, where they both work in Disney World, to meet Steven and me in DC. I contacted the then three remaining justices who had sat on the *Apprendi* court, asking to meet with each of them to discuss the case for this book. Justice Thomas sent me a personal note politely turning down my request. Justice Breyer's assistant called to tell me that the justice had a prior speaking engagement at a judicial conference. I did not hear back from Justice Ginsburg's chambers, but she was battling terminal cancer, and how could I be mad at the Notorious RBG?

And then the COVID-19 pandemic hit, shuttering the United States Supreme Court building and most of Washington, DC, and forcing the Gochmans to cancel their plans. Unable to attend the celebrated National Cherry Blossom Festival in Washington, we settled for the lesser-known "Forsythia Festival" in our backyard in New Jersey. As disappointed as we were, I can't imagine how dismayed the attorneys scheduled to argue cases during the pandemic must have felt. The justices quickly pivoted from in-person to telephonic arguments to protect the health of their more senior members, a sound decision from a public health perspective but a devastating blow to arguing counsel now deprived of their opportunity to appear in person inside the courtroom with all its pomp and circumstance. For some, this would be their only Supreme Court argument. They would never know the terror, wonder, and joy of standing before the altar of the appellate gods.

Supreme Court arguments during the pandemic were conducted via telephone, not video conferencing. This long-distance, voice-only arrangement raised so many questions. Did the marshal call the court to order with the traditional "Oyez! Oyez! Oyez!"? If the justices could not see them on the other end of the phone, did the attorneys for the solicitor general's office bother to wear their formal morning attire? Did the justices wear their black silk robes? Did the Clerk's Office mail the souvenir quill pens to the attorneys who missed their only chance to sit at counsel table?

On the other hand, it's nice to enjoy the home court advantage. Conducting a telephonic argument in the comfort of one's own home or office eliminates so many uncontrollable variables associated with travel to Washington, DC. Arguing counsel need not worry about noisy hotel rooms, reckless parking valets, slippery marble steps, and frizzy hair. Given the choice, however, I'd gladly wrestle with control-top pantyhose and stuff my feet into pointy-toed high heels if the trade-off is arguing in person before the nine justices of the Supreme Court of the United States.

—⚸—

Court TV once had a half-hour cable series called *On Appeal*. Each episode showcased significant civil and criminal cases argued in state and federal appellate courts around the country. The producers of *On Appeal* created an episode about *Apprendi*. They filmed the live argument inside the New Jersey Supreme Court courtroom in Trenton on October 13, 1999, and interviewed the victims of Apprendi's hate crimes, the trial prosecutor Robert Luther, Apprendi's attorney Joseph O'Neill, and me. Production of the *Apprendi* episode was put on hiatus to await SCOTUS's decision. When the *Apprendi* opinion was issued in late June 2000, I called one of the producers of *On Appeal* to let her know. She told me the entire series had been canceled by then due to lack of viewership. Not only did I lose the *Apprendi* case, I have empirical proof that what I do for a living is too boring for television.

The *Apprendi* case itself, however, made a cameo appearance in *Drop Dead Diva*, a scripted legal dramedy airing on the Lifetime channel from 2009 to 2014. In season 6, episode 1, of *Drop Dead Diva*, private defense lawyer Jane Bingum cites *Apprendi v. New Jersey* during a courtroom scene, hoping to convince the trial judge to reduce the length of her client's federal prison sentence. Clearly pleased with herself that the *Apprendi* case popped into her head at exactly the right moment, Jane Bingum cheerfully rattles off the *Apprendi* rule as the federal prosecutor silently fumes. Bingum won her argument, and her client was sentenced to three years in federal prison instead of fifty years.

Despite losing *Apprendi*, I've never experienced any self-recriminations when recalling my argument before the Supreme Court. I still get all goosebumpy when I think about it. I went head-to-head with Justice Antonin Scalia, fielded tough questions from Justice Ruth Bader Ginsburg, and skipped down memory lane with Justice Sandra Day O'Connor. I even heard Justice Thomas speak.

It's hard to explain what it's like to be part of the *Apprendi* revolution, to have my case—*my case!*—result in a landmark United States Supreme Court decision. It is an intoxicating mixture of incredulity that I had the good fortune to argue in the United States Supreme Court, gratitude for the opportunity to do so, and pure childlike glee. I am humbled to have defended the constitutionality of New Jersey's Hate Crime Statute before the nine justices of SCOTUS in Washington, DC. For twenty minutes, it was just them and me. Anne Paskow was right: Supreme Court litigation is a crazy roller coaster ride chock-full of erratic ups and downs and unpredictable twists and turns. Larry Etzweiler was right, too: I had fun.

Winning my case would have been nice, but I'm over that. 'Tis better to have argued in the United States Supreme Court and lost than never to have argued at all.[15] Even Abraham Lincoln lost his only argument in the United States Supreme Court.[16] I wouldn't trade my twenty minutes of time with the nine justices of the Rehnquist court for anything in the world. Writing this memoir has been the optimal way to relive the *Apprendi* argument without the angst of the real thing. There was no time to savor all the little details while caught up in the maelstrom or to envision how it would all play out. Arguing in the United States Supreme Court was this appellate lawyer's dream come true, and I got to relive my dream through writing this memoir. My next book is tentatively titled *Milking It for All It's Worth*.

CHAPTER 23

THE BLACK LEATHER BRIEFCASE I was reaching into when the justices magically appeared from behind the crimson velvet curtains in the United States Supreme Court courtroom at ten o'clock on the morning of Tuesday, March 28, 2000, was purchased specially for the occasion. Sixteen years earlier, in 1984, during my third year of law school, I bought my first leather briefcase at a store in the mezzanine of one of the ill-fated twin towers at the World Trade Center in lower Manhattan on my way to a job interview. All I had brought with me was a manila envelope containing my resume and a writing sample. I needed a more polished and professional look.

The color of the briefcase I purchased was cordovan, which is a rich shade of dark burgundy, similar to the color of the six-inch wood border framing the glass front doors of the Fowlkes family's home in Vineland, New Jersey. If Pantone had announced its color of the year back in 1984, cordovan would have been a front-runner. Cordovan penny loafers and wingtip shoes were everywhere in preppy New York City.

My cordovan-colored briefcase was remarkably heavy when empty. Crammed with books, legal pads, an umbrella, pens, highlighters, the day's edition of the *New York Times*, and an extra pair of pantyhose, it was like slinging a bowling ball bag off one shoulder. I don't know how I dragged that briefcase around in high heels without tipping over sideways.

A year or two later, I replaced the bulky leather briefcase with a practical and lightweight black nylon one. Neither my mother nor my mother-in-law was impressed. Individually and collectively, they offered to buy me a new leather briefcase. I rebuffed their generosity with this compromise: "If I ever have an argument in the United States Supreme Court, I'll buy a leather briefcase." Which I assumed would be never.

But there I was, in early 2000, in need of a leather briefcase. My black nylon one just would not do in the revered United States Supreme Court. The hunt for the perfect leather briefcase became a quest. In what little spare time I had, I scoured department stores and leather goods specialty shops for a briefcase sturdy enough to stand upright on the floor of the courtroom. And it had to have a zipper across the top. I didn't want an awkward flap with a clumsy metal buckle to unclasp and peel open if I needed something from inside the briefcase in a hurry, like a pen, as the justices magically appeared from behind the crimson velvet curtains. I finally found the perfect black leather briefcase with a single zipper across the top. My epic mission for the ideal briefcase deserved an equally epic poem:

> It does not offend me
> To say that *Apprendi*
> Is more about sentence than race;
> But still I must spendi
> Big bucks to buy Fendi
> Or some other fine leather briefcase.
>
> For the one that I use
> Every day for my shoes,
> For my newspaper, lunch, and umbrella,
> Is as old as Methuse
> And I simply refuse
> To use one that's been through such hella.
>
> For I'm off to the Court
> Of Supremes to report
> On why New Jersey's statute prevails.
> And they seem like the sort,
> Or so I have thort,
> Not to overlook minor details.
>
> I'll need killer new clothes,
> Suit, blouse, pumps, pantyhose,
> An ensemble befitting a lawyer.

And I'll look so imposing,
At least while I'm posing
For photos outside in the foyer.

Sandra Day and Ruth G.
Will both wish they were me
When they see me with my perfect hair.
And my adversary
Will concede humbly
When he realizes he can't compare.

Though my hardest I'll try,
If my case goes awry,
If my views and the justices' clashes,
I will hold my head high,
Look 'em dead in the eye,
And playfully bat my eyelashes.

For the thing that will sway
Judges over your way,
Can't be found in any law book.
It's not what you say
That will carry the day,
The issue is how good you look.

So to Charles C. Apprendi,
This message I sendi:
"You haven't a prayer for success."
So, Chuck, don't pretendi
The Court will be friendly,
'Cuz you don't look so good in a dress!

Steven dubbed my ode to my briefcase "Battle Her of the Republic." (Get it? "Her" instead of "Hymn"?) This was the poem I offered to the publisher of the *Green Bag* law journal in exchange for a Justice Sandra Day O'Connor double bobblehead doll, but my more-than-lavish proposal was curtly declined.

I may not own an official *Green Bag* Justice O'Connor double bobblehead doll, but I do have my beloved black briefcase. I carry it with me whenever I give presentations about my excellent United States Supreme Court adventure. The leather has scuffed and softened considerably in two decades, and the bag no longer sits upright on the floor without support. Just like me.

NOTES

PROLOGUE

1. *Apprendi v. New Jersey*, 530 U.S. 466 (2000).
2. "FAQs—General Information," Supreme Court of the United States, accessed March 18, 2022, https://www.supremecourt.gov/about/faq_general.aspx.

CHAPTER 1

1. Donald Janson, "Plan for Klan Rally," *New York Times*, November 18, 1979, https://www.nytimes.com/1979/11/18/archives/new-jersey-weekly-plan-for-klan -rally-in-vineland-stirs-counterplan.html; "Arrest of 22 Klan Members at Jersey Home Foils Group's Plans for Rally," *New York Times*, November 25, 1979, https://www.nytimes.com/1979/11/25/archives/arrest-of-22-klan-members-at-jersey-home-foils-groups-plans-for.html.
2. *1990 Census of Population: General Population Characteristics, New Jersey*, accessed March 18, 2022, https://www2.census.gov/library/publications/decennial/1990/cp-1/cp-1-32-1.pdf, 106, 111.
3. Jessica Peterson, "The Aftermath of a Family's 1994 Nightmare," *Medill News Service*, April 3, 2000.
4. Unless otherwise noted, the facts of the crime and all courtroom dialogue in this chapter are taken from the three official trial court transcripts in *State of New Jersey v. Charles Apprendi, Jr.*, Cumberland County Indictment No. 95-01-46, dated July 24, 1995 (plea hearing); September 5, 1995 (extended-term hearing); and September 29, 1995 (sentencing hearing), as well as from public documents.
5. Peterson, "Aftermath of a Nightmare."

6. In New Jersey, a crime is any offense for which the state's Code of Criminal Justice authorizes a sentence of imprisonment in excess of six months. N.J. Stat. Ann. 2C:1-4a (West 2021). Crimes are classified as first, second, third, and fourth degree. N.J. Stat. Ann. 2C:43-1a (West 2021). First-degree crimes are the most serious, and fourth-degree crimes are the least serious. N.J. Stat. Ann. 2C:43-6a (West 2021).

7. *State v. Barboza*, 115 N.J. 415, 421 (1989).

8. N.J. Stat. Ann. 2C:43-6a(2) (West 1993).

9. New Jersey Public Law 1990, chapter 87, § 4 (eff. August 9, 1990).

10. N.J. Stat. Ann. 2C:44-3e (West 1995).

CHAPTER 2

1. *State v. Apprendi*, 159 N.J. 7, 27 (1999).

2. *Wisconsin v. Mitchell*, 508 U.S. 476, 485 (1993) (quoting 1 W. LeFave & A. Scott, Substantive Criminal Law § 3.6(b), p. 324 (1986)).

3. *Liberty Mutual Insurance Company v. Land*, 186 N.J. 163, 169 (2006).

4. Unless otherwise noted, the facts of the crime and all courtroom dialogue in this chapter are taken from the three official trial court transcripts in *State of New Jersey v. Charles Apprendi, Jr.*, Cumberland County Indictment No. 95-01-46, dated July 24, 1995 (plea hearing); September 5, 1995 (extended-term hearing); and September 29, 1995 (sentencing hearing), as well as from public documents.

5. The rights of crime victims in New Jersey are enshrined in the Crime Victim's Bill of Rights Amendment to the state's constitution, N.J. Const. art. 1, ¶ 22, and are codified at N.J. Stat. Ann. 52:4B-34 to -38 (West 2021). Among the eighteen enumerated rights afforded to crime victims is the right to provide an in-person or written victim-impact statement to the sentencing court detailing the nature and extent of any physical harm or psychological or emotional harm or trauma suffered by the victim, the extent of any loss to include loss of earnings or ability to work suffered by the victim, and the effect of the crime upon the victim's family. N.J. Stat. Ann. 52:4B-36n (West 2021).

6. In New Jersey, as in many other states, a criminal defendant who uses or possesses a firearm while committing or attempting to commit a crime must serve a minimum term in prison before becoming eligible for parole. N.J. Stat. Ann. 2C:43-6c (West 2021). Because Apprendi used a rifle during his crimes, Judge Ridgway imposed a mandatory minimum term of four years on count eighteen of the indictment. On count three (second-degree possession of a firearm for an unlawful purpose), the judge sentenced Apprendi to a maximum term of seven years in prison with a mandatory minimum term of three years. On count twenty-two (third-degree unlawful possession of an antipersonnel bomb), the judge sentenced Apprendi to a maximum term of three years in prison with no period of parole

ineligibility. All three sentences ran concurrently, so Apprendi would serve all three at the same time and not back-to-back. Apprendi's aggregate sentence was twelve years in prison with a parole ineligibility period of four years.

7. Jessica Peterson, "The Aftermath of a Family's 1994 Nightmare," *Medill News Service*, April 3, 2000.

CHAPTER 3

1. With apologies to John Donne.

2. In New Jersey, oral argument is held before a panel of two or three Appellate Division judges at the request of one of the parties. Where there is no request for argument, the court decides the matter on the appellate briefs and the trial record below. N.J. Court Rule 2:11-1(a)(2) (Gann 2021).

3. *Trusky v. Ford Motor Co.*, 19 N.J. Super. 100, 104 (App. Div. 1952).

CHAPTER 4

1. "Criminal Final Charge," in *New Jersey Model Jury Charge (Criminal)* (revised May 12, 2014), https://www.njcourts.gov/attorneys/criminalcharges.html.

2. Nowhere in the United States Constitution does the phrase "proof beyond a reasonable doubt" appear. It was not until 1970 that the United States Supreme Court, in the seminal case of *In re Winship*, 397 U.S. 358, 364 (1970), explicitly held "that the Due Process Clause protects the accused against conviction except upon proof beyond a reasonable doubt of every fact necessary to constitute the crime with which he is charged."

3. *State v. O'Donnell*, 117 N.J. 210, 215 (1989).

4. *Liberty Mutual Insurance Company v. Land*, 186 N.J. 163, 169 (2006).

5. *Pointer v. United States*, 151 U.S. 396 (1894).

6. Ibid., 414–15.

7. Ibid., 414.

8. There are four levels of criminal intent in New Jersey: purposeful, knowing, recklessness, and negligence. N.J. Stat. Ann. 2C:2-2b(1)–(4) (West 2021). The level of criminal intent that the prosecution is required to prove for any given crime is determined by the state legislature and specified in the statute defining that crime. The crime charged in count eighteen to which Apprendi pleaded guilty was possession of a firearm for an unlawful purpose. The New Jersey statute criminalizing this conduct provides, "Any person who has in his possession any firearm with a purpose to use it unlawfully against the person or property of another is guilty of a crime of the second degree." N.J. Stat. Ann. 2C:39-4a(1) (West 2021).

9. "Possession of a Weapon with a Purpose to Use It Unlawfully against the Person or Property of Another," in *New Jersey Model Jury Charge (Criminal)* (revised June 16, 2003), https://www.njcourts.gov/attorneys/criminalcharges.html.

10. *Allen v. City of Los Angeles*, 92 F.3d 842, 850 (9th Cir. 1996).

11. *McMillan v. Pennsylvania*, 477 U.S. 79 (1986).

12. A maximum sentence, on the other hand, is the outermost limit of a criminal defendant's prison term. Most prisoners become eligible for release on parole before reaching the last day of their maximum terms. A prisoner who is not released on parole from state or federal custody must be released on the end date of his or her maximum sentence.

13. 42 Pa. Const. Stat. § 9712 (West 1982).

14. *McMillan*, 477 U.S., 87–88.

15. Ibid., 88.

16. "Bright-Line Rule," Legal Information Institute, Cornell Law School, 2022, https://www.law.cornell.edu/wex/bright-line_rule.

17. *Edwards v. Arizona*, 451 U.S. 477, 484–85 (1981).

18. *McMillan*, 477 U.S., 88.

CHAPTER 5

1. *State v. Manzie*, 335 N.J. Super. 267 (App. Div. 2000), *aff'd by an equally divided court*, 168 N.J. 113 (2001).

2. *State v. Apprendi*, 304 N.J. Super. 147, 153 (App. Div. 1997).

3. Ibid., 155.

4. Ibid., 159.

5. Ibid., 156 (citing *McMillan v. Pennsylvania*, 477 U.S. 79, 88 (1986)).

6. Ibid., 159–61 (Stern, J., concurring).

7. Ibid., 162 (Wecker, J., dissenting).

8. Ibid., 162–163 (Wecker, J., dissenting).

9. Ibid., 167 (Wecker, J., dissenting).

10. N.J. Court Rule 2:12-4 (Gann 2021) sets forth the criteria for granting certification. The Supreme Court of New Jersey will not grant certification unless the appeal presents an unsettled question of general public importance, the appeal is similar to a question presented in another case pending before the state Supreme Court, the decision under review conflicts with any other decision from the same or higher court, the matter calls for an exercise of the state Supreme Court's jurisdiction, or the interest of justice requires review.

11. N.J. Court Rule 2:2-1(a)(2) (Gann 2021).

12. Ibid.

13. *Almendarez-Torres v. United States*, 523 U.S. 224 (1998).

14. 8 U.S.C. § 1326 (1988); *Almendarez-Torres v. United States*, 113 F.3d 515 (5th Cir. 1996).

15. *Almendarez-Torres*, 113 F.3d, 515.

16. Ibid.

17. *Almendarez-Torres*, 523 U.S., 226–227.

18. Ibid., 226.

19. Ibid., 247.

20. Ibid., 242–47.

21. Ibid., 230.

22. Ibid.

23. Ibid., 248–71 (Scalia, J., dissenting).

24. Ibid., 248.

25. Kathy Barrett Carter, "Convict's Attorney Challenges Bias-Crime Law," *Star-Ledger*, October 14, 1998; Michael Booth, "Defense Counsel Challenge Authority of Judges under Hate Crime Act," *New Jersey Law Journal*, October 19, 1998.

26. Booth, "Defense Counsel."

27. Ibid.

28. Ibid.

29. Carter, "Convict's Attorney."

30. Ibid.

31. Booth, "Defense Counsel."

32. *Jones v. United States*, 526 U.S. 227 (1999).

33. 18 U.S.C. § 2119 (1988 ed., Supp. V).

34. *Jones*, 526 U.S., 231.

35. Ibid., 252.

36. Ibid., 248–49.

37. Ibid., 243, n.6.

38. *Jama v. Immigration and Customs Enforcement*, 543 U.S. 335, 351 n.12 (2005).

39. *State v. Apprendi*, 159 N.J. 7, 22–23 (1999).

40. Ibid.

41. Ibid., 20.

42. Ibid.

43. Ibid., 24 (quoting *McMillan*, 477 U.S. at 88).

44. Ibid.

45. Ibid.

46. Ibid., 29.

47. Ibid., 27.

48. Ibid., 26.

49. Ibid., 21.

50. Ibid.

51. Ibid.

52. Ibid., 22.

CHAPTER 6

1. Supreme Court Rule 13.1 (2019).
2. Supreme Court Rule 13.2 (2019).
3. Supreme Court Rule 15.1 (2019).
4. The waiver form is available on the Supreme Court's website: https://www.supremecourt.gov/casehand/waiver.pdf.
5. Supreme Court Rule 15.1 (2019).
6. *Jones v. United States*, 526 U.S. 227, 239 (1999) (quoting *United States ex rel. Attorney General v. Delaware & Hudson Co.*, 213 U.S. 366, 408 (1909)).
7. Ibid.
8. Ibid., 251–52.
9. Supreme Court Rule 15.3 (2019).
10. Ibid.
11. Supreme Court Rule 33.1(g) (2019).
12. Ibid.
13. Ibid.
14. Remarks by Chief Justice William H. Rehnquist (lecture at the Faculty of Law of the University of Guanajuato, Mexico, September 27, 2001), https://www.supremecourt.gov/publicinfo/speeches/viewspeech/sp_09-27-01.
15. *Kansas v. Marsh*, 548 U.S. 163, 185 (2006) (Scalia, J., concurring).
16. Supreme Court Rule 10 (2019)
17. *Hubbard v. United States*, 514 U.S. 695, 720 (1995) (Rehnquist, C.J., dissenting).
18. Supreme Court Rule 10 (2019).
19. *State v. Apprendi*, 159 N.J. 7, 21–22 (1999).
20. *Wisconsin v. Mitchell*, 508 U.S. 476, 485 (1993).
21. *Almendarez-Torres v. United States*, 523 U.S. 224 (1998).
22. Respondent's brief in opposition to petition for a writ of certiorari in *Charles C. Apprendi, Jr., v. New Jersey*, Docket No. 99-478, 8.
23. Supreme Court Rule 24.1(a) (2019).
24. Petitioner's brief on petition for a writ of certiorari in *Charles C. Apprendi, Jr., v. New Jersey*, Docket No. 99-478, i.
25. Respondent's brief in opposition to petition for a writ of certiorari in *Charles C. Apprendi, Jr., v. New Jersey*, Docket No. 99-478, i.
26. *State in the Interest of J.G., N.S., and J.T.*, 151 N.J. 565 (1997).
27. If SCOTUS denied his petition for certiorari, Charles Apprendi had another potential avenue of relief. He could file a writ of *habeas corpus* in the federal District Court for the District of New Jersey, where he could renew his argument that New Jersey's Hate Crime Statute was unconstitutional. 28 U.S.C. § 2254. The losing party could then appeal to the Third Circuit Court of Appeals in Philadelphia,

Pennsylvania. 28 U.S.C. § 2253 (c). From there, the losing party could file a petition for certiorari to the United States Supreme Court and hope that the court granted the petition. Supreme Court Rule 10(c) (2019). So, theoretically, the very same issue could reach SCOTUS through the back door of federal habeas relief, but that would be many years away.

CHAPTER 7

1. Remarks by Chief Justice William H. Rehnquist (lecture at the Faculty of Law of the University of Guanajuato, Mexico, September 27, 2001), https://www.supremecourt.gov/publicinfo/speeches/viewspeech/sp_09-27-01.

2. "About NAAG," National Association of Attorneys General, https://www.naag.org/about-naag/.

3. The four civil cases in which certiorari was granted on November 29, 1999, were: *Robin Free, et al. v. Abbot Laboratories, et al.*, Docket No. 99-391; *Natsios, Massachusetts Secretary of Finance v. National Foreign Trade Council*, Docket No. 99-474; *Donald E. Nelson v. Adams USA, Inc., et al.*, Docket No. 99-502; and *Juatassa Sims v. Apfel, Commissioner, Social Security*, Docket No. 98-9537.

4. *Guide for Counsel in Cases to Be Argued before the Supreme Court of the United States* (October Term 1999), 1.

5. Ibid., 6.

6. Ibid., 5.

7. Ibid., 7.

8. Ibid.

CHAPTER 8

1. Chief Justice William H. Rehnquist, "Oral Advocacy: A Disappearing Act" (Brainerd Currie Lecture, Mercer University School of Law, Macon, GA, October 20, 1983), 35 Mercer L. Rev. 1015 (1984).

2. SCOTUStalk, "SCOTUS Spotlight: Tom Goldstein on 'Hitting Singles' as an Oral Advocate," *SCOTUSblog*, August 17, 2020, https://www.scotusblog.com/2020/08/scotus-spotlight-tom-goldstein-hitting-singles/.

CHAPTER 9

1. "Who We Are," Anti-Defamation League, accessed March 18, 2022, https://www.ADL.org/who-we-are.

2. Brief of amicus curiae, Anti-Defamation League, in support of respondent state of New Jersey in *Charles C. Apprendi, Jr., v. New Jersey*, Docket No. 99-478, 5.

3. James Weinstein, "First Amendment Challenges to Hate Crime Legislation: Where's the Speech?," *Criminal Justice Ethics* 11, no. 2 (1992): 6–20.

4. Brief of amicus curiae, the United States, in support of respondent state of New Jersey in *Charles C. Apprendi, Jr., v. New Jersey,* Docket No. 99-478, 1.

5. Ibid. at 16.

6. For example, N.J. Stat. Ann. 2C:35-5 (West 2021) and N.J. Stat. Ann. 2C:35-10 (West 2021).

7. Supreme Court Rule 26.1 (2019).

8. Supreme Court Rule 26.3 (2019).

9. *State v. Cooke,* 163 N.J. 657 (2000).

10. *State v. Morton,* 165 N.J. 235 (2000).

11. Reply brief of petitioner Charles C. Apprendi Jr. in *Charles C. Apprendi. Jr., v. New Jersey,* Docket No. 99-478, 1.

12. Ibid. at 3.

CHAPTER 10

1. Supreme Court Rule 28.1 (2019).

2. Ibid.

3. Robert L. Stern and Eugene Gressman, *Supreme Court Practice,* 7th ed. (Washington, DC: Bureau of National Affairs, 1993).

4. Robert H. Jackson, *Advocacy before the United States Supreme Court,* 37 Cornell L. Rev. 1, 4 (1951), http://scholarship.law.cornell.edu/clr/vol137/iss1/4.

5. *Miranda v. Arizona,* 384 U.S. 436 (1966); Oyez, accessed March 18, 2022, https://www.oyez.org/cases/1964/759.

6. Supreme Court Rule 28.3.

7. Jackson, *Advocacy before the United States Supreme Court,* 37 Cornell L. Rev., 2.

8. Ibid., 10.

9. Motion by Solicitor General Seth P. Waxman for leave to participate in oral argument and for divided argument in No. 99-478, *Charles C. Apprendi, Jr., Petitioner v. State of New Jersey.*

10. Ibid.

11. Ibid.

12. Ibid.

13. *Guide for Counsel in Cases to Be Argued before the Supreme Court of the United States* (October Term 1999), 4.

14. Ibid., 9.

15. Ibid., 3.

16. At the beginning of SCOTUS's 2019 term, twenty years after the *Apprendi* argument, the court changed its practice to allow arguing counsel two minutes of uninterrupted time at the start of their presentations. *Guide for Counsel in Cases to Be Argued before the Supreme Court of the United States* (October term 2021), 7.

17. William H. Rehnquist, "Oral Advocacy: A Disappearing Art" (Brainerd Currie Lecture, Mercer University School of Law, Macon, GA, October 20, 1983), 35 Mercer L. Rev. 1015 (1984).

CHAPTER 11

1. NAAG Center for Supreme Court Advocacy, https://www.naag.org /our-work/naag-center-for-supreme-court-advocacy/.

2. Georgetown Law Supreme Court Institute, https://www.law.georgetown .edu/supreme-court-institute/moot-court-program/faqs-for-advocates /.

3. *Searight v. New Jersey*, 412 F.Supp. 413, 414–15 (D.N.J. 1976) (internal citations omitted).

CHAPTER 12

1. *Guide for Counsel in Cases to Be Argued Before the Supreme Court of the United States* (October Term 1999), 10.

2. In 1972, the bench was altered from its original straight-line design by cutting it into three pieces and slightly angling the outer two sections from the center section to create a modified C shape so that the justices on either end could see and hear each other. "Building Features," Supreme Court of the United States, accessed March 18, 2022, https://www.supremecourt.gov/about/buildingfeatures.aspx.

3. Free v. Abbott Laboratories, 529 U.S. 333 (2000).

4. *Nelson v. Adams USA, Inc.*, 529 U.S. 460 (2000).

5. Ibid., 468n2.

6. Remarks by Chief Justice William H. Rehnquist (lecture at the Faculty Faculty of Law at the University of Guanajuato, Mexico, Thursday, September 27, 2001), https://www.supremecourt.gov/publicinfo/speeches/viewspeech/ sp_09-27-01.

7. *Guide for Counsel*, 7.

CHAPTER 13

1. "The Court and Its Traditions," Supreme Court of the United States, accessed March 18, 2022, https://www.supremecourt.gov/about/traditions .aspx.

2. Robert H. Jackson, *Advocacy before the United States Supreme Court,* 37 Cornell L. Rev. 1, 13 (1951), http://scholarship.law.cornell.edu/clr/vol37/iss1/13.

3. *Guide for Counsel in Cases to Be Argued before the Supreme Court of the United States* (October Term 1999), 5.

4. *Sims v. Apfel,* 530 U.S. 103 (2000).

5. *Guide for Counsel,* 10.

6. Stanley Kay, "The Highest Court in the Land," *Sports Illustrated,* July 25, 2018, https://www.si.com/nba/2018/07/25/supreme-court-building-basketball-court.

7. Ibid.

CHAPTER 14

1. *Garner v. Jones,* 529 U.S. 244 (2000); *Florida v. J.L.,* 529 U.S. 266 (2000).

2. Supreme Court Rule 5 (2019).

3. Supreme Court Rule 2.1; https://www.supremecourt.gov/about/buildingfeatures.aspx.

4. Unless otherwise noted, the courtroom dialogue in this chapter is from the official United States Supreme Court transcript of oral argument in *Charles C. Apprendi, Jr., v. New Jersey,* Docket No. 99-478, held on March 28, 2000, https://www.supremecourt.gov/pdfs/transcripts/1999/99-478_03-28-2000.pdf. Audio of the argument can be heard at https://www.oyez.org/cases/1999/99-478.

5. Nina Totenberg, "Supreme Court Delays Oral Arguments, Hinting Some May Be Decided Next Term," NPR, April 4, 2020, https://www.npr.org/2020/04/04/827097214/supreme-court-delays-oral-arguments-hinting-some-may-be-decided-next-term.

CHAPTER 15

1. *Brown v. Board of Education of Topeka,* 347 U.S. 483 (1954); *Gideon v. Wainwright,* 372 U.S. 335 (1963); *Frontiero v. Richardson,* 411 U.S. 677 (1973); *Kahn v. Shevin,* 416 U.S. 351 (1974); *Weinberger v. Wiesenfeld,* 420 U.S. 636 (1975); *Edwards v. Healy,* 421 U.S. 772 (1975); *Califano v. Goldfarb,* 430 U.S. 199 (1977); *Duren v. Missouri,* 439 U.S. 357 (1979).

2. Unless otherwise noted, the courtroom dialogue in this chapter is from the official United States Supreme Court transcript of oral argument in *Charles C. Apprendi, Jr., v. New Jersey,* Docket No. 99-478, held on March 28, 2000, https://www.supremecourt.gov/pdfs/transcripts/1999/99-478_03-28-2000.pdf. Audio of the argument can be heard at www.oyez.org/cases/1999/99-478.

3. *Walton v. Arizona,* 497 U.S. 639 (1990).

4. Ibid., 644.

5. Ibid., 644–45.

6. Ibid., 645.

7. Ibid.

8. Ibid., 649.

9. *Pointer v. United States*, 151 U.S. 396, 414–15 (1894).

10. National Archives, https://catalog.archives.gov/id/26921156.

11. *State v. Greeley*, 178 N.J. 38, 46 (2003).

12. Marlene Trestman, "Women Advocates before the Supreme Court," Supreme Court Historical Society, accessed March 18, 2022, https://www.supremecourthistory .org/oral-arguments-women-advocates-before-the-supreme-court/. Belva Ann Lockwood of Washington, DC, holds the distinction of being the first female Supreme Court advocate, arguing 120 years before me, on November 30, 1880.

13. Ibid.

CHAPTER 16

1. Unless otherwise noted, the courtroom dialogue in this chapter is from the official United States Supreme Court transcript of oral argument in *Charles C. Apprendi, Jr., v. New Jersey*, Docket No. 99-478, held on March 28, 2000, https:// www.supremecourt.gov/pdfs/transcripts/1999/99-478_03-28-2000.pdf. Audio of the argument can be heard at www.oyez.org/cases/1999/99-478.

2. "Justice Thomas on Questioning during Oral Arguments," C-SPAN, June 3, 2019, https://www.c-span.org/video/?c4800959/justice-thomas-questioning -oral-arguments.

3. Adam Liptak, "Clarence Thomas Breaks a Three-Year Silence at Supreme Court," *New York Times*, March 20, 2019, https://www.nytimes.com/2019/03/20 /us/politics/clarence-thomas-speaks-supreme-court.html.

4. *Jones v. United States*, 526 U.S. 227, 243 n.6 (1999).

CHAPTER 18

1. Linda Greenhouse, "Justices Consider Hate-Crime Sentencing," *New York Times*, March 29, 2000, www.nytimes.com/2000/03/29/us/justices-consider-hate -crime-sentencing.html.

2. Tony Mauro, "Spring Fever Hits the High Court: As the Session Cranks Up, Justices Get Cranky with Counsel in a Sentencing Case," *Legal Times*, April 3, 2000.

3. Ibid.

4. Ibid.

5. Nancy Ritter, "NJ's Hate-Crime Law Piques U.S. Justices," *New Jersey Lawyer*, April 3, 2000.

6. *Guide for Counsel in Cases to Be Argued before the Supreme Court of the United States* (October Term 1999), 8.

7. Dahlia Lithwick, "Supreme Court Dispatches," *Slate*, March 28, 2000, https://slate.com/news-and-politics/2000/03/supreme-court-dispatches-6.html.

8. Ibid. (emphasis added).

9. "About the Bobbleheads," Green Bag, accessed March 18, 2022, https://www.greenbag.org/bobbleheads/bobbleheads.

10. Ibid.

11. Ibid.

12. *Troxel v. Granville*, 530 U.S. 57 (2000).

CHAPTER 19

1. Remarks by Chief Justice William H. Rehnquist (lecture at the Faculty of Law of the University of Guanajuato, Mexico, September 27, 2001), https://www.supremecourt.gov/publicinfo/speeches/viewspeech/sp_09-27-01.

2. Ibid.

3. Ibid.

4. Melanie Burney, "Court to Tackle Hate Crime Dispute," AP News, March 27, 2000, https://apnews.com/article/a6f828fa7d6ef80d9a0c1d130e2a0a6.

5. *Castillo v. United States*, 530 U.S. 120 (2000).

6. 18 U.S.C. § 924(c) (1) (1988 ed., Supp. V).

7. *Castillo*, 530 U.S., 122.

8. Ibid., 124–31.

9. Ibid., 131.

10. Ibid.

11. *Pointer v. United States*, 151 U.S. 396, 414–15 (1894).

12. N.J. Court Rule 2:6-11(d) (Gann 2021).

13. Supreme Court Rule 25.6 (2019).

14. Supreme Court Rule 26.6.

15. *Hill v. Colorado*, 530 U.S. 703 (2000).

16. *Stenberg v. Carhart*, 530 U.S. 914 (2000).

17. *Dickerson v. United States*, 530 U.S. 428 (2000).

18. *Santa Fe School District v. Doe*, 530 U.S. 290 (2000).

19. *Boy Scouts of America v. Dale*, 530 U.S. 640 (2000).

20. John Paul Stevens, "Some Thoughts about a Former Colleague" (speech, Washington University in St. Louis School of Law, St. Louis, MO, April 25, 2016), https://www.supremecourt.gov/publicinfo/speeches/.

21. www.oyez.org/cases/1999/99-478.

22. The Supreme Court of New Jersey was reversed twice by SCOTUS that week. Two days after the *Apprendi* opinion was released, SCOTUS

overturned a New Jersey decision requiring the Boy Scouts of America to include a homosexual male in its membership. *Boy Scouts of America v. Dale,* 530 U.S. at 640.

23. *Guide for Counsel in Cases to Be Argued before the Supreme Court of the United States* (October Term 1999), 12.

CHAPTER 20

1. *Apprendi v. New Jersey,* 530 U.S. 466, 475–76 (2000).

2. Ibid., 476.

3. Ibid., 490.

4. Ibid., 488.

5. Ibid., 489.

6. Ibid., 499 (Scalia, J., concurring) (emphasis in original).

7. Dahlia Lithwick, "Supreme Court Dispatches," *Slate,* March 28, 2000, https://slate.com/news-and-politics/2000/03/supreme-court-dispatches-6.html.

8. *Apprendi,* 530 U.S., 499 (Thomas J., concurring).

9. Ibid., 520–21 (Thomas, J., concurring).

10. Ibid.

11. Remarks by Chief Justice William H. Rehnquist (lecture at the Faculty of Law of the University of Guanajuato, Mexico, September 27, 2001), https://www.supremecourt.gov/publicinfo/speeches/viewspeech/sp_09-27-01.

12. *Apprendi,* 530 U.S., 524 (O'Connor, J., dissenting).

13. Ibid., 525 (O'Connor, J., dissenting).

14. Ibid., 537 (O'Connor, J., dissenting).

15. SCOTUS ordered the state of New Jersey as the losing party to reimburse Apprendi's attorney, Joseph O'Neill, in the amount of $1,478.30 for the cost of printing the Supreme Court of New Jersey record, plus an additional $300 in clerk's costs, under Supreme Court Rule 43.2 (2019).

16. Maria Newman, "Victim of Hate Crime Calls High Court Ruling a 'Slap in the Face,'" *New York Times,* June 27, 2000, https://www.nytimes.com/2000/06/27/nyregion/victim-of-hate-crime-calls-high-court-ruling-a-slap-in-the-face.html.

17. Ibid.

18. *Apprendi,* 530 U.S. 497.

19. Supreme Court Rule 45.2 (2019).

20. Ibid.

21. Ibid.

22. *State v. Randolph,* 210 N.J. 330, 354 (2012).

23. Maria Newman, "Man's Hate-Crime Sentence is Reduced," *New York Times,* July 21, 2000, https://www.nytimes.com/2000/07/21/nyregion/man-s-hate-crime-sentence-is-reduced.html.

24. Ibid.

25. New *Jersey Public Law*. 2001, chapter 443 § 1 (eff. January 11, 2002); N.J. Stat. Ann. 2C:16-1 (West 2002).

26. N.J. Stat. Ann. 2C:16-1a (West 2020).

27. Phyllis B. Gerstenfeld, *Hate Crimes: Causes, Controls, and Controversies*, 3rd ed. (Thousand Oaks, CA: Sage, 2013).

CHAPTER 21

1. Erwin Chemerinsky, *Supreme Court Review: A Dramatic Change in Sentencing Practice*, 36-NOV Trial 102 (West 2000).

2. *Dickerson v. United States*, 530 U.S. 428 (2000).

3. *Miranda v. Arizona*, 384 U.S. 436 (1966).

4. Justin A. Thornton and Mark H. Allenbaugh, "Apprendicitis: A Troubling Diagnosis for the Sentencing of Hackers, Thieves, Fraudsters, and Tax Cheats," *George Mason Law Review* 9, no. 2 (Winter 2000): 419, 420 n.4.

5. Justice John Paul Stevens, *The Making of a Justice: Reflections on My First 94 Years* (Boston: Little, Brown 2019), 357.

6. Paul Clement, "Justice Stevens at Oral Argument: Often Fatal; Always Kind," *SCOTUSblog*, July 19, 2019, https://www. scotusblog.com/2019/07/Justice -Stevens-at-oral-argument-often-fatal-always-kind/.

7. "Justice John Paul Stevens' 10 Most Influential Opinions," ABAJournal.com, accessed March 18, 2022, https://www.abajournal.com/gallery/stevens_cases/321.

8. Joan Biskupic, "The Center Chair," in *American Original: The Life and Constitution of Supreme Court Justice Antonin Scalia* (New York: Farrar, Straus and Giroux, 2009), 287.

9. Ibid.

10. Ibid.

11. *Walton v. Arizona*, 497 U.S. 639 (1990).

12. *Apprendi v. New Jersey*, 530 U.S. 466, 496–97 (2000).

13. *Ring v. Arizona*, 536 U.S. 584 (2002).

14. Ibid., 593–95.

15. Ibid., 595–96.

16. Ibid., 609.

17. Ibid., 608.

18. *Kimble v. Marvel Enterprises*, 576 U.S. 446, 455 (2015).

19. *Payne v. Tennessee*, 501 U.S. 808, 827–28 (1991).

20. https://corrections.az.gov/public-resources/inmate-datasearch (ADC Number 061210).

21. *Ring*, 536 U.S., 613 (Kennedy, J., concurring).

22. Ibid.

23. Ibid., 610–12 (Scalia, J., concurring).
24. Ibid., 611–12 (Scalia, J., concurring).
25. *Apprendi*, 530 U.S., 537-39 (O'Connor, J., dissenting).
26. *Ring*, 536 U.S., 619 (O'Connor, J., dissenting).
27. Ibid.
28. Ibid., 613–19 (Breyer, J., concurring).
29. Ibid., 612 (Scalia, J., concurring).
30. Ibid., 612-13 (Scalia, J., concurring).

CHAPTER 22

1. *Harris v. United States*, 536 U.S. 545 (2002).
2. *United States v. Harris*, 243 F.3d 806, 807 (4th Cir. 2001).
3. 18 U.S.C. § 924(c)(1)(A); Harris, 536 U.S., 551.
4. *Harris*, 536 U.S., 551.
5. *Apprendi v. New Jersey*, 530 U.S. 466, 487 n.13 (2000).
6. *Harris*, 536 U.S., 562–68.
7. Ibid., 560.
8. *Alleyne v. United States*, 570 U.S. 99 (2013).
9. Ibid., 102.
10. See, e.g., *Ring v. Arizona*, 536 U.S. 584 (2002) (invalidating Arizona's death penalty statute pursuant to the *Apprendi* rule); *Alleyne*, 570 U.S., 99 (the *Apprendi* rule applies to mandatory minimum sentences); *United States v. Booker*, 543 U.S. 220 (2005) (the *Apprendi* rule applies to federal sentencing guidelines); *Oregon v. Ice*, 555 U.S. 160 (2009) (the *Apprendi* rule does not apply to the imposition of consecutive sentences); *United States v. O'Brien*, 560 U.S. 218 (2010) (the *Apprendi* rule applies to the type of firearm used in the commission of a crime); *Southern Union Co. v. United States*, 567 U.S. 343 (2012) (the *Apprendi* rule applies to the imposition of criminal fines); *Hurst v. Florida*, 577 U.S. 92 (2016) (invalidating Florida's death penalty statute pursuant to the *Apprendi* rule).
11. *United States v. Haymond*, 139 S.Ct. 2369 (2019) (the *Apprendi* rule applies to the federal statute governing revocation of supervised release).
12. *Ring*, 536 U.S., 610 (Scalia, J., concurring).
13. Ibid.
14. *North Carolina Law Review* 99 (2021): 1189.
15. With apologies to Alfred Lord Tennyson.
16. "10 Facts: Abraham Lincoln," American Battlefield Trust, accessed March 18, 2022, https://www.battlefields.org/learn/articles/10-facts-abraham-lincoln.

A graduate of the University of Rochester and Cardozo School of Law in New York City, **Lisa Sarnoff Gochman** is a career appellate prosecutor. In 2012, she retired as a deputy attorney general in the New Jersey Division of Criminal Justice in Trenton after twenty-six years of service. She currently serves Of Counsel to the Appellate Section of the Monmouth County Prosecutor's Office in Freehold, New Jersey.